HOW PSYCHOLOG

MW00638256

Psychology is a discipline with global influence but it continues to neglect disadvantaged minorities and to adopt an incorrect model of science. This volume explains what has gone wrong and what steps should be taken for psychology to become a constructive international force. Historically, psychologists have focused only on causal explanations of behavior, neglecting normatively regulated behavior and intentionality. By giving greater importance to context and collective processes, moving from 'societies to cells,' psychologists can better understand and explain individual behavior. Poverty is an extremely powerful context that shapes cognitions and actions, with destructive consequences for disadvantaged individuals. The advocation of 'be happy psychology' and 'resilience' as solutions to problems faced by the disadvantaged leads to entrenched group-based inequalities, with the poor stuck at the bottom. Moving forward, this volume proposes that psychologists should focus on normative systems to ultimately foster a more balanced field of study for the future.

FATHALI M. MOGHADDAM is Professor of Psychology at Georgetown University, where he served as Director of the Interdisciplinary Program in Cognitive Science (2016–2021). He also served as Editor-in-Chief of the American Psychological Association journal *Peace and Conflict: Journal of Peace Psychology* (2014–2021). His extensive publications include about 30 books and 300 papers, and he has won a number of prestigious academic awards.

THE PROGRESSIVE PSYCHOLOGY BOOK SERIES

This book is part of the Cambridge University Press book series, Progressive Psychology, edited by Fathali M. Moghaddam. As the science of human behavior, psychology is uniquely positioned and equipped to try to help us make more progress toward peaceful, fair, and constructive human relationships. However, the enormous resources of psychology have not been adequately or effectively harnessed for this task. The goal of this book series is to engage psychological science in the service of achieving more democratic societies, toward providing equal opportunities for all. The volumes in the series contribute in new and unique ways to highlight how psychological science can contribute to making justice a more central theme in health care, education, the legal system, and business, combatting the psychological consequences of poverty, ending discrimination and prejudice, better understanding the failure of revolutions and limits on political plasticity, and moving societies to more openness. Of course, these topics have been discussed before in scattered and ad hoc ways by psychologists, but now they are addressed as part of a systematic and cohesive series on Progressive Psychology.

HOW PSYCHOLOGISTS FAILED

We Neglected the Poor and Minorities, Favored the Rich and Privileged, and Got Science Wrong

FATHALI M. MOGHADDAM

Georgetown University

CAMBRIDGE
UNIVERSITY PRESS

CAMBRIDGE
UNIVERSITY PRESS

University Printing House, Cambridge CB2 8BS, United Kingdom

One Liberty Plaza, 20th Floor, New York, NY 10006, USA

477 Williamstown Road, Port Melbourne, VIC 3207, Australia

314–321, 3rd Floor, Plot 3, Splendor Forum, Jasola District Centre,
New Delhi – 110025, India

103 Penang Road, #05–06/07, Visioncrest Commercial, Singapore 238467

Cambridge University Press is part of the University of Cambridge.

It furthers the University's mission by disseminating knowledge in the pursuit of
education, learning, and research at the highest international levels of excellence.

www.cambridge.org
Information on this title: www.cambridge.org/9781316513019
DOI: 10.1017/9781009071598

© Fathali M. Moghaddam 2023

First published 2023

A catalogue record for this publication is available from the British Library.

ISBN 978-1-316-51301-9 Hardback
ISBN 978-1-009-06991-5 Paperback

*To the courageous researchers shedding light
on the psychology of social class*

Contents

Preface

I wrote this book because it has become imperative that we rethink psychological science in two major ways. First, we need to rethink our exclusive focus on discovering cause–effect relations, because not all human behavior is causally determined. Rather, most of our behavior is regulated by normative systems, and culture more broadly. Unfortunately, the causal model has been mistakenly adopted even in cross-cultural psychology. Second, we must finally abandon reductionism, the assumption that in order to be a science, psychology has to explain behavior with reference to the most micro units and mechanisms. Instead of moving in the traditional way 'from cells to societies,' I argue for 'from societies to cells' as our framework. As I explain in this book, the causal model and reductionism have had detrimental consequences for psychological science – including the neglect of collective processes generally and poverty and social class specifically.[1] Through this neglect, mainstream psychology has helped *to uphold and even to extend* class-based inequalities.

The rethinking undertaken here is part of a broad effort on the part of different psychologists, whose research is discussed in the forthcoming chapters, to develop psychological science beyond the causal-reductionist model. I argue that this development further strengthens a trend that involves increasing numbers of psychologists, who are bringing more attention to collective processes, social class, and the experiences and interests of the poor.[2] Although no published book matches my description of how we psychologists have failed, a variety of books tackle aspects of this topic. Most such books are either edited collections or focused on social theory.[3] However, there is currently no introductory book that directly addresses the critical need to rethink psychology with respect to the causal-reductionist model.

The chapters in this book are organized to parallel the chapters found in the standard introductory psychology textbooks. In terms of style and content, this book is suitable for readers with no prior experience in psychology. The target audience for this book consists of all those general readers, students, researchers, teachers, and practitioners who want to better understand why and how psychological science needs to change in order to meet its tremendous global potential.

Acknowledgments

This book is inspired by and deeply indebted to those courageous psychologists who are making poverty and social class more central to psychological research and practice. I am also grateful to David Repetto of Cambridge University Press for his support of, and valuable contributions to, the Progressive Psychology series.

CHAPTER I

Why We Must Rethink Psychology

Human behavior is truly puzzling and fascinating. For example, very soon after the start of the 2020 pandemic, supermarket shelves carrying everyday products like hand wipes, toilet paper, masks, and disinfectants were stripped bare. People rushed out and bought everything they could find. This frantic buying and hoarding led to shortages, even in the richest countries in the world.[1] As soon as new supplies reached shops, they were instantly snapped up. Some supermarket shelves remained empty for months. Yet the shortages were almost entirely created by panic-buying and hoarding.

As individuals, we can understand that, in situations like the 2020 pandemic, panic-buying and hoarding only make matters worse. I remember talking with my neighbors when the pandemic started, and as individuals we could agree on how we should behave. But our behavior changed and became 'incorrect' when we became part of the collective. After the panic-buying started, most of us were swept along, rushing to supermarkets and helping to create shortages. But not everyone engaged in panic-buying and hoarding during the pandemic. Some individuals *consciously and intentionally* avoided such behavior.

Because human behavior is varied, complex, and extraordinarily interesting, increasing numbers of people across the world have flocked to *psychology*, the science of human behavior. Psychology is now among the most popular subjects of study for students in universities around the world, and psychologists work as professionals in health, education, business organizations, government ministries, the military, prisons, and many other sectors in all major societies. However, despite this popularity, psychological science has not come close to reaching its potential to help us overcome the enormous challenges we face in changing behavior to improve our conditions.

We can build rockets that take us to the Moon and even Mars, but we are not able to end wars, cultural and institutional violence, poverty, drug and alcohol addiction, and other destructive social problems back here on Earth. We have been able to build super-fast and increasingly efficient computers, but psychological science has not enabled us to end discrimination, racism, sexism, and other injustices. We have the scientific ability to build fantastically efficient, clean, green energy technologies, yet we continue to pollute the environment, make global warming worse each year, and seriously endanger our own future survival on planet Earth. We have been able to increase productivity and create enormous wealth, but more and more of this wealth is in the hands of a smaller and smaller number of individuals, and the poor are falling further behind relative to the superrich. In so many vitally important areas, psychological science needs to become more effective at understanding and influencing collective and individual change. But psychology has a very long way to go to achieve its potential in this regard. There is an urgent need to rethink psychology.

Rethinking has taken place before in the history of psychology. The method of *introspection*, individuals looking inward and reporting on their own mental processes, dominated nineteenth-century psychology but was swept aside by behaviorism early in the twentieth century. The behaviorists argued that, in order to be a science, psychology must exclusively focus on observable behavior; they rejected introspection and the exploration of subjective experience. In the 1950s the behaviorists were pushed aside by the 'cognitive revolution,' which brought the study of the mind back to center stage in psychology. During the twenty-first century, neuroscience has gained considerable influence in psychology, so that the study of the brain in relation to cognition has become far more prominent. Throughout these developments, psychoanalysis has had a profound impact on both academic psychology and wider society, challenging the image we have of ourselves as rational beings and arguing for the important role of irrationality in human behavior.

But the rethinking that took place in the past failed to correct two major flaws that continue to characterize twenty-first-century psychology. These flaws are central to the historically most influential schools: behaviorism, psychoanalysis, cognitive psychology, and now neuroscience. By addressing these two flaws, psychological science will become more attentive to the needs of the poor and issues of group-based inequalities and injustice. The first flaw is the invalid assumption that all human behavior is causally determined and must be explained by discovering cause–effect relations. This is how a leading introductory psychology textbook explains the role of causal determinism: "The scientific approach to anything, including psychology, assumes that we live in a universe of cause and effect ...

scientists assume **determinism**, *the idea that everything that happens has a cause, or determinant, that someone could observe or measure.*"[2] A study of fifteen leading introductory psychology texts showed that they all share this deterministic assumption, that human behavior is causally determined and the goal of psychology is to discover cause–effect relations.[3]

The first major way we must rethink psychology, then, is to reject the invalid assumption that *all* human behavior is causally determined. Of course, some human behavior is explained by cause–effect relations. For example, if I suffer a head injury in a car accident, the blow to my head causes neural damage and results in loss of memory. This is *efficient causation* and works in the same way as gravity causing a book to drop to the ground when I let go of the book in mid-air.[4] But much of human behavior is normatively regulated, in the sense that most of the time most of us intentionally behave in what we interpret as the appropriate way to behave, according to the local culture. However, *we can decide* to behave differently, and there is some diversity in human behavior. For example, some individuals intentionally did not become part of the collective stampede to the shops during the 2020 pandemic.

The attempt to explain all behavior through cause–effect relations leads to serious contradictions, which for the most part remain unacknowledged, particularly inside of mainstream psychology. For example, on the one hand, psychological science tells us that all behavior is causally determined, but on the other hand, the ideology of Western capitalist societies – home to mainstream psychology – gives priority to self-help, individual mobility, and individual responsibility. If the behavior of individuals is deterministically caused by factors beyond their control, if intentionality and free will are an 'illusion' as one prominent psychologist put it,[5] how can the same individuals be held personally responsible for their own actions and outcomes? How can the behavior of a personally responsible individual in a self-help society be causally determined? Indeed, if all behavior is causally determined and there is no free will, how can our moral and legal systems make sense – how can there be 'sin' in religion or 'guilty' verdicts in law courts? (Sam Harris[6] has argued unconvincingly that our morality improves when we accept there is no free will.) As I demonstrate, the solution to this contradiction is to acknowledge that human behavior is of two types: normative and causal. Normative behavior allows for some measure of free will. Thus, psychology is more correctly conceived as the science of normative and causal behavior.

A second common flaw of the major schools of psychology, and of mainstream psychology in the twenty-first century, is *reductionism*: the attempt to explain behavior with a focus on the smallest units possible, moving 'from cells to societies' rather than the antireductionist 'from societies to cells' approach I advocate. Reductionism leads us to look within isolated individuals and even, through the influence of neuroscience, within decontextualized brain processes to discover the 'causes' of behavior such as panic-buying and hoarding (but some neuroscientists have turned to a more dynamic approach to understanding brain and behavior[7]). In mainstream psychology, reductionism has led us to ignore the influence of collective processes and context, which are powerful shapers of individual behavior; collective social processes were the most important factors shaping widespread panic-buying behavior during the 2020 pandemic.

Reductionism has led to extensive use, both in research and in the popular media, of the term hardwiring with reference to (supposedly) fixed behaviors arising from inflexible brain characteristics and/or caused by genes[8]. I refer to this as Type I hardwiring ('I' standing for 'Internal'). But mainstream psychology has not given enough attention to Type E hardwiring ('E' standing for 'External'). External factors, such as material conditions and poverty, that create a context for behavior also serve as a powerful form of hardwiring. But reductionism in mainstream psychology has resulted in this form of influence on behavior to be largely neglected.

In subtle ways, the causal-reductionist model that has dominated psychology is connected to the power structure and class-based inequalities of the larger world. Historically, mainstream psychology is the product of a privileged group in the Western world, and it subtly continues to justify class-based inequalities. The causal-reductionist model means that psychologists interpret class-based inequalities as causally determined by factors existing within individuals, and increasingly within isolated brains. The causal-reductionist model leads us to interpret the plight of the poor as *caused by factors within them*, such as a lack of resilience, motivation, and intelligence. In this way, psychology is not just ideologically biased, *it is itself* part of the larger ideology maintaining the *status quo* and group-based inequalities. Recognizing psychology as ideology is part of the rethinking we need to undertake.

Also, by accepting that much of human behavior is normatively regulated, psychological science necessarily gives more research attention to *normative systems*, the rules, norms, values, and other features of contexts that regulate behavior. As a consequence, the question of who has the economic and political power to shape normative systems, and contexts more broadly, becomes far more central to psychological research and practice.

The behavior of the poor is regulated by normative systems and contextual characteristics that are shaped in large part by economic and political elites.

The rethinking I undertake in this book is in many ways already underway in different (often remote) corners of psychology. This rethinking is to be found in specialized journals,[9] in conference discussions and handbooks,[10] in some parts of books written for advanced researchers.[11] This rethinking has also led to some initiatives that seem promising but still have not created much change, such as the *APA Deep Poverty Initiative*,[12] designed to engage psychological science in efforts to eradicate deep poverty. My goal is to integrate and extend this rethinking in a style that is accessible to a wider audience. My rethinking psychology project focuses on the two themes of causal explanations and reductionism, because I see these as having priority. There are other possible types of rethinking of psychology that I do not discuss in this book, such as rethinking the focus on individual differences rather than treating each person as a distinct case,[13] as is taking place in medical science.[14]

Collective Processes, Poverty, and Social Class

The causal-reductionist nature of mainstream psychology has resulted in inadequate attention being given to collective processes, poverty, and social class. By 'poverty' I do not mean only a lack of material wealth, although the tradition has been for researchers to use material criteria to establish poverty on either absolute or relative terms. *Absolute poverty* is based on the idea of minimum basic rights, while relative poverty relies on ideas about a 'normal' or 'acceptable' standard of living.[15] The systematic study of poverty began with two English businessmen who also conducted social research on poverty. The first was Charles Booth (1840–1916), whose 'poverty maps'[16] used material criteria to conclude that 35 percent of London's population were living in poverty. The second was Benjamin Seebohm Rowntree (1871–1954), who was the first researcher to determine poverty in terms of the minimum income needed to maintain an adequate standard of living, particularly in the areas of nutrition and other basic needs[17] (in the United States the journalist Jacob A. Riis also published influential portraits of poverty in *How the other half lives: Studies among the tenements in New York*, 1890). The tradition established by these early researchers for using material criteria to define poverty is evident in modern programs, such as President Lindon Johnson's (1908–1973) *War on Poverty*, judged to be a success on the basis of narrow material criteria.[18]

As I discuss in forthcoming chapters in this book, the problem of poverty and divisions between social classes has become greater during the twenty-first century. Thus, the need for psychological science to pay closer attention to the experiences of the poor and class-based inequalities has become even more acute.

Plan of the Book

The twelve chapters and the Afterword in this book are organized in line with the chapters found in the standard introductory psychology textbooks, with the exception that the discussion of research methods comes toward the end of this book, rather than in the early part (as found in standard introductory psychology texts).

The continuous theme throughout the chapters is advancing toward a psychology that progresses from 'societies to cells,'[19] from context and macro processes to micro processes. This moves us beyond the causal-reductionist model, which has resulted in an incorrect and incomplete account of behavior. This account is incorrect and incomplete in that it does not give sufficient importance to the role of context, group membership, collective processes, and social class, and it grossly exaggerates the role of intraindividual characteristics (such as resilience, personality, and IQ). As a result of the causal-reductionist model, psychology does not give enough attention to the viewpoint and interests of individuals entrapped by the strong contexts of social class and poverty.

This book is organized in three main parts.

Part I

The six chapters in Part I explore basic psychological processes that are central to human experiences. The main conceptual theme linking these chapters is the *primacy of collective processes in the shaping of individual psychology, looking at behavior from 'societies to cells.'* Collective human processes are foundationally cultural, involving norms, values, rules, symbols, beliefs, and other features of social life that already exist and operate prior to the arrival of the individual in this world, and influence individual behavior in profound ways. The first of these chapters examines how context shapes basic cognitive processes. More specifically, I explore the power of poverty as a context-shaping cognition. Poverty tends to be inherited, and passed on from generation to generation. Cognition has to be understood in the context of this continuous and powerful inheritance. Thus, instead of explaining thinking by focusing on isolated individuals, brains, and brain parts, I give priority to collective processes and relations between people as the key to understanding individual-level cognition.[20]

Intelligence testing is an area in which the claim of neutrality and objectivity by psychological researchers has had a devastating impact on the lower class, as discussed in Chapter 2. I assess and refute the claim that psychological tests are able to measure intelligence independent of experience and culture, that intelligence is basically inherited, and that the United States and other Western societies are now meritocracies, so that an individual's place in the status hierarchy is determined by his or her personal characteristics, particularly IQ.[21] I argue that intelligence tests reflect the values of a stratified education system that perpetuates huge inequalities between the different social classes.

Education is supposed to be a great leveler (as discussed in Chapter 3), a means by which the poor pull themselves up and improve their conditions. But in practice the education gap between the different social classes is widening in major industrialized societies, including the United States. Even when lower class students gain entrance to universities, it is weaker universities, and most of the poorer students do not even have the necessary preparation and resources for the challenge of higher education.[22] These trends have been worsened by the 2020 pandemic[23].

Personality assessment, examined in Chapter 4, has also suffered from the neglect of context. Instruments for assessing personality are developed and used as if personality functions in a vacuum – as if larger society does not exist. Mainstream psychology assumes that 'traits' somehow influence behavior 'independently,' but independence is only possible for more affluent individuals who have the power and resources to exert their personal influence, to 'act out' traits in public. For the lower classes, the key shapers of behavior are the external pressures that force them to conform and obey in line with normative systems put into place by the upper class.

I examine consciousness and free will in Chapter 5, identifying mainstream psychological research on consciousness as 'decontextualized' and pointing out that consciousness has to be understood in a cultural context. Adopting a 'from societies to cells' approach, I argue that the source of consciousness is to be found in collective life and the normative system that is already 'out there' when the individual is born, rather than in the private experiences of individuals. Also, some behavior is normatively regulated and does allow for a certain measure of intentionality.

In Chapter 6, I examine motivation. At the heart of strategies for survival and 'self-help' presented to the poor is the concept of 'psychological resilience.' Mountains of advice are offered as to how the poor can become motivated to spring back from hardships. Of course, recovery is supposed to depend on personal effort and talent, and individual motivation – all in line with reductionism and the self-help ideology. We are told that, in the individualistic culture of twenty-first-century Western societies, a 'pull yourself up' and 'rely on personal effort' strategy is the key to psychological resilience and success. Everybody experiences hardships, but those who have the individual characteristic of 'resilience' thrive even in the face of the harshest challenges, so we are told. The enormous inequalities that persist in the support systems of the different social classes, the context that shapes motivation and resilience, are seldom acknowledged.

Mainstream psychology has focused on individual behavior and given inadequate attention to group and intergroup behavior. Within this neglected field, poverty and social class have remained the most neglected; however, ethnic groups are now receiving more attention. Chapter 7 builds on the scattered but growing research literature on the psychological experiences of different social classes, including experimental attempts to research how 'rich' and 'poor' people (who have been placed in these positions in a laboratory study) make decisions. On the one hand, experimental research provides some evidence that people are averse to inequalities. On the other hand, the empirical evidence shows that in the world outside the laboratory wealth accumulation is becoming even more extreme in the twenty-first century, and the gap between the superrich and the rest is widening.[24] Attention to multiculturalism and the 'celebration of ethnic differences' has not helped poor ethnic minority students achieve parity in educational performance, because the acute and continuing issue of poverty – that detrimentally impacts the poor in all ethnic groups – continues to be neglected in mainstream psychology as well as larger society.

Part II

The three chapters in Part II explore the need for alternatives to the causal-reductionist model in mental health, the justice system, and life in non-Western societies. In Chapter 8, I critically evaluate psychology and mental health. My assessment builds on some of the arguments integral to the anti-psychiatry movement (particularly Ronald Laing, 1927–1989, and Thomas Szasz, 1920–2012), because of the priority they give to context in explaining human behavior. But, unlike leaders in the anti-psychiatry movement, I accept the need for drug therapy in some instances. However,

I am particularly critical toward the contemporary positive psychology movement and twenty-first-century trends that I label 'be happy' psychology. The danger is that the poor (across all ethnic groups) will be persuaded to arrive at compensation for economic inequalities through 'be happy' psychology, and reductionist 'self-help' solutions more broadly.

The (in)justice system is examined in Chapter 9. There has been innovative psychological research on justice and perceptions of injustice, as well as the relationship between procedural and distributive justice. There are now numerous books and entire journals dedicated to the psychology of justice.[25] However, the link between the psychology of justice and life experiences of the poor needs far more attention. The poor have very different experiences in the (in)justice system and are far more likely to look through prison bars from the wrong side.[26] As things stand, money, resources, and connections help create a justice system for the middle and upper classes but an injustice system for the lower class.

The non-Western world is another context in which causal-reductionist psychology has brought far more benefits to the upper class compared to the rest of society, a topic examined in Chapter 10. The 'wholesale' exportation of causal-reductionist psychology to non-Western societies has taken place with almost no attention to the actual needs of the masses in non-Western societies.[27] The assumption that cross-cultural psychology would address this problem has proved to be invalid, because cross-cultural psychology has shared the causal-reductionist model of mainstream psychology. The question of 'what would be an appropriate psychology for non-Western societies?' has seldom been asked and almost never addressed.[28] Like the poor in Western societies, the poor in non-Western societies have concerns that arise from problems such as food insecurity, extreme lack of resources, and powerlessness, issues not faced by more affluent individuals and not given enough attention in mainstream Western psychology.

Part III

The claim that psychology as a discipline is neutral in large part rests on the assumption that the research methods of psychology are culture-free and unbiased. This claim is critically evaluated and found to be invalid in Chapter 11; my discussion is in line with a broad movement to progress beyond traditional quantitative research methods.[29] The research methodologies adopted in psychology are manufactured within a given historical time and place; they are shaped by a particular set of cultural assumptions and values.[30] For example, the most commonly used research method in psychology continues to be the laboratory,[31] through which, typically, individuals are studied in isolation. The laboratory method arises out of the causal-reductionist model of human behavior, reflecting strong cultural biases. The results of studies using mainstream psychology research methods are questionable (particularly in terms of reliability, validity, and generalizability) when considered in the larger global context. Indeed, as the controversy of replication demonstrates,[32] these results are even questionable within the narrow confines of Western societies.[33]

Revolution has often been considered as a solution to the problems of class-based inequalities and poverty. In Chapter 12, I consider why in practice revolutions have failed to bring about full or 'actualized' democracy and justice.[34] As discussed extensively by Pareto[35] and others, revolutions typically replace one elite with another but do not end the resource and power disparities between the different social classes. The limited psychological research related to revolution has focused on the factors that lead to collective mobilization and make regime change possible. However, this research focus does not benefit the poor, because in most cases regime change simply leads to one set of rulers or a single dictator replacing another without decreasing social class inequalities and improving the plight of the poor[36].

From the perspective of the poor, the most important research questions regarding revolutions are not just about regime change but about why it has not been possible to change the behavior of both leaders and the masses to progress toward actualized democracy. Revolutions come with promises of better worlds, but in order to achieve such worlds the cognitions and actions of both leaders and the masses have to change in the required manner. Very importantly, the behavior of leaders has to change to enable and encourage a more open, just society. But such changes are limited by *political plasticity*,[37] the malleability of political behavior, a topic that is highly important from the perspective of the poor but has received too little research attention from psychologists.

The future of psychology as a normative and causal science is briefly explored in the Afterword. The perspective presented is from societies to cells, with the emphasis on how individual psychology is shaped by collective processes and context. Psychological science must become capable of understanding both the normative systems that regulate behavior and the cause–effect relations that in some instances causally determine behavior.

To sum up, this brief book critically examines and rejects the causal-reductionist model and argues that we need to rethink psychology. By reframing psychology as the science of both normative and causal behavior, the spotlight shifts to collective processes and context in shaping individual experiences. This perspective leads to a more accurate understanding of the *common* plight of poor people across all ethnic groups and enables psychology to better contribute to improving the human condition, in both Western and non-Western societies.

PART I

Psychological Processes

> [S]ocial class positioning influences all aspects of everyday interactions – how to talk, if to talk and when, whom to trust, whether or not to plan or risk, what can or cannot be done, how to belong, and who to be.

To the above highly insightful analysis by Hazel Markus and Susan Fiske[1] we can add: Social class positioning also influences all aspects of cognition, intelligence, personality, health, justice, and everyday experiences broadly. Indeed, social class is one of the most profound and significant determinants of human psychology, and it deserves to receive far more attention in mainstream psychology. The six chapters in Part I contribute to remedy this shortcoming in psychological science.

Reductionism born out of assumptions about how American society is meritocratic and based on free and open competition between individuals, is the most important factor leading mainstream psychology away from social class. Mainstream psychologists continue to work from micro to macro, from cells to societies, and to give inadequate attention to context. In an effort to break out of reductionism, the chapter topics in Part I include basic psychological processes central to mainstream psychology, including cognition, intelligence, personality, consciousness, motivation, and group life. In each chapter, a mainstream topic is examined through an alternative approach. An overriding outcome is the realization that contextual factors, such as social class, should be more central to our psychological explanations of human behavior.

CHAPTER 2

Cognition and Decision-Making in Societal Context

The master, in his cook's uniform, stationed himself at the copper; his pauper assistants ranged themselves behind him; the gruel was served out; and a long grace was said ... The gruel disappeared; the boys whispered to each other, and winked at Oliver; while his next neighbours nudged him. Child as he was, he was desperate with hunger, and reckless with misery. He rose from the table; and advancing to the master, basin and spoon in hand, said somewhat alarmed at his own temerity:

"Please, sir, I want some more."

This famous passage from Charles Dickens's novel *Oliver Twist* depicts a scene in which the starving Oliver Twist dares to ask for more food from the school official, a "fat, healthy man" who turns pale in response to Oliver's audacity.[1] The malnourished children at Oliver's workhouse crave, think, and dream about food. Their minds are preoccupied with hunger and daily survival, not learning. Under their miserable living conditions, these starving children are not able to compete with well-nourished children who enjoy the support of relatively luxurious homes, schools, and neighborhoods.

Unfortunately, in the twenty-first century, large numbers of children share Oliver's experience of hunger, in both Western and non-Western societies, including in the United States.[2] Around the world about 800 million people have continued to suffer hunger over the last few decades.[3] The political 'anyone can make it' argument would have greater validity in a context where the lower class receive adequate nourishment, as well as health, legal, educational, and professional opportunities and support. But in the current situation, this argument is completely invalid because inequality has been increasing and opportunities for upward mobility are extremely limited for lower-class individuals. As Eldar Shafir has pointed out, "A major contribution of the behavioral sciences has been a deeper appreciation of the power of context to shape thinking and behavior. When situations are mild, people's traits and dispositions can shape what they do, but as contexts grow more powerful, individual differences become less relevant. And poverty is a powerful context."[4]

The idea that poverty and lack of food influence cognitive functioning seems obvious, but the causal-reductionist approach of mainstream psychology has resulted in such 'obvious' points being neglected, as part of the larger neglect of context. In order to highlight the role of context on cognition, as an illustrative example in this chapter I focus on poverty, cognition, and decision-making. My goal is not to provide an exhaustive review of research in this area but to use key research examples to reveal how poverty can influence cognition and decision-making. At the same time, I accept that experimental studies, particularly those conducted in laboratories and with WEIRD (White, Educated, Industrialized, Rich, Democratic) samples (discussed in Chapter 5 of this text), do not capture the full impact of poverty on behavior in the 'real world' outside. The scant earlier research on this theme includes studies by Jerome Bruner (1915–2016), showing that poor children compared to rich children overestimated the size of more valuable coins,[5] and research on how starvation impairs biological and psychological functioning, such as problem-solving.[6] However, mainstream psychology text books have shamefully neglected questions about the relationship between poverty and behavior. For example, how does poverty influence sensations, perceptions, motivations, attention, memory, attributions, attitudes, stereotypes, and other basic psychological processes? There are scores of widely used, expensive, glossy textbooks that introduce millions of students to the discipline of psychology every year, but 'poverty and psychology' is a neglected topic in these textbooks. According to the reductionist ethos underlying twenty-first-century mainstream psychology, individuals are self-contained, independent, and factors within them shape behavior.

The widening wealth divide in the twenty-first century[7] provides an even more urgent need for psychologists to give greater attention to research on poverty and cognition. Poverty directly and indirectly increases *cognitive load*, the 'burden' that performing a particular task imposes on the cognitive system of a learner.[8] This comes about through the influence of different aspects of poverty. For example, deprivation in cognitive stimulation in the home environment (particularly in the early years) can detrimentally influence neural structures[9] and *executive function*,[10] the problem-solving resources we can put into action for managing ourselves to achieve a goal. These resources enable us to self-regulate and direct attention toward carrying out tasks.

Poverty impairs cognitive functioning even in tasks that ostensibly are unrelated to finances. The hard evidence compels us to recognize that the relationship between poverty, cognition, and decision-making is circular: Poverty leads to impaired cognitive functioning, which in turn perpetuates poverty.[11] The implication is that psychology has a key role to play in overcoming poverty – a role that can only be taken up by rejecting the reductionist 'anyone can make it' argument in the context of enormous and rising resource and educational inequalities.

The academic achievement gap is widening not just between the elite and the rest but also between people with different levels of wealth located across the entire socioeconomic continuum. That is, the achievement gap had widened not only between children from families with incomes in the ninetieth percentile and the fiftieth percentile but also between children from families with incomes in the fiftieth percentile and tenth percentile.[12] Thus, inequality is spreading, as wealth concentration continues to increase.

There are indications that, if current trends continue, inequality is going to increase even more around the world. In countries as widely different in political rhetoric as the United States, China, the United Kingdom, and Russia, wealth concentration is increasing.[13] In so-called 'Communist China,' political power is used to amass riches, so that numerous members of China's parliament have personal fortunes of over $320 million.[14] Along with the global trend of wealth concentration is the global spread of 'individual responsibility' and 'self-help' as explanations for how society works and how the rich and powerful become rich and powerful through personal effort and talent. In this sense, an inefficient form of capitalism has triumphed,[15] because in many different countries around the world, monopolistic forces are being allowed greater freedom to shape events and human behavior. Under the guise of 'free market,' enormous monopoly organizations (Apple, Google, Amazon, and the like) are 'ruling the world.'[16] Labor unions have become weaker[17] and a 'gig economy'[18] mentality is becoming more influential, particularly among the young, so that unstable part-time employment with little or no benefits (such as retirement and health insurance) is becoming the norm even among young people with university education.

The research on cognition and poverty leads us to re-evaluate current trends in major societies. The disadvantaged situation of children living in poverty starts to impact performance very early, well before the age at which students take college entrance examinations. Well before the age of ten, the majority of children growing up in poverty already have fallen behind in the education race. Their impoverished conditions mean that from birth they are competing with at least one hand tied behind their backs.

This chapter is organized into three main parts. Section 1 explores how people see poverty and the consequences of such perceptions. Section 2 examines the direct and indirect impact of poverty on cognitive performance and decision-making. Section 3 explores cognition, decision-making and poverty through a contextual lens, by considering the larger context of individual behavior.

Perceptions of People Who Are Poor

> We don't want our tax money going to welfare queens. You know, the type who have four, five, six children so they can get more and more government money without ever having to do real work.

The man who made this declaration to me emphasized his points by waving a thick forefinger in the air, as we waited in line to board our plane at Dulles Washington International Airport. Heather Bullock and her associates have pointed out that "Welfare recipients are among one of the most hated and stereotyped groups in contemporary society,"[19] and the man in front of me was emphatically confirming this research finding.

"We don't need no welfare queens driving Cadillacs bought with our money, running away from work," he added dogmatically. I started to explain to him that the stereotype of the 'welfare queen driving a Cadillac' is false,[20] but the line moved on and we were soon wedged into our seats in different sections of the plane.

How people perceive people who are poor and explain poverty are important in a number of ways. This particular gentleman believed that people are poor because of their individual characteristics, specifically poor individuals are lazy and irresponsible, and any monetary support they receive only makes the situation worse, by encouraging them to evade 'real work.' In particular, he focused on poor women, which is in line with general tendencies in the US population, as Bullock and her colleagues have noted: "In the United States, classist stereotypes about the characteristics and behaviors of poor people are pervasive. In particular, women receiving public assistance are stereotyped as lazy, disinterested in education, and promiscuous."[21]

In the context of societies giving priority to self-help and individual responsibility, many people believe that those who have wealth are successful because of their individual talents. Correspondingly, people who are poor are stigmatized and those on welfare are looked down upon. Through political rhetoric and what Ange-Marie Hancock[22] describes as the *politics of disgust*, people who are poor are shunned, positioned as lazy, lacking talent and drive, and in general deserving their low status. As Wendy Williams[23] notes, "poverty is viewed as a moral failing by the public because it indicates that individuals have not worked hard enough." A consequence of believing the poor to be 'undeserving' is opposition to the 'safety net' (such as unemployment insurance, health services for the poor, child support), which is under attack in many major societies. Negative attitudes toward people who are poor have subtle but foundational influences on the poor themselves.

How People Who Are Poor Are Impacted by Stereotypes

The reductionist and misleading 'anyone can make it' value system dominating the United States and some other major societies impacts people who are poor,[24] so that "the stigma of poverty includes the feeling of being viewed as a societal burden, lazy and unmotivated. Such 'welfare stigma' ... can lead to cognitive distancing ... and underperformance ... among the poor, including foregoing important benefits to which they're entitled."[25] Although historically the stigma of poverty has not received enough attention from psychologists,[26] gradually the pervasiveness and significance of this topic is being recognized by more researchers.[27]

Perhaps the most devastating impact of the stigma of poverty is on 'capacity to aspire' among people who are poor.[28] Received wisdom tells us that people who are poor remain poor in part because they fail to have high enough aspirations, which stunts their motivation to strive for higher goals. Research shows that the negative consequence of low aspirations is far more serious for people who are poor, because they remain poor – whereas affluent individuals with low aspirations benefit from a support system, which includes both material and social networking support, to keep them in a comfortable situation.[29]

A very useful framework for better understanding low aspirations and other psychological characteristics of people who are poor is the research pioneered by Claud Steele,[30] on *stereotypes,* inaccurate and exaggerated generalizations about groups, and *stereotype threat,* the feeling of threat group members experience, that in a given situation they may behave in a way that confirms the negative stereotype about their group. Stereotype threat research proposes that widely known and collectively shared group stereotypes have insidious and often undetected impacts on the behavior of individual group members. According to this perspective, for example, in the academic test setting, including in schools and universities, anxiety and threat would be raised by the gender stereotype suggesting that women have lower ability in mathematics than men and by the racial stereotype suggesting that African Americans are less intelligent than White Americans. The more important and 'high stakes' the test setting, the greater the anxiety, threat, and impaired performance experienced by individual group members under the cloud of a particular stereotype.

In tightly controlled experiments, the subtle impact of stereotypes has been demonstrated on African Americans,[31] women,[32] and even White males.[33] The common procedure of these experiments has been to test the performance of the members of minority and majority groups, on topics such as mathematics, under varying levels of stereotype threat, manipulated in a number of ways. For example, stereotype threat level has been manipulated in tests by either mentioning that the test measures mathematical ability or presenting the test as not measuring individual differences in ability. African Americans and women scored lower on tests when they were told that the tests measure an ability, such as in mathematics, relevant to the common stereotype about their group.

These stereotype threat studies are even more impressive because the African Americans and women participants were selected to have high abilities in the test topic. This shows, for example, that even women high on mathematical ability scored lower when stereotype threat was high in a math test context. The power of stereotype threat was also demonstrated when White males scored lower on math tests in a test condition where a comparison was invoked with Asians (stereotyped to have exceptionally high math ability). Thus, although White males are generally conceived as being an advantaged group, stereotype threat led them to score lower in mathematics in a test setting where the comparison with Asians was invoked.

The concept of stereotype threat has also been extended to social class.[34] The point of departure for this research is the puzzle of why one of the best predictors of the educational achievement of children is the socioeconomic status of parents[35]. A host of different factors have been examined as possible causes. For example, there is evidence that genetic factors play some part in the relationship between parental socioeconomic status and children's educational achievement (also, see Chapter 3 of this book).[36] However, genetic and environmental factors interact, and the influence of genetic factors tends to be manifested through context. In addition to genetic factors, some other explanations have been put forward for lower educational achievement among the poor, such as a lack of ability to pay for education programs, inadequate nutrition and health among poor children, and cultural differences between social classes leading to lower motivation among the poor to do well in education. In addition to these factors, stereotype threat represents another possible explanation for the lower performance of poor children in education. The possible role of stereotype threat in education begins with the treatment of, and expectations from, people who are poor in education contexts. Even in schools, there tend to be subtle differences in the treatment of children who are poor compared to relatively affluent children by teachers and others.[37] Children who are poor are treated less favorably in schools and tend to have a lower level of information and social skills passed on to them from their parents, family members, neighbors, and social connections generally regarding 'how to get on' in school.[38]

The parents and family of more affluent children are not only better educated but also better informed about education and how to make progress in school. 'Test-taking' is part of the family culture of the middle and upper class es, whereas people who are poor are less familiar with schooling, test-taking, and educational advancement. In this sense, the school setting, particularly the educational examination setting, is more of a threat to children who are poor, just as stereotypes of people who are poor are more negative. In support of this perspective, Jean-Claude Croizet and Theresa Claire found that children who are poor scored lower than children from a relatively affluent background in a test when it was described as a measure of verbal intellectual ability, but children from poor and relatively affluent backgrounds scored the same when the test was *not* presented as a test of ability.[39]

A major reason for children from poor backgrounds experiencing stereotype threat in educational contexts has to do with what children from more affluent backgrounds have in terms of cultural familiarity, appropriate social skills, and role models. Children from more affluent backgrounds have family members, family friends, and neighbors who have successfully completed university degrees and are successful professionals. They include school teachers and school principals, university professors, researchers, and university administrators, as well as other professionals in the education sector. These children grow up knowing that it is normal for their family members to succeed at schools and universities. They learn to view educational progress as part of what routinely happens in everyday life. These children from more affluent backgrounds will know family members who have multiple university degrees, some from highly competitive universities. As they grow up, the talk at the dinner table is about cousins, older siblings, and children of family friends preparing for and succeeding in university entrance exams. They soak up the social skills needed for educational success and the role models surrounding them point to high educational aspirations. These are all absent in the lives of lower-class children.

For most lower-class children, universities and other educational institutions represent unfamiliar, threatening contexts. The teachers, principals, counselors, professors, deans, and other professionals who work in educational institutions are from outside the circles of their families, friends, and neighborhoods. Like the police, lawyers, and judges the poor encounter in the justice system, these are people who have power over them, set the rules they live by, and punish them when 'deemed necessary.' But they are not from their group; they are part of the world of children from more affluent backgrounds, who are at ease socializing with university-educated professionals and who fully expect to graduate from universities themselves.

It is important to point out that greater access to elite universities by African Americans and other minorities does not necessarily solve the problems of the poor in education. First, as William Bowen and Derek Bok showed in their groundbreaking work *The Shape of the River*,[40] most African American students at elite universities are themselves from an affluent background. These affluent students do not experience the culture shock that hits poor White, Black, and Hispanic students when they enter elite universities. Second, as Anthony Abraham Jack has argued in *The Privileged Poor* (minorities from a financially disadvantaged background who are given the opportunity of attending elite universities), "Access alone is not enough for fostering inclusion and generating mobility."[41] The privileged poor in elite universities live a dual reality: On the one hand they are learning the rules for life among the privileged class, but on the other hand they "still know what it feels like and what to do when the eviction notice gets taped to the front door or when the sound of gunshots precedes the spray of bullets."[42] Students from poor families have been shown to face similar challenges in other countries.[43] This is not just an 'American problem' but one faced by lower-class children around the world.

Poverty, Cognitive Performance, and Decision-Making

Poverty impacts the cognitive performance and decision-making of people who are poor both indirectly and directly. Indirectly, the impact of poverty on cognitive performance and decision-making is through the shaping of the larger context in which cognition takes place, such as the characteristics of the family. More directly, poverty impacts cognitive performance and decision-making through the very important role the scarcity of money plays in cognition among the poor.

Indirect Impact of Poverty on Cognition and Decision-Making

[C]ontext is prioritized for lower-class individuals. Disposed to relative resource scarcity and diminished rank, lower-class contexts expose individuals to increased external social influences on the material conditions of their lives – less safe neighborhoods, threats of job instability, resource fluctuations in schools – that constrain their actions and limit their social opportunities.[44]

Michael Kraus and colleagues, quoted above, have identified ways in which the poor are constrained by the strong contexts in which they live. Relative to more affluent people, the poor lack power, connections, and influence and are to a greater degree impacted by contextual forces they have little or no control over. The outcome is that the poor have a reduced sense of personal control and are less inclined to invoke individual agency to explain events.[45] This is in line with research showing that individuals who report being of a higher social class also have a higher sense of control in different domains of their lives.[46] This relationship is to a degree circular, so that poverty tends to lead to a lower tendency to prioritize personal agency, which in turn tends to prevent individuals from climbing out of poverty. This circular route matters, because it can result in a 'poverty trap' from which individuals find it extremely difficult to escape.

A powerful indirect impact of poverty on cognitive performance is through food insecurity. This impact comes about through a number of paths. In families experiencing food insecurity, parents are more likely to suffer depression, stress, and irritability and as a result be less responsive to the needs of children. Inadequate nutritional intake is likely to result in children being less alert, less attentive, and more distracted. Being thirsty and hungry leads us to be more attentive to cues related to drink and food.[47] In addition, when a family has to concentrate their monetary resources on trying to buy enough food, educational equipment and services become a low priority. In 2016 about 22 percent of adults in the world suffered severe or moderate food insecurity, the breakdown of food insecurity in regions being: 56.03 percent in Africa, 18.74 percent in the Americas, 8.09 percent in Europe, and 18.79 percent in Asia.[48] Almost 16 million US households

(12.3 percent of the total) experienced food insecurity in 2016. Poorer students on US campuses also suffer high levels of food insecurity.[49]

Food insecurity is more likely to lead to harsh negative consequences for families with young children.[50] These families are less experienced with parenting and their children, being younger, are more vulnerable in the face of stress and disruptions generally. Research has shown food insecure families with preschool children to be characterized by more severe parental physical and mental health problems, as well as greater conflict. Not surprisingly, when families do not have enough to eat, the parents are more likely to become irritable and aggressive and to have arguments and fight.[51] This has a negative impact on young children in particular. In one study of children at nine months, two years, and preschool, food insecurity resulted in unfavorable socioemotional skills (and hyperactivity problems in particular), as well as lower readiness for reading and math learning, in kindergarten[52].

Direct Impact of Poverty on Cognition and Decision-Making

> [P]overty may favor behaviors that make it more difficult to escape poverty.[53]

The poor often engage in behaviors that perpetuate poverty. For example, the poor fail to take advantage of programs that could benefit them[54] and borrow money under conditions, such as very high interest rates, that are not to their advantage.[55] The causal-reductionist approach of mainstream psychology leads us to interpret such behaviors as arising from intrapersonal characteristics, with explanations such as 'the poor make wrong decisions because they are not so smart.' But an alternative explanation for such behavior is the indirect influence of poverty, such as through food insecurity as discussed above. An alternative explanation particularly influenced by the research of Sendhil Mullainathan and Eldar Shafir is through the direct impact of poverty on cognitive style.[56] From this perspective, having too little money directly and persistently shapes how we think and act – often for the worse.

In a series of experiments, poor and relatively affluent participants were presented with different scenarios involving monetary expenses, then asked to carry out computer-based tasks that measure cognitive function.[57] For example, one scenario involved car repairs that required low or high payments. Results show that poor participants, but not affluent ones, did less well on cognitive tasks when they had thought about a car repair scenario involving high costs. In a very creative field study that tested the same idea, sugarcane farmers in villages in Tamil Nadu, India, were given cognitive tasks before and after the sugarcane harvest. Before the harvest, these farmers typically face financial pressures, but they have more money after the harvest and face lower financial pressures. Results show that the farmers performed better on cognitive tasks after the harvest, when they had more money.

Not having enough money to pay the rent at the end of the month, or the electricity bill, or the car repair bill, or gas for the car, intrudes into and dominates everyday thinking. A lack of money and the immediate demands of costs that have to be covered mean that attention is not given to issues that are often even more important in the long term but can be avoided for now – such as saving money and investing in education and health. Going to the dentist and getting treatment for a cavity is put off because it can be, while money is borrowed from a payday lender at an exorbitant interest rate (sometimes well above 200 percent).

There is strong empirical evidence showing how scarcity, having too little, directly and detrimentally influences how people problem-solve – that is, how context shapes cognition. In a series of controlled experiments, research participants were randomly assigned to be 'poor' or 'rich,' with respectively smaller and larger budgets distributed to them as 'paychecks' across the different rounds of a game (e.g., they played *Family Feud*).[58] Participants used their paychecks to earn points in the different rounds; any resources that were unspent at the end of a round could be treated as 'savings,' moved forward, and used in the next game. Under some conditions, participants could also borrow when they had nothing left from their paychecks. Several experiments involved scarcity of time rather than money, so that the poor participants had less time than rich participants to make their decisions. Scarcity of both monetary and time budgets resulted in less optimal decisions. Poor participants were more depleted of energy by the tasks, engaged in more counterproductive borrowing (they actually performed better when they could not borrow), and focused more on the present and neglected the future. This is in line with research demonstrating that individuals are less effective decision-makers when they are under a larger cognitive load. For example, when individuals are busy on a harder memorization task (e.g., having to remember seven digits instead of one), they are less effective at completing arithmetic tasks, less risk-taking (thus losing opportunities to gain), and more impatient for money.[59]

But it can also be argued that scarcity does not just bring a higher cognitive load, it also brings some (so-called) benefits to poor people. For example, there is some evidence that the poor are better at remembering prices, noticing hidden taxes, and making better use of scarce resources.[60] However, surely most, if not all, poor people would forgo these 'benefits' of being poor and be ready to give up such 'advantages' in order to reap the benefits of more affluent life conditions.

A Contextual Explanation of Cognition, Decision-Making, and Poverty

When researching the goals and aspirations of lower-class parents with young children, it is essential that we consider the wider context of their behavior. Sometimes these parents express a hope that their children will become medical doctors or lawyers. The same parents often verbally report that education is extremely important for the future of their children. However, what lower-class parents often lack is a behavioral style, social and knowledge skills, and basic advice and know-how that match these middle-class values. For example, they are not able to provide their children with educational opportunities, such as after-school enrichment classes, summer educational programs, computers and books, and other educational equipment, or even a quiet, undisturbed place for their child to do schoolwork at home.

The economic conditions of the lower-class limit and shape their behaviors, often leading to a gap between their espoused values and goals and their actual behavior. To take the example of education for the young, on the one hand, lack of money means that the poor are not able to provide the material conditions (e.g., private space to do homework) and tools (e.g., personal computer for each child, after-school tutors) necessary for their children to compete on a level playing field with children from more affluent families. On the other hand, poverty and low education mean that parents do not have the social connections, skills, know-how, or the professional training and experience necessary to guide their children through the competitive educational system.

Of course, a small number of children from lower-class families who have extraordinarily high intelligence and talent do succeed despite the odds against them, and these few 'tokens' serve to validate the (unfair) system: 'See, she comes from a poor background and made it to a top university. Anyone can make it if they try hard enough and have the talent!' These token students find themselves in classes with token professors.[61] While Black, Latinx, and Native American students make up 52 percent of all students in postsecondary education, only 11 percent of full-time faculty are from these ethnic groups.[62] But, while there is at least some debate around the question of why there are so few ethnic minority faculty in higher education, almost no attention is given to the question of why there are so few tenure-track faculty in higher education from an economically deprived background. Rather than discussing poverty and class-based inequalities, focus is placed in a so-called 'culture of poverty,' thus distracting from economic inequalities.

The distinction between rhetoric and action, the values people express and their actual behavior, is highly important when we consider heated controversies[63] around the concept of 'a culture of poverty.' This concept stems from the seminal contribution of Oscar Lewis to our understanding of the thoughts and actions of the poor.[64] Lewis conducted research on poor families in Latin America and reported that as a result of their difficult life conditions, the poor develop counterproductive, dysfunctional behaviors that are part of a so-called 'culture of poverty.' For example, the poor fail to make long-term investments and act impulsively for short-term gratification. Through the influence of Daniel Patrick Moynihan (1927–2003) and others in President Johnson's administration (1963–1969), the concept of a culture of poverty was extensively applied to explain the plight of African Americans and other deprived minorities in the United States. Moynihan's perspective, reflected in the following quote, ignited considerable controversy: "[A] community that allows a large number of men to grow up in broken families, dominated by women, never acquiring any stable relationship to male authority, never acquiring any set of rational expectations about the future – that community asks for and gets chaos. Crime, violence, unrest, disorder – most particularly the furious, unrestrained lashing out at the whole social structure – that is not only to be expected; it is very near to inevitable. And it is richly deserved."[65]

The 'culture of poverty' concept faces severe criticism from those who argue that this is yet another example of 'blame the victim,' wherein the poor are now blamed for their own plight.[66] But an alternative and perhaps more fatal shortcoming of the culture of poverty explanation is that it does not distinguish between values and actions.[67]

The expressed attitudes and values of individuals often do not match their actions, in part because their material conditions do not allow them to act in accordance with their expressed attitudes and values. For example, a study of attitudes related to pregnancy among 961 young Black and White young women showed an unexpected pattern of differences.[68] On the one hand, young Black women had less positive attitudes toward nonmarital sex, sex without contraception, and nonmarital child bearing; they also expressed less desire for sex over the next year. But there was a difference between attitudes and expectations. Young Black women were more likely to expect sex without contraception, and they expected more positive outcomes if they became pregnant out of wedlock. In line with expectations, nonmarital fertility rates among unmarried Black women are higher than among unmarried White women.[69] This is another reminder of the criticism that the 'culture of poverty' thesis does not distinguish between attitudes and values on the one hand and actions on the other hand.

As Kecia Johnson and Karyn Loscocco argue, "it is common, even among Black leaders, to see the solution to 'marriage problems' as a question of adapting to White middle-class norms."[70] But adapting to White middle-class norms is extremely difficult for the poor, because they do not have the material benefits of the White middle class. Poor individuals are often able to accurately identify and express the attitudes and values that are 'correct' according to White middle-class norms, but their material conditions do not allow them to live out these attitudes and values – even if they want to. Poor White, Black, and Hispanic parents can express attitudes and values supportive of their children becoming medical doctors, lawyers, and engineers, but in practice a lack of resources (material and nonmaterial) prevent them from taking the necessary action in order to fulfill such expressed attitudes and values.

Thus, in order to explain the expressed attitudes and actual actions of individuals, we need to consider the larger context. This context includes the resources and capabilities individuals have (or lack) for realizing their expressed attitudes and goals. Critics will contend that I have exaggerated the impact of context, treated poverty as deterministic, and neglected the role of individual and collective resilience.[71] In response, I point out that while a small group of individuals do break out of poverty and move up the status hierarchy, these exceptional 'token' individuals should not blind us to the injustice of the enormous and growing group-based inequalities that characterize major twenty-first-century societies.

Concluding Comment

[P]roblems due to impoverished experiences and environments arise in very early childhood, even in utero. The biological embedding of adversity occurs early in development, and a failure to promote emotional and cognitive progress in infancy can lead to lifelong deficits in cognitive and emotional capacity ... Simply moving to a better neighborhood has a significant impact on children's long-term chances of success, increasing their college attendance and earnings.

Eldar Shafir[72]

Despite the need for more research on the psychology of poverty, and despite poverty being a neglected topic in the glossy texts used to introduce psychology to millions of students around the world, the existing evidence clearly demonstrates the powerful impact of poverty on human cognition and decision-making. Poverty establishes an extremely strong context, shaping the behavior of individuals from even before birth – right up until death. From the earliest years when children learn what poverty means through practices and words ("No! We don't have the money to buy crayons or pencils or books. You can't have a computer! We have to pay the rent and we need the money for car repairs!"), poverty acts as a huge cognitive load that impairs decision-making. Poor people are forced by their powerlessness to waste more of their time waiting for basic services and doing nothing but wait in line,[73] another way in which their lives are different and deserve special attention. Poverty and social class must become a *central* topic of research in psychological science and a major theme in introductory psychology courses and the glossy texts used to introduce psychology to new students.

CHAPTER 3

Mis-measuring Intelligence and Justifying Educational Inequalities

Through intelligence testing, the causal-reductionist model of mainstream psychology has had the seldom-acknowledged political consequence of supporting the idea that the lower class and the ruling upper class are born to be where they are, at the bottom and at the top rungs of society. In line with this is the causal-reductionist claim that intelligence is for the most part causally determined by inborn factors and that intelligence tests are objective measures of intelligence independent of culture and the background of test-takers. The wider implications of these assertions have also been developed by some researchers at different times since the nineteenth century.[1] For example, one such (wrong-headed!) implication is that some kind of selection policy needs to be implemented (through immigration restrictions, sterilization campaigns, and other means) to protect against the decline of intelligence in 'our group.' In the twenty-first-century age of populist authoritarianism and strongman leadership,[2] this ethnocentric and racist message is once again gaining support among some politicians and their extremist supporters – a dark reminder of events in the 1930s when ideas about groups with superior inborn intelligence and the 'need' for selective breeding were advocated and put into practice, resulting in genocide.

Mirroring the contents of the standard introductory psychology textbooks, I dedicate an entire chapter to intelligence, which has a complex, expansive, and controversial place in the history of psychology and continues to have a largely detrimental influence in areas such as education and immigration. I provide an alternative introductory account of intelligence, pointing out the implications of the causal-reductionist model for intelligence research. Far from achieving 'neutral' and 'objective' measures, psychological research on intelligence has been biased by political motivations, including those of some leading researchers themselves.

This does not mean that all research on intelligence and its hereditary roots is politically biased or that research on the biological basis of intelligence should not be supported. Of course, intelligence is shaped through an interaction of hereditary and environmental factors. But genetic factors achieve their influence through contextual characteristics. What we have learned from the science of *epigenetics* is that genes are not just possessed or absent but also turned 'on' and 'off' by biochemical signals and environmental conditions broadly. Consequently, individuals may (or may not) possess favorable genes that are activated, or not activated and remain dormant. Environmental conditions such as food insecurity and stress, particularly during the early years of development (including in the womb), will have long-term consequences for individuals by impacting genetic activation patterns. Genes are dependent on context and the old 'nature vs. nurture' debate is a fallacy because the two are interdependent and best envisaged as one.[3] As leading researchers in epigenetics have proposed, it is simply incorrect to argue that a certain percentage of intelligence is predetermined by genes because the environment plays an important and complex role in gene expression, so that development becomes *probabilistic*.[4]

Intelligence Testing in Societal and Historical Context

Each year, the profile report issues by the College Board systematically reveals that Scholastic Assessment Test (SAT) scores are strongly related to parental income … The very rich get the best scores, the very poor the lowest.

Jean-Claude Croizet and Mathias Millet[5]

Intelligence is one of the most controversial and challenging research topics in the history of psychology. This becomes clear when we consider how we should interpret the relationship between three important variables: scores on intelligence tests as indicated by the Intelligence Quotient (IQ), scores on the Scholastic Assessment Test (SAT) still used by many competitive universities to select students, and socioeconomic status (SES) – mainly based on parental income. There is strong evidence that scores on IQ and SAT tests are highly correlated.[6] SAT scores and SES are also highly correlated: In 2009, each 10–70 point increase in SAT scores corresponded to $20,000 additional parental income.[7] This trend is in line with who gains entrance to selective universities: Only about 3 percent of students getting into the most selective 146 colleges come from the economically disadvantaged.[8] Since the time of Alfred Binet (1857–1911), the French pioneer in intelligence test construction, it has been known that more affluent people score higher on intelligence tests than the poor.[9] Consequently, there is general agreement that IQ, SAT, and SES are interrelated. The challenge and controversy are about how these relationships can best be explained and acted on.

Particularly from the perspective of people who are poor, it makes an enormous difference how we explain the relationships between IQ, SAT, and SES. This is because different interpretations of these relationships have widely different policy implications for how we do or do not help poor people. For example, if we believe the claim that IQ is largely inherited and is the main determinant of SAT and SES, then the implication is that certain individuals are biologically born to enter into the best universities and to enjoy high social class (SES) but also that certain other individuals are biologically excluded from elite universities and doomed to remain lower class.

In the early twenty-first century there has been a surge of overly simplistic research arguing that IQ is largely inherited,[10] as well as that IQ is the key determinant of both SES and SAT:[11] that our genetic makeup shapes our intelligence and this in turn determines performance both on the SAT test and in the competition to climb up the ladder of success in the larger society.[12] From this perspective, lower-class people are in their 'inferior' position basically because they were 'born that way.' The dominant role of inherited factors implies that lower-class people are *not* going to be helped in significant ways by social programming, such as *Head Start* and other similar programs designed to enrich the environment. A long line of researchers, from Francis Galton (1822–1911), Cyril Burt (1883–1971), Arthur Jensen (1923–2012), and Philippe Rushton (1943–2012) to contemporary researchers such as Richard Herrnstein, Charles Murray, and Robert Plomin, have interpreted intelligence as largely inherited.

But some twenty-first-century researchers on the 'heredity side,' such as Plomin, tend to be more sensitive to the controversies surrounding intelligence testing and the political implications of hereditary interpretations of individual differences on intelligence.[13] For example, on the one hand Plomin writes that "Both education and social class are substantially correlated with intelligence,"[14] and he sees the root 'cause' of these associations to be inherited factors. He also argues that "Life is an intelligence test,"[15] and the reason why some individuals do better than others in education, at work, and at climbing up the social class ladder is because they are more intelligent and intelligence is largely genetic (the gene is treated as if it operates in a vacuum, an issue I return to later in this chapter). On the other hand Plomin acknowledges that findings from research on heredity and intelligence have been used to implement policies highly detrimental to minorities, including forced sterilization, but he argues that scientists should not be blamed for the misuse of what he sees to be 'objective science.' His basic message is: 'I am a scientist. I only deal with the objective facts. Don't blame me for the policies others develop on the basis of my research findings.'

It is vitally important to understand the positioning attempted by Plomin and others, giving priority to the genetic basis of intelligence: First, they are trying to position their research as politically neutral and objective, as 'science in search of the truth.' Second, they are positioning IQ and SAT tests as objective and neutral. Similarly, they attempt to position the education system as objective and neutral – and by extension the social class system, which they claim to be open, competitive, and shaped by intelligence. Indeed, in their famous book *The Bell Curve: Intelligence and Class Structure in American Life*, Richard Herrnstein and Charles Murray argue that American society is becoming a meritocracy based on inherited intelligence, "with the underclass mired ever firmly at the bottom and the cognitive elite ever more firmly anchored at the top."[16] From the perspective of these researchers, society is open and meritocratic, with intelligence (as measured by IQ/SAT) being largely inherited and determinant of where in the social hierarchy individuals are located.

But there also thrives an alternative perspective based on an alternative scientific research tradition, positioning the standard IQ tests and the SAT as highly biased in favor of the rich. Researchers in this scientific tradition strongly reject the claim that society is open and meritocratic and that success in university entrance exams is based on inherited IQ. For example, Robert Sternberg, a leader in research on intelligence, sums up the university testing system in this way: "The system of selective college admissions, for the most part, is based on tests geared to favor US middle- and upper-middle class students, not students of the working class, or of different cultures, who may not have had comparable opportunities."[17] In an extensive report subtitled "How Higher Education Reinforces the Intergenerational Reproduction of White Racial Privilege," Anthony Carnevale and Jeff Strohl identify parental education as "the strongest predictor of a child's educational attainment and future earnings."[18]

Rather than look inside individuals for biological or other differences, this alternative scientific tradition looks *outside* individuals to the role of social, cultural, and political structures in re-producing social class and other group-based inequalities.[19] The predominance of young people from higher SES backgrounds in higher education, and particularly at the most prestigious universities, is explained not by reference to biological differences but by the enormous advantages provided by their affluent parents. Among higher-class families, attending an elite university is part of the inheritance passed on to the next generation; it is part of 'who we are.' The role of elite universities in family tradition and identity construction is well known and reflected in the wider culture; in F. Scott Fitzgerald's novel *The Great Gatsby*, this is how Gatsby constructs his identity: "I am the son of some wealthy people in the Middle West – all dead now. I was brought up in America but educated at Oxford, because all my ancestors have been educated there for many years. It is a family tradition."[20] In fabricating his identity, Gatsby is using the norms of the wider culture and signaling his elite status by referencing his 'family tradition' of being educated at Oxford. In contrast to this, the identities and traditions of working-class youth exclude them from going on to higher education – that is part of 'who they are.'

In the rest of this chapter, I discuss three major themes in intelligence research: (1) the claim that intelligence is being measured independent of culture, (2) the measurement of intelligence through biological markers, and (3) the twins method as a faulty 'gold standard' in research. Then, I critically assess the invalid 'intelligence is declining' claim. This claim has important policy implications, because it has been used to justify restricting immigration from certain parts of the world, as well as to control reproduction by certain ethnic/racial groups. In the final major section of this chapter, I critically reexamine intelligence in societal context.

Major Themes in Research on Intelligence

The major themes of twenty-first-century research on intelligence can be traced back to the pioneering studies of Galton, which took place in the causal-reductionist tradition. These themes include: attempts to develop tests of intelligence independent of culture, the measurement of intelligence through biological markers, and the use of the 'twins method' to distinguish between the contributions of nature and nurture in shaping intelligence. There is another theme lurking in the background, only sometimes explicit but always continuous from the time of Galton to the present: the assumption of biological superiority of certain people, so they are 'naturally' more intelligent and 'born to rule.'

Galton was the first to develop the concept of *eugenics*, the selective breeding of humans toward a 'better' human stock. The idea of 'selective breeding' became influential in the United States and some European countries, as reflected particularly in Nazi ideology and practices.

Unfortunately, in some respects we have returned to the same theme in the twenty-first century, with authoritarian leadership, extremist nationalism, and 'racial supremacy' emerging as major themes in politics (in Western societies, 'racial supremacy' equates with white supremacy, whereas in Narendra Modi's India it equates with Hindu supremacy,[21] and thus the espoused 'superior group' varies across societies). These authoritarian movements have historically equated nationhood with 'racial purity.' This is reflected in the idea that the United States is a 'White nation,'[22] as well as in President Trump's preference to have immigrants from Norway over 'shithole' countries.[23]

The Claim That Intelligence Is Measured Independent of Culture

Throughout the history of modern psychology, it has been assumed that intelligence tests measure intelligence independent of the personal background and experiences of the individual being tested. For example, if teenager 'A' has grown up homeless on the streets of Mumbai and never attended school and teenager 'B' has grown up in a highly affluent family in New York and attended elite schools, it has been assumed that intelligence tests assess their intelligence independent of their backgrounds. This assumption has held constant, even though the nature of the tests has changed.

In 1880 Galton became the first Western researcher to try to measure intelligence under standard conditions (the Chinese had attempted to measure intelligence under standardized conditions to develop efficient administrative systems from about 1300 years ago[24]). Galton believed that intelligence is largely inherited and reflected in sensory capacity, such as reaction time. By the end of the nineteenth century Galton's focus on physical measurements had been pushed aside and overtaken by the ideas of Binet, who measured intelligence through a focus on higher cognitive capacities, such as problem-solving and memory. For most of the twentieth century, it was Binet's influence that shaped intelligence testing, but as I explain later in this chapter, in the twenty-first century the Galtonian tradition of focusing on physical measurements has returned.

Binet established a tradition of intelligence tests being extremely similar to the kinds of tests children encounter in mainstream schools. This is not surprising, when we consider that Binet became involved in intelligence test construction in 1904 after accepting an invitation to help better identify 'subnormal children' in French public schools. Through collaboration with Theodore Simon (1873–1961), in 1905 Binet developed a test with questions that increased in difficulty with the age of the child. Examples of questions for each age are: age four, copy a square; age five, name basic colors; age six, count thirteen pennies; age seven, repeat five digits; age eight, count backwards from twenty to one. Binet's intelligence test was adapted for the United States population and became the Stanford–Binet intelligence test in 1917. In this way, the tradition continued of intelligence tests being closely associated with academic work and tests in schools. Clearly, those who experienced a certain kind of education would enjoy an advantage when taking the Stanford–Binet and other similar intelligence tests.

One of Binet's most important innovations was to establish performance norms for each age group. This required distinguishing between chronological age and mental age; a child's chronological age could differ from her or his mental age. For example, consider eight-year-old Sara who performs on Binet's test as well as the average ten-year-old. This means that the Sara has a chronological age of eight but a mental age of ten. The IQ, introduced by William Stern (1871–1938), is computed by dividing mental age by chronological age and multiplying by 100 (in this case, Sara's IQ is 10 divided by 8, multiplied by 100 = 125. Since IQ is standardized to have a mean of 100, Sara's IQ is 25 above the mean).

The growth of the intelligence testing industry was greatly influenced by the First (1914–1918) and Second (1939–1945) World Wars. Millions of recruits, some of them illiterate, had to be assigned quickly to different types of work toward the war effort. There was a need for tests that could rapidly assess the intelligence of large groups of recruits. During the First World War two intelligence tests, the Army Alpha and the Army Beta, were developed for use with literate and illiterate recruits respectively and were administered to about 1.7 million individuals. This opened the way at the end of the war (1918) for the development of a variety of intelligence tests and their extensive use in the military, in education, and also in industry.[25] This also opened the way for the results of mass-administered intelligence tests to influence government policies, such as the 1924 Immigration Act. This act restricted immigration from certain parts of the world (e.g., China) on the grounds that the intelligence level of the American population would decline if people from 'low intelligence populations' are allowed to enter the country.[26] This claim was (and is) bogus, racist, and politically motivated: The 'lower score' of Chinese and other immigrant groups was because of lack of appropriate educational training and language proficiency (of course, racist policies were also influenced by factors beyond intelligence, such as economics and group identities). Social norms have changed and, ironically, the same Asian groups are being stereotyped as 'superior' (particularly in quantitative skills) in the twenty-first century.

The Measurement of Intelligence through Biological Markers

Evolutionary theory as developed by Charles Darwin (1809–1882) has had a profound influence on both scientific research and the larger world, but there have been different interpretations of what its implications are for topics such as intelligence. For example, it could be argued that from an evolutionary perspective intelligence must be considered in relation to environmental conditions, because the intelligence of organisms (including different groups of humans) is reflected in how successfully they adapt and function in their different ecological conditions. However, Galton adopted a very different perspective, preferring to believe that Darwin's theory of evolution implies that intelligence must be inherited. In other words, Galton ignored the important role given to context in Darwin's theory of evolution. He attempted to demonstrate the inherited nature of intelligence through his research, which included measures of perception, audition (sense of hearing), sensitivity to touch, reaction time, and various other physical characteristics, used as indicators of intelligence.

Galton had considerable influence through his research project entitled *Hereditary Genius* (1869),[27] despite this research being deeply flawed.[28] Galton was a gifted innovator in correlational methods and he computed that eminent people in England were related to one another at a rate above chance. He jumped to the conclusion that this correlation means intelligence is inherited. Of course, it could also mean that eminent people benefit from the same upper-class family upbringing, and they share and pass on their environmental advantages within and across generations. Central to Galton's idea that 'eminent people' inherit high intelligence is the assumption that eminent people share certain physical characteristics, such as large head size.

The Galtonian tradition of searching for biological markers of intelligence continues strongly in the twenty-first century. We can usefully conceptualize twenty-first-century research on the neurobiology of intelligence in two categories, concerning studies that attempt to, first, pinpoint genetic sources of intelligence and, second, identify brain neural networks and brain volume associated with intelligence.

With respect to the first type of study, some progress is being made particularly through the use of larger samples in genome-wide association studies (GWAS) to better identify genes that seem to be associated with intelligence.[29] For example, recent studies have involved samples of over 100,000 individuals.[30] Interestingly, although the influence of hereditary factors seem to change over the course of life, there is stability in some of the same genes that are associated with intelligence.[31] However, the general consensus is that, although associations are indicated, no single gene or even small group of genes is identified as determining intelligence.[32] Thousands of genes and hundreds of loci have been implicated,[33] and this is probably a fraction of those actually involved. Leading researchers summarize the situation in this way: "[I]ntelligence is a highly polygenetic trait where many different genes would exert extremely small, if any, influence, most probably at different stages of development."[34]

Research on brain areas and brain volume associated with intelligence was initiated in the nineteenth century, particularly in France, Britain, and Russia.[35] The tradition continues today of examining the brains of eminent individuals, such as Vladimir Lenin (1870–1924), in search of what makes them 'gifted.' For example, after his death a study was made of Albert Einstein's (1879–1955) brain, showing his parietal lobe to be different from a comparison group with normal intelligence.[36] Of course, to demonstrate that a special characteristic of Einstein's brain is causally determining his genius, we would also need to account for the numerous other individuals who have the *same brain characteristic as Einstein but do not produce* the theory of relativity, or anything close to it. However, there is evidence that brain volume and cortical thickness are positively associated with intelligence (this is also true for chimpanzees[37]). There is also evidence that particular types of brain neural network efficiency are associated with higher intelligence.[38] Focusing on brain network efficiency seems to be a fruitful path, as research suggests general intelligence cannot be attributed to one specific brain region.[39]

Fortunately, there is now a trend to avoid simplistic interpretations of genetic research, in the context of the 'epigenetic turn,' which means adopting a relational and contextual concept of gene. Research is starting to show more details of how adverse life experiences, such as poverty, can modify gene expression,[40] as well as how heritable variations can arise purely from environmental effects, without mutations in DNA sequences playing a role.[41] Hector González-Pardo and Marino Pérez-Álvarez argue that an important implication of epigenetics for psychology is that "the hereditary percentages attributed to genes and environment, as in the case of intelligence quotient … are no longer valid."[42] Genes and environment are meshed into one; it is invalid and misleading to discuss their influence separately – as has been attempted through twins research.

The Twins Method As a Faulty 'Gold Standard'

Galton was the first researcher to systematically study twins with the intention of proving the inherited nature of intelligence. His research was undertaken before the basic principles of genetics became known through the discoveries of Gregor Mendel (1822–1884)[43]. However, Galton's research led him to conclude that identical twins are more similar to one another than fraternal twins in both mental and physical characteristics, even when they live apart. He concluded this must be because of their greater biological similarities. After Galton, a long line of researchers has taken up the mantle of 'genetic determinism and intelligence,' determined to prove that intelligence is basically inherited. In some cases, their political goals have led them to manufacture false data to try to make their case. For example, the 'eminent' British psychologist Sir Cyril Burt (1883–1971) supposedly amassed a large data set using twins, 'demonstrating' that intelligence is largely inherited. But much of Burt's data was fabricated.[44] The Cyril Burt case underlines the controversial and political nature of intelligence as a research topic.[45]

However, it is essential that we keep separate the controversies associated with research on biology and intelligence (heightened by issues surrounding eugenics, Nazi and neo-Nazi movements, and modern race-based extremist ideologies) from the twins method as a tool in research. How objective is this tool? Twenty-first-century research includes large samples of monozygotic (genetically identical) and dizygotic (genetically different) twins. It is assumed the twins method is the 'gold standard' for distinguishing the contributions of hereditary and environmental factors in human behavior. A close examination of the twins method shows it to be far from perfect (related to this, I later reexamine the tradition of 'nature vs. nurture' debates).

Researchers in support of a hereditarian argument point out that monozygotic twins reared together resemble each other on various characteristics (such as intelligence) more than do dizygotic twins reared together. They argue this similarity arises because of the greater genetic similarity of monozygotic twins. This conclusion assumes that reared-together monozygotic and dizygotic twin pairs experience equal environments: an assumption that has been strongly contested.[46] Critics have argued that monozygotic twins live in environments that are much more similar than do dizygotic twins because, looking identical, they are treated more alike, expected to behave more alike, and socialized to behave more alike.[47] The more similar environments of monozygotic twins act as a confound in twins studies, making it invalid to assume only a genetic cause for the greater similarity.

We also need to be cautious in interpreting the finding that monozygotic twins reared apart show a high level of similarity. On the surface, it would seem that being reared apart means their environments are different and so their similarities must be caused by genetic factors. However, in key respects (as I explain below) the environments of monozygotic twins reared apart tend to be similar, as shown by the New Zealand psychologist James Flynn through his discussion of the 'multiplier effect.'[48]

Consider the example of monozygotic twins Michael and Clive, separated at birth so they grew up as members of different families in different American cities. Michael and Clive both grew up to be exceptionally tall and fast compared to other children. From childhood, they received elite basketball coaching and a lot of encouragement to excel in basketball from teachers, other students, and of course their families. They were both recruited to play in local basketball teams in their early teens. They both played for their high school basketball teams, where they received the best training available, as well as time and resources to improve in basketball. In other words, at each step the 'inborn' abilities of Michael and Clive were reinforced, supported, and built upon. The environment acted as a *multiplier*, increasing the difference between the twins and other children they grew up with. The initial advantage of being tall and fast was multiplied into a huge advantage by enriched environments. The multiplier effect also operates on children with other initial advantages, such as mathematical or musical abilities.

A critical rethinking of gene–environment interactions is taking place, particularly through epigenetics – the so-called "last nail in the coffin of genetic determinism."[49] The environment of monozygotic twins is very similar, but even small contextual differences lead to differences in gene expression, so that "monozygotic twins ... can have very different morphological and psychological traits, as well as different vulnerability to diseases that arise in their lifetime."[50] Rather than genetic determinism, research on intelligence needs to incorporate lessons from epigenetics and explore the complex but highly important role context plays in gene expression.[51]

The Bogus 'Intelligence Is Declining' Claim

The intersection of intelligence testing and politics has repeatedly culminated in a concern for 'protecting the intelligence of our group,' through either eugenics or immigration policy or some other 'selection' strategy. In his book *Inquiry into Human Faculty and Its Development* (1883), Galton distinguished between positive and negative eugenics. Positive eugenics meant encouraging people with higher intelligence to have more children; negative eugenics meant discouraging those with lower intelligence from having children. By the beginning of the twentieth century, eugenics was a national movement in the United States, Britain, and Germany.[52] In the United States, the first eugenic sterilization law was enacted in Indiana in 1907, and in 1927 such laws were upheld by the US Supreme Court. A *Eugenics Record Office* was established (1910) in Cold Spring Harbor, New York, to collect information and train eugenics field officers. Mass sterilization programs were planned by eugenics leaders in the United States. This was all with the support of eminent US citizens, including John D. Rockefeller, Alexander Graham Bell, and (former president) Theodore Roosevelt. The growth of the eugenics movement in the United States meant that "For all their early success, German eugenicists were becoming worried that their American counterparts were surpassing them."[53]

The horrors of Nazi Germany and the Second World War meant that, for a while at least, eugenics lost respectability. However, this has not ended sterilization programs in different Western and non-Western countries.[54] Nor did the decline of public support for the eugenics movement result in an end to the argument that 'our group needs to be protected against low intelligence others.' Once again, this argument is being driven by advances in genetics research; witness the twenty-first-century mass media discussions about 'designer babies.' There is again popularity in the idea that more intelligent people can have more and 'better' children, in line with Galton's idea of positive eugenics. But Galton's 'negative eugenics' implies that there is also a need to protect the ingroup against mixing with lower intelligent people. Of course, this makes immigration a hot button issue for those concerned with the intelligence genepool. This is how Herrnstein and Murray use contemporary language to argue a point that echoes the Galton creed:

> Putting the pieces together – higher fertility and a faster generational cycle among the less intelligent and an immigrant population that is probably somewhat below the native-born average – the case is strong that something worth worrying about is happening to the cognitive capital of the country.[55]

In the twenty-first century, through populist authoritarian leadership in the United States and around the world, we are once again experiencing the revival of racist language in discussions of immigration policy. This racist language manifests itself in the actions of White terrorist nationalists murdering people in order to prevent the 'invasion from Mexico.' An example is the terrorist attack in El Paso, Texas, August 3, 2019, that killed twenty-one people and seriously injured many others. This racist language also reflects the sentiments of Herrnstein and Murray, arguing that "something worth worrying about is happening to the cognitive capital of the country." Of course, this 'worry' reflects a number of assumptions: including that that there is a decline in population intelligence in countries such as the United States because of too many immigrants from 'low intelligence' countries and the related assumption that tests of intelligence measure intelligence independent of culture and background experiences.

What Is the Flynn Effect and Why Does It Matter?

> When the average person takes the … Wechsler or Stanford-Binet IQ tests, they score at 130 compared to norms set 100 years ago. This puts the average person at that time at 70 against today's norms.
>
> James Flynn[56]

Herrnstein, Murray, and other hereditarians, going all the way back to Galton, need not have worried about the 'intelligence gene pool being weakened.' Despite mass immigration from countries such as Mexico, and despite (supposedly) 'low intelligence' women having more babies than (supposedly) 'high intelligence' women, the data demonstrates that IQ scores have been *rising, not falling*. This substantial and sustained rise in IQ scores, referred to in the quote above, is known as the *Flynn effect. This rapid rise in IQ test scores cannot be explained by genetic changes.*

A number of different environmental factors contribute to the Flynn effect. For example, better nutrition and health are probable contributors to people doing better on intelligence tests. However, the most important contributors are probably the 'testing culture' experienced by recent generations, with younger people getting more and more practice in taking intelligence-type tests. As Western-style education expands around the world, and as a larger number of people become more familiar with mass-testing using intelligence-type tests, IQ scores rise.

Clearly, through private education and personalized educational programs, affluent families give their children a huge competitive advantage in education in general and in taking intelligence-type tests (including the SAT and similar tests). Herrnstein, Murray, and many other hereditarian researchers have made the invalid assumption that the rich score higher on intelligence-type tests, and make up the majority of students in the elite universities, because they have inherited higher intelligence. The correct interpretation is that the rich score higher on intelligence-type tests and dominate the elite universities because they can provide their children, from birth, with the enriched environment and intense, disciplined, expensive training that lead to such success. This correction also leads to a different and more valid conceptualization of intelligence, as discussed below.

Rethinking Intelligence in Societal Context

Although the concept of IQ suggests that intelligence is unitary and captured by one index, from at least the start of the twentieth century Charles Spearman (1863–1945) and others researched different types of intelligence. Spearman proposed the idea that in addition to a general intelligence factor, referred to as 'g,' there are multiple specialized intelligences, referred to as 's's.'[57] I return to this point later in this chapter). Another influential distinction was made by Raymond Cattell (1905–1998) between *fluid intelligence* (gf), the ability to reason and use information, and *crystalized intelligence* (gc), information, skills, and knowledge acquired through education and experiences.[58] The search for multiple intelligences has been pushed forward by Sternberg,[59] Howard Gardner,[60] and others researching practical intelligence, emotional intelligence, Machiavellian intelligence, and cultural intelligence, among other types of intelligences.[61] The idea that there are multiple types of intelligences highlights the role of the context and the question: what kinds of intelligence are nurtured, supported, and encouraged in different people in their different roles?

The example of women and intelligence demonstrates the pivotal role of context. Until the 1960s, "universities set limits to the number of females they would admit. For example, under Stanford's quota system, three males were accepted for every female."[62] In 1965, men were awarded 65 percent of bachelor degrees, but the situation dramatically changed, after legal reforms forced universities to abandon quotas for women.[63] By 2004, women were awarded 58 percent of all bachelor degrees in the United States. Along with this change, conceptions of women's intelligence changed: A century ago the stereotype of women was that they could not cope with higher education challenges, but now women are successfully competing against men in higher education. In areas such as mathematics, however, research is showing that cultural factors supporting gender inequality still act as impediments to the performance of women.[64]

The case of Maryam Mirzakhani (1977–2017) provides a vivid illustration of the powerful impact of environmental conditions on intelligence.

Mirzakhani is the first (and to date the only) woman to win the Fields Medal (the equivalent of the Nobel Prize) in mathematics. She was born in Iran but left to study in the United States and won a professorship at Stanford University. Mirzakhani is an example of the many outstanding successes Iranian women have achieved *outside* Iran in science and other fields, when they are given equal opportunities to demonstrate their intelligence. But within Iran, women are held back by reactionary and backward laws supporting male domination and, not surprisingly, the equivalents of Mirzakhani do not flourish there. The highly different levels of achievements of Iranian women inside and outside Iran highlight the power of contextual conditions to shape 'intelligence.'

In many societies over the last century, women have come to enjoy greater equality of opportunity, and they have flourished as a result. Women did not change biologically over the last century, their genetic characteristics do not account for their dramatic improvement in performance in higher education – from being almost invisible in universities to being the majority (interestingly, in 1904 Spearman concluded that with regard to general intelligence, "In adult life, there would seem no appreciable difference between the two sexes"[65]). It was the change of contextual characteristics that enabled women to succeed in higher education: Women adopted the belief that they are able to compete academically with men, and legal obstacles were erased so that women could compete on a more level playing field. The same dramatic contextual changes are needed to enable children from lower-class families to compete more fairly in education – this realization comes after we overcome the causal-reductionist approach of mainstream psychology and recognize the power of contextual factors.

Children from poor families (of all ethnicities) suffer huge disadvantages in educational competition. Family wealth is the deciding factor in explaining the Black–White educational achievement gap.[66] More broadly, the differences between educational achievement of children from high-income and low-income families have been increasing in both lower schools and higher education.[67] This has led some researchers to discuss educational inequality as 'inherited' and educational opportunity for all as a myth.[68] Of course, extraordinarily talented individuals do break out of their deprivation and rise up, to be pointed at as token examples of how the American Dream is still alive. But such tokens are the exception, not the rule. The increasing wealth gap between social classes and the increasing parental spending on children (by those who have money to spend) is making it even more difficult for lower-class children to successfully compete in education.[69]

Thus, children from poor families face both blatant and more subtle challenges. As an example of a more subtle challenge, Bettina Spender and Emanuele Castano have demonstrated that one of the factors leading low-SES students to perform badly in testing situations is the stereotyping and stigmatization suffered by low-SES Americans.[70] This is an example of the well-known phenomenon of stereotype threat, "when members of a stigmatized group perform poorly on a task because they fear confirming negative stereotypes that are associated with their ingroup."[71]

Concluding Comment

> My so-called inventions already existed in the environment – I took them out. I've created nothing. Nobody does. There's no such thing as an idea being brain-born; everything comes from the outside.[72]
> Thomas Edison (1847–1931)

The causal-reductionist model underlying mainstream psychology has led to intelligence being conceived as largely inherited and residing within individuals. This is tied to the assumption that society is open, and individual success depends on personal effort and talent. Americans in particular overestimate the level of personal freedom and mobility across classes.[73] The mainstream perspective overlooks the power of context. The standard IQ tests are able to predict individual success to some degree: Individuals identified by mainstream tests as exceptionally talented before the age of thirteen continue to excel in their university and professional careers.[74] But, as we have discussed in this chapter, poverty also serves as a powerful context and predictor.

Reflecting back, clearly the political biases and motivations of researchers, sometimes extending to outright falsifications, have influenced psychological research on intelligence. Second, the enormous historical shifts in our conception of the intelligence of women and other groups (e.g., the Chinese) and the rise of IQ scores (the Flynn effect) must serve as a warning for us to take into full consideration the powerful impact of context on 'intelligence,' and more generally on performance in education. Third, epigenetic research has opened new possibilities for exploring the subtle and sophisticated ways in which environmental factors can bring into play, or keep dormant, genes that are possessed (or absent). Yet again, this development heightens the importance of context in what is manifested and measured as 'intelligence.'

CHAPTER 4

Personality and the Power of Context

At the heart of both scientific psychology and 'layman' psychology is the concept of *personality*, which in mainstream psychology refers to something within a person, a 'cause,' that makes his or her behavior consistently the way it is. Emphasizing both consistency in behavior and causal mechanisms, an influential introductory personality text defines personality as "an individual's characteristic patterns of thought, emotion, and behavior, together with the psychological mechanisms – hidden or not – behind those patterns."[1] The fame and influence of historically important psychologists such as Sigmund Freud (1856–1939), B. F. Skinner (1904–1990), Carl Jung (1875–1961), Carl Rogers (1902–1987), and Abraham Maslow (1908–1970) derive in large part from their personality theories. The most influential bodies of research in twenty-first-century psychology include ideas about personality, such as the proposition that the main dimensions of personality are universal (a topic we discuss later in this chapter). Psychological ideas about personality have entered into our everyday language, so that we routinely use terms such as ego, repression, and extroversion in our daily lives.

But the subject of mainstream psychology has remained largely limited to what I term *System M ('Micro') personality*, which focuses on intrapersonal characteristics as the cause of consistencies in behavior. More attention needs to be given to what I term *System E ('Extended') personality*, which sees contextual macro processes and particularly social class as the source of consistencies in behavior. Whereas System M explanations assume that individuals are born with certain profiles of openness to experience and other traits, System E explanations propose that contextual conditions, such as being born into families possessing or lacking wealth, power, and status, influence certain profiles of openness to experience and other traits. Second, socialization in families from different social classes influences personality, through the learning of social-class related values, goals, motivations, and processes such as self-stereotyping.[2] Third, the members

46

of different social classes are judged, by themselves and others, according to the stereotype standards for their class. They will self-ascribe and be ascribed personality characteristics differently based on their class memberships. Thus, whereas System M personality assumes that personality is 'self-contained' and shaped by factors within individuals, System E personality proposes that context and factors such as social class, status, and power afford different personality characteristics. In this chapter I critically examine both System M personality and System E personality as conceptual frames, demonstrating that both are needed and must be included in psychological research.

My focus on the importance of System E personality is in line with research supporting the 'shifting standards model,'[3] which proposes that "People hold (and often share) stereotypes of groups, and when called on to make judgments of individual group members, those stereotypes affect the standards used to render subjective evaluations on stereotype dimensions."[4] For example, a lower-class employee is evaluated as 'very good' on the criterion of 'conscientiousness' as a worker but does not receive bonus money, even though his manager is judged only 'good' on 'conscientiousness' but does receive bonus money. Research suggests that judgments on characteristics such as conscientiousness shift across social categories – the lower-class employee may be perceived as 'very good' compared to other lower-class employees but, as a group, lower-class employees can be stereotyped as much lower on conscientiousness than middle-class managers. Consequently, a manager who is only 'good' is meritorious enough to receive a bonus. In this way, the characteristics ascribed to individuals depend on their *group memberships*.

System M Personality

The point of departure for mainstream psychological research on personality is the consistent patterns of behavior that (are assumed to) arise from within individuals and operate mostly at the interpersonal level. System M personality has a long history and is reflected in typologies of personality (described below), which use discrete categories ('either/or' categories), and have evolved over thousands of years. Typologies often involve assumptions about the relationship between physical features and personality. The most historically important of these, influential for about 1,500 years, was the classification system of Hippocrates (c. 400 BC), as adapted by Galen (c. AD 200). Types of temperament were assumed to be determined by the relative presence of four fluids: the melancholic (depressive) type produced

by excess of black bile; the choleric type (quickly angered, aggressive) produced by too much yellow bile; the sanguine type (vibrant and cheerful)
resulting from excess of blood; and the phlegmatic type (leisurely, calm)
produced by too much phlegm. This approach of linking physical characteristics to temperament is reflected, for example, in Shakespeare's Julius
Caesar (1.ii.192–195), when Caesar identifies Cassius as looking like a dangerous person:

> Let me have men about me that are fat,
> Sleek-headed men and such as sleep a-nights.
> Yond Cassius has a lean and hungry look,
> He thinks too much; such men are dangerous.

Typologies have continued to influence conceptions of personality in
the modern era. William Sheldon (1898–1977) introduced three body
types with associated personality characteristics:[5] the easy going and
sociable *endomorphic*, the introspective and creative *ectomorphic*, and the
assertive and energetic *mesomorphic*. More recently, a distinction between
personality Type A (competitive, combative, impatient, driven) and Type
B (relaxed, care free, leisurely in outlook) evolved out of the research of
Meyer Friedman (1910–2001) and Ray Rosenman.[6] The usefulness of this
typology has been shown in the health arena; for example, Type A individuals are more prone to develop coronary heart disease.

Idiographic and Nomothetic Approaches

A challenge taken up by modern researchers is to develop an understanding
of personality based on scientific research methods. A chapter on 'research
methods for studying personality' is a standard part of twenty-first-century
texts on personality.[7] However, dilemmas persist as to what are the best
scientific approaches to studying personality. For example, the *idiographic*
approach treats each individual as an independent case with unique characteristics, living in a distinct ecological niche nobody else can occupy (the
idiographic approach is in line with patient-specific treatments in medical
practice[8]). In contrast, the *nomothetic* approach attempts to understand
personality by examining trends in (often large) groups and collectives of
individuals, focusing on common characteristics.[9] While critics of mainstream psychological research, particularly humanistic psychologists, insist
each person must be studied and treated as a unique case, mainstream
research on personality adopts the nomothetic rather than the idiographic
approach.

The nomothetic approach provides broad generalizations about personality characteristics based on data reflecting trends in large collectives. However, the distinct characteristics of particular individuals are neglected. For example, Dr. Hunter has completed a study with 1,000 participants on the relationship between shyness and depression among teenagers. Mary is one of the teenage participants who completed the questionnaires in this study. Dr. Hunter's findings allow her to come to conclusions about the relationship between shyness and depression in teenagers generally, but she is not able to report on Mary specifically. It may be that Mary is an outlier among the sample of participants and is not accurately described by the general findings of Dr. Hunter's study. In order to get an accurate picture of the relationship between shyness and depression in the case of Mary specifically, Dr. Hunter would need to undertake an idiographic study.

Sources of Data on Personality

Mainstream psychology also faces a dilemma concerning sources of data about personality. The vast majority of data used as the basis of personality assessment measures is derived through verbal reports, usually with individuals reporting on their own characteristics. For example, participants are asked to use a continuous scale ranging from '1' (not at all) to '9' (to a great extent) to rate the degree to which they see themselves as 'ambitious,' 'friendly,' 'open-minded,' 'outgoing,' and 'fearful.' A similar technique is to present full sentences, such as "I am shy around other people" and to ask participants to rate the extent to which the sentence accurately describes them. David Funder refers to this as 'S' ('self-report') data.[10] This contrasts with an alternative, very rarely used method: asking somebody who knows the person to report on her characteristics. Funder refers to this as 'I' data and reports a high match between 'S' and 'I' data because the way most people describe themselves is similar to how they are described by others.[11] He also identified two other sources of data about personality: life outcomes or 'L' data (concrete facts about a person, such as "have you ever been arrested?") and observed behavior or 'B' data (observations of a person's behavior in or outside a laboratory).[12]

Our ideas about personality would be more reliable and valid if we include all the four different types of data listed above, but the vast majority of personality research relies solely on self-report or 'S' data. We have known at least since the 1970s that what people say only predicts their behavior under very specific conditions, such as when verbal expressions are being attended to, and are based on correct information and experience.[13]

However, these conditions are difficult to meet and often people do not act in accordance with their own words, and they later change their words to fit their actions.[14] Both cognitive dissonance theory and self-perception theory predict that under certain conditions people do change their words to fit their own actions – this is in line with a lot of research showing that often cognition and action are not logical or rational.[15] We are motivated to deceive ourselves about ourselves while at the same time retaining the illusion of objectivity. We allocate attention in a biased way to make sure we 'notice' information that reflects positively on ourselves, and we remember in a biased way so that the past casts a favorable light on us.[16] Thus, the method of using self-report as a basis for our understanding of personality has major shortcomings.

Traits and Their Complications

Central to mainstream personality research and major personality tests is the idea that personality is characterized by certain *traits*, consistent tendencies in behavior, such as narcissism, neuroticism, and aggression. Whereas typologies are categorical (e.g., in classical typology from ancient times, a person was categorized as melancholic, choleric, sanguine, or phlegmatic), traits are continuous dimensions. For example, 'agreeableness' is assumed to be a dimension, with individuals located somewhere on a continuum from extremely low agreeableness to extremely high agreeableness. The dominance of the trait approach is seldom questioned in twenty-first- century psychology, but two questions are worth critically exploring. First, how many traits should we use to capture personality? Second, are traits causes, consequences, or simply verbal reports reflecting societal norms?

With respect to the number of traits, one could claim that there are as many traits as there are words to describe behavior. Over the last century there have been major research efforts to identify the most important traits. Gordon Allport compiled a list of 18,000 such words;[17] he then used logical and intuitive means to reduce these words to three categories from the most to the least pervasive and foundational: cardinal, central, and secondary traits. Allport gave more importance to the idiographic approach, treating each person as unique.

In contrast to Allport's strategy, most twenty-first-century trait researchers give priority to the nomothetic approach and rely almost exclusively on *psychometrics*, techniques for measuring psychological phenomena using large data sets. These measurement techniques have come about through the development of statistical procedures, such as correlation, factor analysis and regression, as well as far more powerful computers capable of analyzing much larger data sets.[18] Raymond Cattell (1905–1998) used psychometric techniques to explore major themes in personality (such as forceful–submissive, reserved–outgoing, worried–confident) as a basis for his widely used Sixteen Personality Factor Test (16PF). Hans Eysenck (1916–1997) concluded on the basis of psychometric research that personality is centered on three dimensions: introversion/extroversion (reserved, introspective vs. outgoing, sociable), stability/neuroticism (level of anxiety), and impulse control/psychoticism (levels of impulsivity and sensitivity in relationships).[19] The Eysenck Personality Questionnaire measures these dimensions of personality.

In recent decades, research by Warren Norman (1930–1998) and others has led to the proposition that all human personalities are characterized by the 'Big Five' personality traits:[20] openness to experience, conscientiousness, extroversion, agreeableness, and neuroticism (OCEAN).[21] These traits are proposed as universal: that is, the personality of all human beings is assumed to be characterized and 'captured' by these five traits. However, below I raise a number of questions as to the logic of traits and the way they are supposed to function.

First, traits are assumed to be consistently present in individuals, but they can disappear in some circumstances. For example, imagine you attend a funeral and are introduced for the first time to Joe, a friend of your extended family. You and Joe stand next to one another throughout the funeral ceremony, then shake hands and say goodbye when the ceremony ends. After the funeral, another family member asks you, "What did you think of Joe? He is such an extrovert! Always telling jokes. He really is hilarious! Did he make you laugh?" You answer, "No, he was very quiet. I guess he didn't have much to say." Of course, Joe was quiet and 'not being hilarious' because he was attending a funeral. But mainstream psychology proposes that Joe is high on extroversion in all circumstances – this is a trait he carries with him in all circumstances.

Second, are traits causes of behavior, or are they the consequences of other factors, or are they best conceptualized as being outside causal chains? For example, if Jane is described as 'shy,' is shyness a cause of Jane's style of behavior or an effect of some hidden, underlying factors within Jane? Or should we avoid conceptualizing Jane's shyness as being part of a causal chain of her behavior? Unfortunately, both in everyday life and in psychological research, causal language has been used to describe traits and behavior, but in a rather muddled way. For example, we describe Jack as aggressive in the way he interacts with others. Jack has an "aggressive style," we comment, treating 'aggressive' as a behavioral *consequence*. Then when we witness Jack push his way in front of another person waiting in line, we explain that Jack's action was *caused* by his aggression. In this way, aggression is both cause and consequence.

A close analysis of the way researchers discuss traits reveals the same circularity. For example, Cattell distinguishes between *surface traits*, clusters of observable actions that are associated with one another, and *source traits*, the underlying causes of surface traits.[22] Eysenck distinguishes between *habits*, observable responses, *traits*, such as being shy or aggressive, and *types*, such as being introverted or extroverted. In Eysenck's system, habits form the basis of traits, and traits form the basis of types. However, the models constructed by Cattell and Eysenck do not really escape circularity and thus remain unconvincing. What are conceived by them as 'surface' and 'habits' could be reconceptualized as causes rather than effects – as people act in certain ways, they watch themselves act and regulate their beliefs about themselves according to their actions.[23]

Researchers have also searched for genetic causes of personality.[24] As we would expect from epigenetic research, in the area of personality research also, gene expression has been found to be influenced by environmental factors in highly complex ways. For example, in a meta-analytic study involving 805 independent samples and 127,685 participants, dopamine genes were found to be linked to extraversion and neuroticism traits but only in environments with high climatic demands (such as very hot climates).[25] Also, the influence of genes on personality is through both environmental influence and interaction with (probably numerous) other genes.[26] Although some aspects of personality are probably influenced by genetic factors, personality is also in important ways influenced by their contextual conditions, a topic I turn to later in this chapter.

System E Personality

The essence of higher class position is the expectation that one's decisions and actions can be consequential; the essence of lower-class position is the belief that one is at the mercy of forces and people beyond one's control, often, beyond one's understanding. Self-direction ... is possible only if the actual conditions of life allow some freedom of action, some reason to feel in control of fate. Conformity ... is

the inevitable result of conditions of life that allow little freedom of
action, little reason to feel control of fate.

Melvin Kohn[27]

[B]y and large, psychologists have tended to leave the study of social
class to sociologists, usually regarding social class as a variable to be
statistically controlled for, if they attend to class at all.

Joan Ostrove and Elizabeth Cole[28]

There is a remarkable contrast between the acknowledgment by some
researchers that social class shapes personality, and the observation by
other researchers that social class is a neglected topic in psychology. Given
the enormous psychological literature on personality,[29] it is disappointing
that more research attention has not been given to personality and social
class.[30]

Although in the twenty-first century there is still too little research
directly on social class and personality, a number of psychologists, such as
Susan Fiske of Princeton University and others,[31] have given more systematic and serious research attention to social class. In addition, a number
of leading theories of intergroup relations have stimulated research on
psychological processes underlying group-based power and resource
inequalities.[32] This turn toward psychological research on social class comes
at a time of, and is probably stimulated by, increasing resource inequalities
and extreme wealth concentration.[33]

The shift toward greater wealth inequality is historic, as discussed in
earlier chapters of this text and well documented by Thomas Piketty.[34] At
the start of the nineteenth century, US society was more egalitarian than
European. But wealth inequality grew rapidly in the United States from
the 1950s: From 1979 to 2016 the share of wealth in the hands of the richest 0.1 percent doubled to 20 percent. While the income of the richest
Americans has also increased at a much faster rate than middle-class and
lower-class incomes, US government tax policies have further widened
wealth inequalities. The billionaire Warren Buffett famously declared that
he pays a lower tax rate than his secretary, and this is true for the richest
400 Americans who pay an average tax rate of 23 percent compared to the
average of 25 percent paid by low-income Americans. Tax policy has helped
to bring about *The Triumph of Injustice* in the United States, as Emmanuel
Saez and Gabriel Zucman document. Under these conditions, a few (but
not nearly enough) psychologists are giving more attention to social class.
More research is needed to explore the relationship between social class and

personality, treating social class not as a 'cause' of personality but as a means through which personality comes to be normatively regulated.

In this section I will elaborate on System E personality by explaining how social class influences different patterns of behavior in people of different social classes. Rather than interpreting personality as an 'effect' resulting from 'causes' such as 'traits,' I explore personality as patterns of behavior regulated by three main features of social class: first, material conditions; second, normative systems; third, patterns of cognition.

The Role of Material Conditions

Rich and poor live in physically separate worlds. These worlds are kept apart by money – the poor cannot afford to step foot into the world of the rich, except as servants, gardeners, kitchen workers, cleaners, nannies, and the providers of various other services. The rich live in neighborhoods that exclude the poor as residents, they belong to exclusive social and sports clubs, they go shopping in places and eat at restaurants that only they can afford, and they send their children to expensive schools that only allow some token but talented 'privileged poor' kids to enter (but still be in a disadvantaged position vis-à-vis the rich students[35]). When they travel, the rich sit in their own private jets and yachts or in exclusive first-class sections of trains. Even when they go to sports stadiums, concert halls, and nightclubs also attended by 'ordinary people,' they sit in reserved areas kept exclusive by high prices. Studies of the segregation of social classes clearly reflect this pattern: Money isolates the rich around the clock.[36] As Christopher Ellis has noted, "certain types of contextual and geographic arrangements render the lifestyles of wealthy and poor essentially disconnected from one another, with the consequence that wealthy citizens rarely if ever need to see lower-income citizens if they choose not to."[37]

The rich also experience the material world in ways that are different from the poor. The holidays they take, the cars they drive, the clothes they wear, the food they eat … every aspect of their material lives are luxuriously different. Perhaps no aspect of the different lives of the rich is more important than the superior health care they receive,[38] which is one factor leading to much longer lives for the rich.[39] A report by the *National Bureau of Economic Research* found that the gap in life expectancy between Whites and African Americans was 7.1 years in 1993 but declined to 3.4 years in 2014; however, "Study after study has found that SES differences have been widening in recent decades, whether SES is measured by educational attainment or by income."[40] Most studies have found that the rich live 10–15 years longer than the poor – and the gap is increasing. The poor typically work in physically demanding and dangerous conditions, without adequate health care and insurance.[41]

The material life conditions of the poor impact their personality development. For example, extended experiences of childhood poverty increase the probability of maladaptive behavior, such as aggression, emotional instability, disobedience, and poor cognitive functioning at school.[42] Also, the probability of taking up a leadership position is limited by persistent experience with poverty during childhood.[43] Thus, in the debate on the question of whether 'leaders are born or made by circumstances,' research clearly points to childhood poverty as being an important factor in limiting the probability of lower-class individuals from becoming leaders. A major factor in these developmental processes is simple nutrition: Children who experience persistent poverty are often deprived of the nutritional support needed for optimal brain development,[44] and this deprivation impacts the kind of person they become – including their personalities.

The Role of Normative Systems

The behavior of the poor is regulated by normative systems (norms, rules, stereotypes, values) that severely limit their social behavior. Living on low incomes severely restricts the range of activities the poor can engage in – as documented in books such as *Nickel and Dimed*,[45] recounting the experiences of a relatively affluent writer who spent a year doing menial jobs for minimal wage. She reports her constant struggles to simply survive. More money gives the rich greater choices and a wider range of activities to engage in; having little money, the poor consistently have little choice in what they can do. Moreover, as we discussed in Chapters 2 and 3, poverty leads people to constantly focus on how to cope with lack of money, how to pay for the rent, food, and other basic needs, and how to overcome everyday difficulties, such as getting to work and other essential places, when there is not enough money to 'buy your way out of trouble' (such as having a car that urgently needs repairs). Poverty places strict restrictions on how an individual behaves, and this is one way in which the persistent patterns of behavior that come to be labeled as 'personality' are in important ways shaped by social class.

Michael Kraus and colleagues have extensively studied differences between rich and poor in social behavior.[46] Their 'inequality maintenance' model of social class brings attention to how social class membership is communicated to, and identified by, other people. Through the communication of tastes and preferences in food, music, literature, leisure, clothing, and the like, individuals signal their social class membership, and others (most of the time) correctly interpret these signals and assign individuals to particular social classes. For example, first impressions based on the type of shoes a person is wearing,[47] as well as small facial cues such as positive affect and superior health,[48] provide accurate perceptions of social class. Research shows that another cue commonly and accurately used to gage social class is language – a classic study on this was carried out not in 'class-ridden' London but in 'class-free' New York city.[49] Not only does the language of New Yorkers indicate social class, but at least some New Yorkers tend to vary their language depending on the social class of their interlocuter.

Thus, subtle and not-so-subtle patterns of behavior are fairly accurately used by people as indicators of social class. The assignment of another person to a particular social class has important implications for how that individual is viewed, particularly through influencing cognitive processes and the triggering of stereotypes.

The Role of Cognition

Style of cognition is central to personality, and research demonstrates that social class shapes cognition in important ways.[50] The perception of social class triggers stereotypes that are detrimental for the poor: A multinational study (thirty-seven samples in twenty-seven countries) showed cross-=cultural consistency in the poor being judged to be less competent (but 'warm') relative to the rich.[51] In the US context, the stereotype of the poor as 'lazy' influences education policy and serves to justify class-based economic inequalities.[52] Negative stereotypes of the poor and preferences for the rich (as more hard-working, deserving, talented) are part of the wider culture of contemporary societies and, not surprisingly, children are socialized from an early age to adopt and use such stereotypes.[53]

Stereotypes of higher- and lower-class people have important consequences for behavior in everyday life. Stereotypes of social classes can detrimentally impact the performance of poor children on (supposedly) 'objective' educational tests, in subjects such as mathematics (this relates to our discussions in Chapters 3 and 4)[54]. Such stereotypes are triggered by symbols of social class, clothing being an important example. When participants in a study were randomly assigned to conditions where they wore lower-class, neutral, or upper-class clothing, those wearing upper-class clothing achieved more profits and made fewer concessions in a negotiation task; also, their testosterone levels increased.[55] (This is in line with research showing that dominance is associated with testosterone levels.[56]) Clearly, perceiving oneself as upper class, even temporarily in an experimental setting, can bring changes not only in actions but also some biological processes.

Perceptions of social class membership also influence feelings of deservingness and the 'natural' basis of class-based inequalities.[57] Individuals who endorse class-based resource inequalities tend to see a biological basis for class membership: They believe that the members of 'superior' classes have superior genes.[58] Experimental evidence also shows that those who belong to the upper class, even temporarily and by chance in a laboratory setting, tend to justify class-based inequalities and explain them by reference to dispositional characteristics of individuals rather than contextual factors.[59] When the relative status of individuals was experimentally manipulated, those who were high status were less supportive of more egalitarian resource redistribution.[60] This is in line with intergroup theories that predict those who become part of the ruling class are the strongest endorsers of the current unequal hierarchy and power system.[61]

In conclusion, social class membership shapes in important ways consistent patterns of cognitions and actions in individuals – what I have termed *System E Personality*. Very importantly, the patterns of behavior that we identify as 'personality' are not neutral; they are closely linked to our social class memberships. Research evidence clearly demonstrates that social class membership influences the biases people show during interactions with others, treating upper-class individuals as more competent. Those who perceive themselves as part of the upper class come to see their wealth and status advantages as justified by their genetic and other dispositional characteristics and come to behave with greater confidence and authority.

Concluding Comment

What we come to identify as the personalities of individuals, their consistent styles of behavior, arise in large part from the roles they play and their group memberships in the wider society, particularly their social class, and the wealth, power, and status they possess. The personality we manifest is largely shaped by our circumstances and the style of behavior we are permitted to manifest. In rethinking the psychology of personality, we must give more importance to context, through developing the psychology of System E personality alongside the traditional System M personality.

Psychological research on social class has expanded in the twenty-first century, illuminating how social class membership brings about certain personality styles. This new perspective assumes a greater role for contextual conditions in shaping the style of behavior manifested by individuals. The conclusion is that what mainstream psychology terms individual 'personality' would be very different if Jane grows up as the daughter of a lower-class family living in cramped, polluted, rented housing and continuously facing financial hardships, as opposed to an affluent family who provide her with luxurious conditions and choices. Growing up as a member of the upper rather than lower class, Jane would literally become a 'different person' in her style of behavior.

CHAPTER 5

Consciousness: Decontextualized and Contextualized Approaches

Explain consciousness.

This is the challenge thrown out by Hilary, an aspiring psychology student, to her hard-nosed tutor, Spike, in Tom Stoppard's brilliant play *The Hard Problem*.[1] For dramatic effect, Stoppard (using a term coined by the philosopher David Chalmers[2]) titles his play in the singular, identifying consciousness as 'the hard problem.' However, it is more accurate to say there are two 'hard problems' to explain: first, *consciousness*, being aware of things inside and outside oneself and, second, *free will*, the ability to choose between alternative courses of action.

I distinguish between two foundationally different approaches to understanding consciousness and free will. The first focuses on *decontextualized consciousness and free will*, on the assumption that all human beings experience consciousness and free will in the same manner and that group membership (such as social class) and context are unimportant in how consciousness and free will develop. This decontextualized approach fits in with mainstream psychology research, which is mostly conducted with samples from WEIRD (White, Educated, Industrialized, Rich, Democratic) populations, studied in contexts with little variation – on the assumption that contexts are unimportant.[3]

Causal-reductionism is in line with a *decontextualized approach*, explaining consciousness and free will by finding causes within individuals and/or treating consciousness itself as a cause of behavior.[4] But this approach has led to unsatisfactory accounts and outcomes,[5] such as the rejection of conscious will (a topic I return to in this chapter). Second, the decontextualized approach does not address the relationship between the social and group characteristics of individuals and the nature of consciousness and free will. For example, there are likely to be very important differences between the consciousness and free will developed by individuals born into and socialized in the context of extremely rich families as opposed to extremely poor families. This is in line with arguments made by Michael Kraus and colleagues: "[L]ower-class individual's system of knowledge is characterized by a sense that one's actions are chronically influenced by external forces outside of individual control and influence ... In contrast, upper-class contexts prioritize the individualized self. Disposed to environments of relatively abundant material resources and elevated rank in society, upper-class individuals are free to pursue the goals and interests they choose for they choose for themselves."[6] I argue for the need to study *contextualized consciousness and free will*, giving particular importance to the context in which the individual is being socialized.

Rather than treating consciousness and free will as context-independent and as 'caused' by factors, or serving as 'causes' to determine other factors, I follow a Vygotskian tradition and argue that consciousness and free will are *emergent properties of societies entering into individuals, and individuals entering into societies.*[7] As Roy Baumeister and his colleagues have argued, "conscious thought allows the individual's behavior to be informed by social and cultural factors."[8] Importantly, the social and cultural factors informing the conscious thoughts of different individuals vary – particularly across social classes.

Thus, I argue that the source of consciousness and free will is 'out there' in the social world, not in the individual, nor the brain or brain parts, nor neural networks, nor individual cells, nor biochemical processes within the individual. Of course, the biological characteristics of individuals are all necessary for the development of consciousness and free will – *they are enablers.* However, to explain consciousness and free will, we must look first at the larger culture. It is through socialization and becoming a participant within this larger culture, with social class as one of its most important components, that individuals emerge with consciousness and the capacity to act as intentional agents.

In the first part of this chapter I discuss the traditional decontextualized explanation of consciousness and free will. In the next part, I examine contextualized consciousness and free will, with a focus on the relationship between US culture and mainstream psychology, as well as the role of social class in shaping consciousness and free will.

Decontexualized Consciousness and Free Will

In the first part of this chapter, I discuss the long tradition of psychologists studying consciousness and free will in a decontextualized manner. That is, the characteristics of the context and the group memberships of individuals are ignored, and the research focus is exclusively on the consciousness and free will as detached experiences. This tradition is associated with the (assumed) advantages of reductionism in psychology: isolating and reducing phenomena in order to simplify and make research more manageable. After all, consciousness is extremely complex, pervasive, and at the heart of all our experiences: It is only when we are under anesthesia and when we are in dreamless sleep that consciousness vanishes. As pointed out by William James (1842–1910), consciousness involves us attending to some thing(s) to the exclusion of others:

> [C]onsciousness is at all times primarily a *selecting agency*. Whether we take it in the lowest sphere of sense, or in the highest of intellection, we find it always doing one thing, choosing one out of several of the materials so presented to its notice, emphasizing and accentuating that and suppressing as far as possible all the rest. The item emphasized is always in close connection with some *interest* felt by consciousness to be paramount at the time.[9]

The 'selecting agency' nature of consciousness functions in a way that is similar to *working memory*, the memory system concerned with immediate conscious experience. Chris Frith has proposed that "we can equate the contents of consciousness with the contents of working memory."[10] But the idea that there are different levels of consciousness suggests that consciousness is more expansive than working memory.

We usually think of consciousness as 'all or none,' either being conscious or not conscious of an experience. However, some research has focused on the experiences of patients with abnormal consciousness, such as being in a *coma*, when the brain shows a steady but low level of activity and no response to stimuli, or a *vegetative state*, when there is very limited response to stimuli. This research suggests that consciousness is not 'all or none' in all cases. For example, consider the case of a young female patient in a vegetative state as a result of a road traffic accident, who could not respond with overt action to commands, 'imagine you are playing tennis' or 'visiting all the rooms of your house,' nevertheless showed neural responses indistinguishable from healthy volunteers.[11] In this case, neural activity indicates the patient was conscious of, and responding to, the commands but not able to carry out corresponding physical movements.

Studies of *metacognition*, thinking about thinking, also suggest different levels of consciousness. An example is the 'tip of the tongue' phenomenon, which "involves a failure to recall a word of which one has knowledge."[12] Roger Brown (1925–1997) studied this phenomenon by reading to research participants definitions of infrequently used English words and asking them to try to recall the words. The findings show that before recalling the words, participants often had correct ideas about key features, such as the number of syllables and some letters in the missing words. In some cases, such word features are remembered, but the word is not correctly recalled and remains on the 'tip of the tongue.' Different levels of consciousness are implied by this research.

A number of techniques have been developed to try to distinguish between neural processes associated with consciousness. A frequently used method focuses on *binocular rivalry*, involving the presentation of different stimuli – for example, a house and a face – to the left and right eye. Participants in this research do not report seeing a mixture of a house and a face but a constant shift every few seconds between seeing a house or a face. This brings us back to William James's point (quoted above) that consciousness serves as a 'selective agency,' focusing our attention on some things to the exclusion of others.

The idea of 'levels of consciousness' adds further complexity to the 'nonphysical' experience of consciousness. How can a sense of awareness, a psychological experience, arise from the brain, a biological entity? Peter Hacker has described this as an example of a 'bogus mystery'[13] – a mystery created by the researchers themselves (I discuss this point further in the last part of this chapter). Further, he has criticized the reductionist neuroscience approach to trying to solve this puzzle: This involves examining the association between behavioral correlates of consciousness, usually in the form of self-reports or simple actions (such as tapping a finger), and neural processes simultaneously detected in the brain.[14]

But as to research on the neural correlates of consciousness, two different lines of thinking have emerged. One view is that the search for the neural correlates of consciousness should continue until sufficient information is gathered and the puzzles of consciousness are solved. A recent review by leading researchers suggested we have not reached this goal, but some progress has been made: "[N]o single brain area seems to be necessary for being conscious, but a few areas … are good candidates for both full and content specific NCC (neural correlates of consciousness)."[15] Thus, although gaps still remain in our knowledge, from this perspective, research on the neural correlates of consciousness is on the correct path. An alternative perspective is represented by critics such as Hacker, who argue that research on the neural correlates of consciousness is on the wrong path: "The quest for the neural correlates of consciousness is misconceived, since there is no one thing called 'consciousness', but many different things."[16] In the second half of this chapter, I put forward a contextualized perspective on consciousness and free will, which, instead of looking inside individuals, interprets consciousness in relation to the external context.

The Causal Model, Consciousness, and Free Will

The logical outcome of a decontexualized, causal-reductionist model of behavior is that individuals do not choose to behave in one way or another, but various factors cause individuals to do what they do. This view must lead to a rejection of the conscious will.[17] Indeed, conscious will must be interpreted as a fallacy, an illusion – as indicated by the title of an influential book, *The Illusion of Conscious Will*,[18] reflecting the logical position one reaches through the decontexualized, causal model of mainstream psychology.

Despite extreme ups and downs of different schools and perspectives in the history of psychology, the causal model and its implications for conscious will have remained a stable part of mainstream psychology. Behaviorism, psychoanalysis, cognitive psychology, and now neuroscience have all adopted a causal model, respectively assuming 'stimuli,' 'irrational factors in the unconscious,' 'cognitive mechanisms,' and 'brain mechanisms' to serve as the causes of behavior.[19] Although later schools rejected some basic tenets of behaviorism, they remained loyal to the view that behavior is causally determined and free will is an illusion. This perspective is clearly spelled out in B. F. Skinner's novel *Walden Two*, by a character who represents the mainstream psychology point of view on causation and freedom: "I deny that freedom exists at all. I must deny it – or my program would be absurd. You can't have a science about a subject matter which hops capriciously about."[20] This perspective, that a science of psychology is only possible if we adopt a causal, deterministic perspective, is very much reflected in mainstream twenty-first-century psychology.[21] Below I discuss an example of research underlying this viewpoint.

Example of Research Underlying the Rejection of Conscious Will

In the 1980s Benjamin Libet (1916–2007) and his associates,[22] following a decontexualized tradition, conducted highly influential studies that were interpreted as questioning conscious will. This research focused on the *readiness potential*, an unconscious build-up of electric activity inside the brain prior to a conscious decision to take an action.[23] The basic elements of this research are as follows: Participants were asked to carefully monitor a clocklike apparatus so they can recall exactly when they made a decision to flex their finger and/or the wrist of the right hand. They were free to take the flex action at any time they felt inclined; thus, they were engaging in "self-initiated voluntary acts."[24] As participants made their decisions and carried out flexing actions, their brain activities were also recorded to detect changes in the brain area associated with muscle movements (the motor cortex). The findings showed that participants announced the decision to flex about 200–300 ms before the action, but the readiness potential (motor cortex activity prior to start of flex movement) was 300–800 ms prior to the reported decision. This finding was replicated by others and interpreted to mean that the brain begins producing a voluntary movement before we are explicitly aware of it.[25]

As Libet and his associates explained, in their view "the brain evidently 'decides' to initiate or, at the least, prepare to initiate the act at a time before there is any reportable subjective awareness that such a decision has taken place. It is concluded that cerebral initiation even of a spontaneous voluntary act ... can and usually does begin *unconsciously*."[26] This is in line with the determinism underlying mainstream psychology, in the sense that behavior is assumed to be determined by cause–effect relations outside the control of individual free will. Thus, taking a decontextualized approach, mainstream psychology arrives at the conclusion that individuals do not have free will.

Even within the tradition of decontextualized research, the interpretation of Libet's research has been seriously challenged. For example, a challenge came about through research led by Aaron Schurger,[27] who examined *spontaneous* fluctuations in neuronal activity (driven by mechanisms within neurons or interactions between neurons). These are circumstantial patterns, like movements in stock markets or weather patterns, with no intention behind them. The patterns of brain activity recorded by Libet and colleagues were not reflecting 'intentions'; nevertheless the participants were more likely to take flex action when the circumstantial brain activity pattern reached a high. We can extend this idea to various everyday situations, such as the act of reaching for a cup of coffee while reading: "If you set the cup of coffee within reach with the idea of drinking it, then sooner or later you will probably reach for it and take the next sip. However, why did you reach for it at the precise moment that you did and not, e.g., 500 ms earlier or later?"[28] The answer provided by Schurger and colleagues is that spontaneous fluctuations in neural firing (devoid of intentions) could reach a high point and tip the scale toward the action of reaching out for the cup of coffee (or flexing the finger and/or wrist) at that particular time. Subsequent research has shown that a certain level of neural activity is necessary for action,[29] and this can happen either on purpose or randomly. That is, the neural activity can arise as a result of irregular or spontaneous fluctuations but also because of building intentionality in the decision-maker.

Working within the traditional decontexualized model, Moritz Braun and colleagues conducted an extensive meta-analysis of Libet-style experiments.[30] Their research shows that "the evidence base of the most crucial of Libet and colleagues' findings appears thinner than anticipated in light of the substantial scientific work that built on it."[31] Others working within the decontexualized tradition have pointed out that participants in Libet's study had already made up their minds to participate in the study and take a particular action, and "the brain has an increased activity prior to is awareness of a conscious decision to physically perform it; but the presence of the readiness potential does not constitute a causally sufficient condition for the performance of the action."[32] The various criticisms of the Libet-style experiments led to the view, even among those working within the decontexualized tradition, that it is "time to lay the Libet experiment to rest."[33]

However, there are important limitations to trying to understand consciousness and free will in a decontexualized manner. First, the contents and nature of consciousness and free will that is socialized within individuals depend a great deal on the circumstances in which they are brought up. Consider the case of two sixteen-year-old white girls, both born and raised in Boston, United States. Clare is a member of an upper-class family, with a long tradition of education at elite schools in the United States, the United Kingdom, and France. She already has plans to attend St. Andrews University, where Prince William met Kate Middleton, then study law at an American Ivy League school before joining her uncle's law firm. Through private lessons, hard work, and a strong sense of purpose and discipline, Clare speaks four languages and has excellent grades. Jane was born into an impoverished lower-class family, constantly being forced to move from place to place because of debts. From about the age of twelve, Jane often missed school in order to earn some money at a food market, and she will get a full-time job as soon as she can officially leave school. She is a hard worker and seems to have the potential to get high grades, but her teachers do not have a good sense of how well she could do at school, because she is absent so often. Jane feels forced by her family circumstances to ignore school and try to work as much as possible to make money.

Clearly, the very different life conditions and experiences of these two sixteen-year-old girls will develop within them a sense of consciousness and free will that is in foundational ways different. For example, if we ask Jane about free will, she will probably say she is doing the only thing she can do – try to make money to support herself and help her family. On the other hand, huge family wealth and resources give Clare a sense of having choice and being in charge of her own life. Jonathan Kozol has described the 'savage inequalities' that characterize the educational systems catering to poor and affluent children,[34] but we should add that such savage inequalities are all-inclusive and pervade all aspects of the experiences of children who are poor versus affluent – including their sense of consciousness and the free will they enjoy.

Second, a decontextualized understanding of consciousness and free will leads to a position that is unsatisfactory and against common sense; it contradicts the assumptions underlying all major legal and moral (religious and secular) systems. Without the assumption of some measure of free will, the existing legal and moral systems become nonsensical. How can an accused be judged to be guilty of a crime if he or she does not have free will? A murderer could simply respond, "Yes, I killed that woman and took her money. However, my personality traits and other causal factors led me to kill and rob. I did not choose to do what I did. I don't have conscious will. You can't blame me – you have to blame the causes of my behavior." Similarly, religious systems would have to abandon the idea of 'sin,' because without conscious will, how can there be sin? In his or her defense, the person accused of committing a sin would simply respond, "I had no choice, you can't blame me, like all other humans I have no free will!"

However, rather than debate the characteristics of consciousness and free will within the confines of a decontextualized tradition, I next turn to discuss a contextualized approach.

Contextualized Consciousness and Free Will

I argue that consciousness and free will emerge in individuals through socialization, and the characteristics of context influence this process in important ways. I begin by discussing human biological characteristics as *enablers*, factors that are necessary but not sufficient for the emergence of consciousness and free will. Next, I consider the powerful context represented by US culture and values for shaping how mainstream psychology conceptualized consciousness and free will. The United States continues to represent the First World of psychology, the sole superpower, and the characteristics of mainstream psychology are in important ways shaped by US culture and values (this topic is discussed in greater depth in Chapter 10 of this text). The neglect of social class in mainstream psychology reflects this US influence. In the final section, I discuss the influence of social class on how consciousness and free will develop in individuals.

Human Biological Characteristics Enable Consciousness and Free Will

The newborn infant has the biological *potential* to develop into a functional human being, but as Sharon Fox and associates point out, this potential only provides a framework: "Although our genetic code provides an important foundation for early development, it must be understood as a framework upon which many environmental factors influence future structure and function."[35]

Of course, for individuals to emerge through socialization with consciousness and free will, they need to have independent bodies, with brains, cells, biochemical processes, and all of the material characteristics of individual humans. These material properties of individuals are necessary, but they are not sufficient and they do not 'cause' consciousness and free will. Similarly, human society is necessary but not sufficient for, nor is it a cause of, consciousness and free will. In essence, consciousness and free will are not explained through cause–effect relations.

Hardwiring and the Biological Framework: My highlighting the role of context does not mean I am adopting a Lockean *Tabula Rasa* approach to human development, arguing as the radical behaviorists did that humans are born as 'blank slates' on which life experiences can write anything. We are born with some hardwiring, and this has been elaborated by various schools. For example, Gestalt psychologists demonstrated how our perceptions are structured by a number of inborn principles of organization, such as similarity, good continuity, and proximity.[36] From the 1950s the influence of behaviorism has declined. A key turning point was Noam Chomsky's famous review of B. F. Skinner's behaviorist account of language learning,[37] which showed that the 'blank slate' model of infants at birth is incorrect.[38] For example, humans are born "specially designed" to learn languages.[39]

Neural networks and the firing of neurons are patterned. Some of these patterns are already set at birth and many others are learned through experiences and are changed over the lifespan, and particularly over the first 1,000 days. One extreme indication of this is provided by cases of feral children, who have lived in isolation from human contact from a young age.[40] A famous example is the *Wild Boy of Aveyron*,[41] who survived in isolation in the woods near Aveyron, France, during his early childhood and (re)joined human society in 1800 (probably) when he was in his early teens. He was taken to Paris and attracted a great deal of attention from scientists, because he seemed to present an opportunity to test ideas about the 'noble savage' and the inherent characteristics of humans raised in nature rather than in society. Unfortunately, as with other cases where a child has not learned language by the critical period of around puberty, the *Wild Boy of Aveyron* did not learn language or successfully adjust to life in society (he died in 1828).[42] The *Wild Boy of Aveyron* did not lack consciousness, but living in the wild he developed a consciousness that was very different from that which would have developed if he had grown up as a member of French society at that time.

Thus, the human biological entity at birth has the *potential* to develop consciousness and free will, similar to how this biological entity is preprogrammed with the potential to learn language (the role of biological factors in human behavior is discussed more in-depth through attention to epigenetics in Chapter 3 of this text). Just as the particular language a human individual acquires depends on his or her surroundings, the particular form of consciousness and free will acquired also depends on surroundings. A person who grows up in China and learns Mandarin Chinese also acquires consciousness and free will through the surroundings. In essence, it is through our interactions with others, starting from our interactions with our mothers and our surroundings while we are still in the womb, that we acquire a certain form of consciousness and free will.

From a mainstream perspective, a question arises: If consciousness and free will evolve out of participation in collective life, then what lies behind consciousness and free will? Mainstream psychology looks for causal explanations, attempting to peek behind the curtain and identify hidden mechanisms behind consciousness and free will. But in this, as in other types of behavior, there is no 'behind,' there are no 'hidden causes.' Individuals enmeshed in the life of a community 'live out' a form of consciousness and free will that arises through their participation. They carry with them a form of consciousness and free will, which is their behavior in everyday social life. There is no causal agent behind the 'playing out' of consciousness and free will.

The US Context, Consciousness, and Free Will

Among the most important neglected topics in mainstream psychology is how American ideals have shaped consciousness, resulting in a celebration of individual mobility and an absence of consciousness about social class membership.[43]

Celebrating the Self-Contained Mobile Individual: The cowboy movie is a quintessentially American art form (Robert Bellah and his associates point out, "America is ... the inventor of that most mythical individual hero, the cowboy, who again and again saves a society he can never completely fit into."[44]. In classic cowboy films such as *Shane* (1953, starring Alan Ladd) and *Unforgiven* (1992, starring Clint Eastwood), the hero is self-contained, independent, and mobile, an individual on the move who enters the scene alone, fights the good fight and defeats the 'bad guys,' then exits alone. This theme of the self-contained, mobile individual is central to American culture and American literature; for example, in F. Scott Fitzgerald's quintessentially American novel *The Great Gatsby* (1925),[45] Gatsby moves by himself from being poor to being fabulously wealthy. On the way to wealth and fame he fabricates a new identity and pursues his dream through both social and geographical mobility.

Cross-cultural studies of individualism–collectivism have demonstrated that the United States consistently measures as the most individualistic major society.[46] Research on the theme of 'bowling alone' (rather than going bowling in a group with neighbors, family, or others) shows that Americans are literally more and more likely to go bowling alone, less engaged in community activities and organizations, and less connected to group life.[47] Whereas in the United States membership in and ties to all kinds of groups, including Girl Guides, Boy Scouts, neighborhood organizations, and the like, have declined, major societies that remain more collectivistic, such as India, maintain stronger ties between individuals and families, neighborhoods, and collectives in general. Even if Americans now belong to Internet-based 'electronic communities' rather than mainstream communities, the relationship between individuals and collectives in America underscores the American ideal individual independence and mobility.

These 'bowling alone' trends are in line with the 'self-help,' 'individual responsibility,' 'anyone can make it in America' political ideology pervasive in America. The *American Dream* encapsulates this ideology: the idea that American society is open and anyone can make it in America through hard work and personal effort. Robert Putnam has pointed out that historically Americans have been less concerned with equality of income and wealth and more concerned with equality of opportunity and social mobility,[48] "that is, whether young people from different backgrounds are ... getting on the ladder at about the same place and, given equal merit and energy, are equally likely to scale it."[49]

My claim here is *not* that American society actually is open, or that social mobility actually is high in America, or that the American Dream is alive and functioning. The evidence suggests quite the opposite: Social mobility in the United States is lower than most 'class ridden' European countries and in practice the American Dream is "in crisis."[50] Rather, my claim is that irrespective of the actual health of the American Dream, popular belief in self-help, individual responsibility, and individualism in general is strong in the United States. Acting on individualistic beliefs, Americans overestimate the level of social mobility in the United States.[51] It is this popular belief that is being reflected in cross-cultural measures of individualism–collectivism, reporting American society to be highly individualistic.

American Ideals and Mainstream Psychology: American individualism has had a profound influence on the development of mainstream psychology in the United States and around the world. As Edward Sampson and other critics have argued,[52] mainstream psychology reflects the American ideal of self-contained individualism; the findings emerging from this psychology reflect, and are limited by, the cultural and historical values of the United States. The most important of such values reflects the *embryonic fallacy*, the idea that from conception to death individuals determine their own destinies.[53] The outcomes for each person are determined by factors within themselves; the motivation, talent, resilience, and other personal characteristics within each person shape their destinies.

An example of the influence of individualism in mainstream psychology is in the role given to cognition in general and to IQ in particular, in shaping individual behavior and longer-term achievement. With respect to cognition, Sampson has noted, "the cognitive perspective in psychology, by virtue of the primacy it gives to the individual knower and to subjective determinants of behavior, and though appearing to reveal something fundamental and invariant about the human mind, represent a set of values and interests that reproduce the existing nature of the social order."[54]

Sampson's claim can be illustrated through the example of mainstream psychological perspectives on intelligence, which is discussed in detail in Chapter 3 of this text. On the one hand intelligence is viewed in mainstream psychology as something shaped by factors within individuals, particularly heredity; on the other hand, intelligence is seen as shaping the status, role, and success of individuals in the larger society. The outcome is a reinforcement of individualism, individual responsibility, and the 'self-help' ideology broadly. By implication, rich and powerful people are rich and powerful because of their intelligence and other dispositional characteristics, rather than because of their inherited wealth or other contextual factors. A glaring example of the rich and powerful attempting to position themselves as 'self-made' is the case of Donald Trump. Prize-winning investigative journalists have demonstrated that inheritance played a dominant role in Trump's wealth, whereas in his political campaigns he has attempted to position himself as a self-made billionaire.[55]

Social Class, Consciousness, and Free Will

[T]he experience of social class as an intergroup and structural phenomenon has received comparatively little attention in psychology.
                                                    Keefer, Goode, and Van Berkel[56]

As Keefer and colleagues (quoted above) report, social class is a neglected topic in mainstream psychology, despite social class serving as a powerful contextual factor that shapes how individuals perceive and behave in the world. For example, Keefer and colleagues report that compared to the members of lower social classes, those of higher social classes perceive class boundaries as more permeable. This perception of society being 'open' obviously serves to interpret their own higher class as 'deserved' on the basis of their personal merits. Social class provides a powerful context in which consciousness and conceptions of free will take shape. As Michael Kraus and Nicole Stephens have argued, "social class is not simply a trait of individuals. Instead, social class is rendered meaningful through the contexts that people inhabit over time."[57]

The context of social class actively shapes the developing brain and individual behavior from early infancy.[58] Children born into poverty often experience conditions of severe environmental pollution, food insecurity, and other forms of deprivation, which can have detrimental long-term impact. As pediatricians Sarah Cusick and Michael Georgieff explain, "Early life events, including nutritional deficiencies and toxic stress, can have differential effects on developing brain regions and processes based on the timing, dose, and duration of these events."[59]

Social class has an impact on basic cognitive processes, including language and memory skills, within the first two years of life.[60] The social class differences found in cognitive abilities later in life (discussed in Chapters 3 and 4 of this text) have their roots in this early period of life. Most importantly, children learn to adapt their behavior to the expectations of the environment. When children as young as four years old perceive themselves to be in a context of higher inequality, they behave in less prosocial ways.[61] Among adults, greed and selfish behavior are shown more when society is more unequal.[62]

The early and continued impact of social class is one of the main reasons why the performance of students in college admissions and higher education continues to be seriously influenced by social class, despite efforts by universities to avoid this outcome. A *New York Times* headline decries "The persistent grip of social class on college admission,"[63] despite the SAT and other tests being made optional by many competitive universities. But the powerful impact of social class is from the earliest days of life,[64] many years *before* the age at which students take the SAT and other such tests. In many respects, the first five years of life are the most important in the competition to gain entrance to elite universities.

Also relevant to success in education is research examining how different social classes nurture different conceptions of the self. Nicole Stephens and colleagues argue that individuals socialized in lower-class families develop more interdependent selves, whereas those socialized in higher-class families develop more independent selves.[65] It is the independent self that is more in tune with, and leads to success in, the culture of higher education and professional work.

Studies of lower-class youth show how being mired in poverty shapes their consciousness. For example, Amanda Roy and colleagues conducted studies of lower-class youth in the Chicago area.[66] These young people perceived the world through a prism of violence, oppression, and economic disparities. But these youth were not passive in response to the physical, structural, and cultural violence surrounding them. They critically reflected on the injustices of their situation and attempted to participate in change, for example, by posting on social media and voicing their opinions.

Research shows complex differences in the attitudes of young people growing up in poor versus affluent families. For example, material goods are even more important to the happiness of young people growing up in poor families in an affluent society.[67] It seems that lacking material resources results in poor youth becoming more focused on material resources than affluent youth. In turn, this greater materialism may serve as a factor in higher juvenile delinquency among poor youth,[68] crime providing one of the very few avenues to material wealth for poor youth.

If the source of consciousness and free will is in the larger society, then we should expect some cultural variation in the conception of the person, together with the conception of consciousness and free will characterizing persons. This expectation contradicts mainstream psychology, which focuses on assumed universals in personality traits (discussed in Chapter 4 of this text). But the proposition that the concept of the person varies across cultures has been strongly supported by the groundbreaking research of Richard Shweder and others for at least the last half-century.[69]

Concluding Comment: Adopting the 'Societies to Cells' Perspective

The causal-reductionist tradition has resulted in a decontextualized approach to studying consciousness and free will. The 'neural correlates of consciousness' are examined as if they are material entities we can point to as evidence for what really 'causes' consciousness. Similarly, 'free will' is examined as if it will be found in a brain part, or a gene, or some other physical entity we can point to as the 'cause' of (an assumed absent) free will. Behind all of these wrong paths is the priority given in mainstream psychology to the supremacy of the individual and the causal-reductionist account of behavior.

The supremacy of the individual brings us back to US ideals about individual liberty and mobility – the ideal of the American Dream, the American West, the American cowboy who roams freely on the range, enters the town alone, fights the good fight, and leaves alone to disappear into the Western skyline. The destinies of these mobile individuals are assumed to be determined by themselves: Whether they become super-rich or remain poor is 'up to them.' They move independent of the larger political and economic system. This independence and free movement, this self-contained individualism, is a myth that has shaped mainstream psychology and its decontextualized explanations of consciousness and free will (the dominance of the American model of individualism in main-stream psychology is further discussed in Chapter 10 in this book, with a focus on psychology in non-Western societies).

A contextualized approach to studying consciousness and free will treats the biological characteristics of humans as enablers, in a process where contextual characteristics, particularly social class, have important roles in the form of consciousness and free will that emerge within the individual through socialization processes. Children born into poor families, facing serious food and other shortages from the earliest stage of life, and experiencing impoverished, violent neighborhoods and schools will develop consciousness and free will that is different from children born into afflu-ent families, socialized in dynamic environments designed for maximum cognitive enrichment.

CHAPTER 6

Motivation and Resilience: Self-Help Myths and the Reality of Invisibility

Motivation, what activates, sustains, and directs behavior, is an important topic in mainstream psychology. All the major mainstream introductory psychology textbooks have a chapter on motivation (sometimes coupled with the topic of emotion). Nor is interest in motivation new; it has been present throughout the history of modern psychology, particularly focusing on work motivation.[1] But the vast body of psychological research on motivation has been shaped by the causal-reductionist model. Sandra Jovchelovitch and Vlad Glaveanu point out that, despite the variety of research approaches to studying motivation, "Most motivational theories assume that motivation 'comes' from the individual, is acted upon by the individual and serves specific functions at the individual level."[2] In this chapter I present an alternative introduction to motivation, building on and integrating critical voices already active in rethinking the psychology of motivation. I also explore the political and ideological function of the reductionist, individualistic focus in motivation research – which I argue serves to maintain the status quo, with its huge and growing social class inequalities.

To better understand the larger political function of the individualistic bias in motivation research, it is useful to consider developments in a related area of research. In the twenty-first century, the topic of *resilience*, the ability to deal with and bounce back from challenging situations with minimum stress, has also attracted considerable attention in mainstream psychology.[3] Motivation and resilience are linked through a concern with what makes individuals more successful. It is assumed that the drive to do well and the ability to withstand difficulties arise from intrapersonal characteristics. Despite some attention to building up resilience in collectives,[4] the focus of resilience research has remained firmly on the individual and has even become more reductionist by moving to 'neural resilience' and brain processes.[5] Thus, the trend in research on resilience is in keeping with the causal-reductionist approach of mainstream psychology in general and motivation research specifically. What activates, sustains, and directs behavior, and the ability to deal with and bounce back from challenging situations with minimum stress, are all seen as determined by individual (and now brain) level processes.

The main concern of research on motivation and resilience is not just individual performance but more specifically individual performance in the work context.[6] Underlying this research trend is a foundational assumption about human beings: that they are hard-wired to be selfish, to work best when striving for individual profits and benefits. The concern is that if work – and social and professional life more broadly – is not orga-nized around individual motivation and individual profits, then *social loaf-ing* will result.[7] The assertion is that people will be less motivated to work when they are working for the 'common good' and for 'collective benefits/ profits' than when working for their personal benefits/profits (this topic is further discussed in Chapter 12). Mainstream psychology implicitly or explicitly sides with this argument, by keeping the focus on intraindividual processes, individual motivation, and individual resilience.

In the first part of this chapter, I discuss the discipline of psychology as an ideology, characterized by reductionism and serving a social and politi-cal function of supporting the status quo. The reductionism of mainstream psychology, particularly in domains such as motivation and resilience, is in line with the individualism of the American Dream. We shall see that the reductionist, individual-focused approach of mainstream psychology has helped to perpetuate belief in the American Dream. Of course, from some political perspectives, this has been an extraordinarily important, essential, and necessary function – not only in the United States but also in some other parts of the world. Mainstream psychological research has at least implicitly helped to maintain the focus on the individual and perpetu-ate the myth that society is a meritocracy, that competition is on a level playing field, and that individuals find their 'natural' place in the status hierarchy based on individual talent, hard work, and motivation.

Related to the discussion on motivation, I critically examine research on resilience, which has experienced considerable growth in the twenty-first century (but not without criticisms[8]). Psychological research on resilience has given importance to dispositional characteristics (such as self-esteem), continuing the reductionism that is characteristic of mainstream psychol-ogy. I present an alternative perspective on both motivation and resilience, looking from 'societies to cells,' giving priority to macro societal and col-lective processes.

Whereas from a mainstream psychology perspective motivation and resilience are important as dispositional (intrapersonal) features of indi-viduals, from an alternative perspective, the most striking feature of life among the lower class is not individual motivation or resilience but *invisibility*, going about daily life without being noticed. The vast majority of lower-class people are in life conditions, including their jobs, where if they do have high motivation and resilience, it will not actually change much for them financially or politically.

Mainstream Psychology as Ideology

[I]n the US corporate and very conservative religious groups have sought to use populist rhetoric and to win "popular" support by extolling the weak state, while at the same time being deeply involved in mandating strong control over the curriculum so that it purposely *excludes* anything that raises questions about their largely unquestioned ideological or religious beliefs, thus reminding us once again of the importance of absent presences, of what is missing as well as what is there, in the curriculum.[9]

Michael Apple's analysis of *Ideology and Curriculum* (the source of the above quotation) highlights the importance of 'absent presences,' what is missing as well as what is present in a discipline, such as psychology. For example, a main argument in this volume is that class-based inequalities and in particular perspective and experiences of the poor are not adequately represented in mainstream psychology. The entire topic of poverty and its impact on behavior (see Chapter 2 of this text) is given far too little attention, for example, in introductory psychology texts used to teach tens of millions of new students about 'the science of behavior.' In this and other important ways, the discipline of psychology functions as a reductionist ideology, providing us with a skewed worldview, a very biased lens, through which to interpret the world, both by what it includes and by what it excludes.

What psychology includes is priority to the individual and intrapersonal (and increasingly brain) processes as the 'cause' of behavior. Mainstream psychology encompasses the *embryonic fallacy*, the assumption that as soon as life begins, the individual becomes the source of psychological experiences (discussed in Chapter 5).[10] This reductionist bias has been enhanced through developments in neuroscience, so that it is not the individual but the brain, brain parts, and their characteristics that are now more a focus. Related to this, the *mereological fallacy* is also commonplace (discussed at more length in Chapter 11 of this text). That is, the properties of whole persons are attributed to parts of the brain.

Reductionist neuroscience has enhanced and justified the pro-elite biases in mainstream psychology in a number of ways.[11] Most importantly, reductionist neuroscience provides 'advanced technology' and 'scientific terminology,' serving to bolster the legitimacy of mainstream psychology. For example, brain imaging technology and terminology (electroencephalography, EEG; functional magnetic resonance imaging, fMRI; positron emission tomography, PET; etc.) have enhanced the image of a reductionist approach in psychology as legitimate. From an ideological perspective, reductionist neuroscience matches the dominant individualistic ethos of mainstream psychology, by providing 'facts' that 'demonstrate' intraindividual processes to be the 'causes' of behavior.

The ethos perpetuated by reductionist neuroscience is in line with, and has been perpetuated through, the popular media in capitalist democracies.[12] Results from neuroscience studies are represented and disseminated in the popular media with a focus on three central themes, all pointing back to the brain as the main source of behavior: the brain as capital or resource that needs to be boosted; the brain as a source of group-based differences, such as between 'normal' and 'abnormal' people and between men and women; and the brain as biological proof of social phenomena.[13]

Within this reductionist story, there is a neglect of the relatively small (but growing) number of studies that have pointed to a bigger picture by examining poverty and the brain. This body of research points to how poverty detrimentally impacts early brain development and also what interventions might be effective toward alleviating this impact.[14] Neuroscience research on the impact of poverty on cognitive development can help put the spotlight on the detrimental consequences of poverty, as well as flaws in the supposed 'meritocratic system' of the United States and other major societies. How can there be a 'level playing field' and 'equality of opportunity' when poverty has such devastating impact on cognitive functioning?[15]

Topics Absent in Psychology

Social class and poverty, then, are important examples of topics that are largely absent in mainstream psychology. Other topics not given adequate attention are the psychology of democracy and dictatorship, global warming, wealth inequalities, political power and powerlessness, and invisibility. I am not only arguing that mainstream psychology neglects such topics because it is influenced by ideological bias; rather, I am pointing out that mainstream psychology *is* ideology. This is in contrast to received wisdom, which tells us that mainstream psychology is 'science,' and a generator of 'neutral psychological facts.'

The main function of psychology as ideology is to support and fortify the political status quo, with its growing class-based inequalities.[16] This is achieved first and foremost through mainstream psychology, reinforced by reductionist neuroscience, stubbornly insisting on behavior being causally determined by factors within individuals and increasingly within brain processes. In this way, *individuals* are held responsible for their outcomes. This contrasts with research that shows social class shapes how people value characteristics such as self-direction in their children, and this trend is consistent across countries with different political systems and cultures.[17]

Mainstream psychology claims to stand 'apart from' political biases, on a platform of objectivity. In fact, it is not science that guides mainstream psychology but, rather, hidden political ideology. Reductionism is adhered to, irrespective of various 'crises' inside and outside psychology. If mainstream psychology was actually guided by science and not ideology, then it would be changed by such 'crises.' Neither the 'replication crisis' of psychology in the twenty-first century (which arose because many published studies are not replicable[18]) nor the 'social psychology crisis' of the late twentieth century (which arose because of attacks on both the research methods and research topics of social psychology[19]) has had any serious or lasting impact on the tenets of mainstream psychology.

The 'crises' in psychology do not have a major impact on mainstream psychology precisely because the main societal function of mainstream psychology is not scientific but ideological, and this function has not changed – not even when large numbers of the 'facts' produced by psychology prove not to be replicable. This ideological role of mainstream psychology remains neglected. For example, defenders of mainstream psychology have put forward various explanations and interpretations of why the replication crisis has come about, such as the need for more 'open science' and the need to take steps to avoid 'cognitive biases' among researchers themselves,[20] on the assumption that the function of mainstream psychology really is to arrive at objective facts. If only we can be less biased and more open about how we do research, the replication crisis will subside – so the argument goes. But this completely misses the point: Mainstream psychology functions to legitimize the existing social and political order. That is why topics such as poverty and the perspectives of the lower social classes are still largely absent or reduced to reductionist, intrapersonal characteristics when they do get a mention in mainstream texts.

My argument that mainstream psychology serves as ideology echoes arguments made by others. In his brilliant analysis of modern psychology, Edward Sampson argues that the value system and reductionism of cognitive psychology lead it to serve as an ideology that justifies the existing social order with its many inequalities and injustices.[21] Moreover, cognitive psychology serves to bolster *false consciousness*, a view of group membership and class-based inequalities that is divorced from objective reality and serves to perpetuate inequalities and elite rule. Sampson's arguments regarding how certain ideologies (in this case, cognitive psychology) justify the existing system were later developed in greater depth and detail through system justification theory.[22]

The concept of system justification is derived from the concept of false consciousness, reflecting the proposition that "ideas favoring dominant groups in society prevail because these groups control the cultural and institutional means by which ideas are spread. As a result, social and political realities are distorted systematically by the ideological machinations of elites."[23] Education and research institutions, as well as research fields such as psychology, are a central part of the 'cultural and institutional means' through which ideas are spread. In line with Sampson, then, I interpret the discipline of psychology as ideology.

However, I am not suggesting there is a conspiracy among psychologists to serve such a political function. Psychological researchers do not consciously strive to support the status quo. Rather, I am pointing out that, first, mainstream psychology is dominated by the United States. Second, mainstream psychology is exported from the United States to the rest of the world. Third, particularly in the United States, but also to a large degree in other capitalist countries, people are socialized to interpret the world through a causal-reductionist lens, which gives highest priority to individualism and individual-based meritocracy. Reductionist neuroscience has served to strengthen this trend, so that the 'causes' of behavior are now depicted as not just individuals but brains and neural networks. Like other people socialized in the United States and other capitalist societies, psychologists are influenced to adopt a reductionist interpretation of behavior, and this is clearly evident in mainstream psychology.

Motivation, Resilience, and the American Dream

> Americans are today divided about how much (if at all) income and wealth should be redistributed ... On the other hand, we are less divided about the desirability of upward mobility without regard to family origins ... The roots of this primal commitment to equality of opportunity are deep and diverse.
>
> Robert Putnam[24]

[C]hildren's prospects of earning more than their parents have faded over the past half-century in the United States. The fraction of children earning more than their parents fell from approximately 90% for children born in 1940 to around 50% for children entering the labor market today ... most of the decline in absolute mobility is driven by the more unequal distribution of economic growth in recent decades, rather than by the slowdown in GDP growth rates ... If one wants to revise the "American Dream" of high rates of absolute mobility, then one must have an interest in growth that is spread more broadly across the income distribution.

Raj Chetty and colleagues[25]

There is a disparity between the beliefs of Americans that upward mobility is an essential part of the American Dream and the economic reality that upward mobility is less likely in the twenty-first century in the United States than it was half a century ago. The harsh reality of lower upward mobility has resulted in, on the one hand, claims that the American Dream is alive and well in Canada, Scandinavia, and some other places *outside* the United States. As a *Washington Post* headline put it, "Finland's Prime Minister Sanna Marin says the American Dream is best achieved in Nordic countries."[26] On the other hand, this has led to attempts by politically right-wing institutions in the United States to cast doubt on the research showing lower upward mobility.[27] In the context of these interweaving trends, psychological science has played a very important role, for the most part serving to justify the status quo in favor of the upper class.

Research demonstrates that people who perceive higher levels of social mobility show a greater tendency to defend the current system,[28] with its class-based inequalities. The individualistic focus in mainstream psychology helps to bolster the idea that individual characteristics matter most in determining social status. Those who actually experience upward social mobility also become stronger defenders of the existing system.[29] But irrespective of individual experiences with social mobility, the impact of mainstream psychology is to firmly keep the focus on intrapersonal characteristics as determining the fate of individuals.

Individual Resilience

In the twenty-first century, the individualistic focus of psychological research on motivation has been enhanced by research on resilience, with priority on the characteristics of individuals that are assumed to cause them to spring back from adversity. The concept of resilience has its roots in the domains of physics and engineering and was transferred to explain human behavior at a later stage.[30] (But in engineering resilience is a property of structures and systems, whereas in mainstream psychology it is assumed to be a property of elements/individuals.) As psychological research on resilience has expanded, the focus has firmly fixed on individual performance.[31] It is assumed to be so much better if individuals can be trained to be resilient from a young age to deal with poverty, for example. Thus, in the *Handbook of Resilience in Children*, we read that it is important to study resilience in the belief that "every child capable of developing a resilient mindset will be able to deal more effectively with stress and pressure."[32] Of course, poverty is an important example of such 'stress and pressure" that it is assumed individuals can be trained to withstand, through cognitive training, for example.[33]

Psychological research on resilience has focused particularly on training individuals to have greater resilience (a number of critics have noted this individual and intraindividual focus and lack of attention to context[34]). This is exemplified by the approach taken by Martin Seligman; as we would expect from Seligman's positive psychology (discussed in Chapter 8 of this text), he assumes optimism in individuals to be the key.[35] The main thrust of this approach to poverty is: If we can get individuals to think more positively and to withstand stress, they will be able to better tolerate and perhaps dig themselves out of poverty, or at least be happy in poverty.

But some researchers have taken an even more extreme reductionist approach, focusing on the neural correlates of resilience.[36] The implication is that problems such as poverty can be fought by training individuals to develop 'neural resilience.' Dante Cicchetti and Jennifer Blender warn of the danger of reducing resilience to biological processes: "In the context of resilience, we do not wish to convey or encourage the reduction of resilience to biological processes ... reducing psychological phenomena to components of genetic, neuroanatomical, neurochemical, or neurophysiological factors dismisses the great impact that experience has on these processes."[37] Despite such warnings, the larger body of neuroscience research continues on a reductionist path, including on the topic of resilience.

Poverty Still Largely Absent from Mainstream Psychology

There are enormous numbers of studies on how individual motivation and individual resilience can be strengthened, on the assumption that the poor are poor because they personally lack motivation and resilience rather than because of contextual factors – such as being born poor! More attention needs to be given by psychologists to styles of thinking that justify social-class inequalities, as such research is illuminating. For example, consider research on psychological processes and poverty,[38] specifically focused on social *attributions*,[39] inferences about causes. These studies show a tendency for poverty to be blamed on individual characteristics, particularly among more affluent people.

The most sophisticated psychological approach to poverty was developed by Bernard Weiner and colleagues,[40] who adopted an attributional framework. This analysis makes two novel contributions that go beyond the received wisdom that politically right-wing individuals tend to blame the poor for their poverty (e.g., laziness), while politically left-wing individuals tend to explain poverty by attributing causes to contextual characteristics (such as lack of educational and job opportunities). Weiner and colleagues point out that by persuading people to feel sympathetic toward the poor, we increase the likelihood of aid being provided. But in the context of the enormous volume of research in mainstream psychology, there are still very few psychological research studies on the poor.

The most comprehensive research on the experiences of the poor themselves was conducted for the World Development Report 2000/2001 and included as participants 60,000 poor people from 60 countries.[41] This detailed study of how the poor see the world reflects the relative material deprivation suffered by the poor. Very importantly, these studies also reveal painful awareness among the poor of how their voices are *not heard*, their needs *are ignored*, their social networks and political influence *are weak*, their situation seems to be *getting worse* rather than better, and they remain *invisible to those in power*. Just as the poor and their needs are invisible in the larger world, they remain largely invisible in mainstream psychology.

Poverty and Invisibility

Whether we are present ... or not present, no one will take notice.[42]
Collective expression from a group of poor men, Foua, Egypt

A striking feature of poverty is that it is characterized by what I call *invisibility*, being treated as a nonperson. In order to better understand invisibility, it is useful to start with the most extreme and obvious examples, such as found in the relationship between royalty and servants. Like most royal palaces, those of King Ludwig II (1845–1886) of Bavaria were designed to minimize interactions between the servants and the king. For example, the servants were not allowed to use staircases used by his majesty. But Ludwig went a step further: In Linderhof Castle (near Oberammergau, Bavaria) Ludwig had a dining table that rose up and down, from one floor of the palace to another, so the servants were able to serve dinner without being seen or seeing his majesty. The servants were invisible. In twenty-first-century societies, lower-class individuals are often invisible, in part because they lack status, power, and resources. They move around, as cleaners, drivers, waitresses, gardeners, and so on, as if they do not exist. They are the shadow armies that invisibly keep the world turning. They are only noticed when they do not perform their jobs satisfactorily or commit crimes against middle- and upper-class members. Invisibility as experienced by the poor results in a further lack of attention to their needs and interests.

The invisibility of the poor and that of the superrich are in some respects similar but in some other respects very different. For example, the superrich and the poor are both physically separated from the rest of society, so they live in spaces far removed from everyone else. In a literal sense, these groups are not seen. The superrich separate themselves through the exclusivity of their homes, schools, clubs, neighborhoods and shopping centers, private planes, and yachts. The poor find themselves separated, pushed out of sight into certain neighborhoods, schools, shopping centers, and buses and other forms of transportation. Thus, invisibility through physical separation is common to both the superrich and the poor. But there are key differences. First, the superrich are invisible by choice, but this is not a choice for the poor. Second, when the superrich actually are present they become noticed, whereas the poor are very often present (to serve the rich) but remain unnoticed.

The political clout of the superrich, their luxurious and often ostentatious presence, means that they suck oxygen from the space they occupy. The rich display resilience because their wealth and power ensure that when present they are noticed and catered to. Everyone attends to them, meets their needs, bends over backward to make them happy. When their limousines, jets, and yachts come into view, they become the center of attention. But the armies of the poor – the cleaners, the maids, the gardeners, the garbage collectors, the kitchen helpers, and so on – are often invisible even when they are present. The poor are trained to serve in silence and without being noticed.

Acts of nonconformity, disobedience, rebellion, riots, make the poor visible,[43] but the norm for the poor is to remain invisible.[44] This is documented by studies of the poor in different parts of the world, such as research on poor women in South Asia: "So invisible were these women that even a private non-governmental organisation working for gender

empowerment and human rights ... had overlooked them in its projects."[45] But the poor are also in important respects invisible in the United
States and other affluent societies. Consider the invisibility of the enormous numbers of the poor who work as cleaners, service providers, and so
on in the homes, organizations, offices, restaurants, daycare centers, senior
homes, gardens, social clubs, and streets of the affluent but are taken for
granted – not noticed unless they do something wrong.

Alternative Perspectives on Motivation and Resilience

> Poor people are caught in a web of multiple and interlocking deprivations.[46]

In what are probably the most extensive crossnational studies ever conducted exploring the experiences of poor people, Deepa Narayan and
colleagues (quoted above) identified 'multiple and interlocking' ways in
which poor people suffer deprivation. The child born into a lower-class
family is immediately disadvantaged in nutrition, health, housing and
neighborhood quality, environmental pollution, security, social support,
transportation, schooling, political representation, and so on. These types
of disadvantage are 'interlocking,' in the sense that it is extremely difficult
to improve the lives of children in any one of these areas without making
improvements in other areas. For example, improvements in schools are in
large part dependent on improvements in neighborhoods, security, political representation, health services, and so on.

   The interlocking deprivations confronting lower-class children are
not completely impenetrable – a few very exceptional individuals break
through and move out of poverty. These individuals become the 'stars'
who are pointed out on university campuses, in business organizations,
in political parties, on sports fields. These individuals serve as the tokens
that 'demonstrate' that the system 'works' and really is open. As Bligh
Grant points out, "from a structural perspective, the principal function
of a token is to maintain the belief that upward mobility is possible."[47]
Consider, for example, this appreciative account of Oprah Winfrey:

> The journey of Oprah Gail Winfrey from Hattie Mae's pig farm in Missis-
> sippi to the pinnacle of wealth, power, and success in American television is
> a journey we must all admire.[48]

Of course, we must all admire the case of Oprah Winfrey because at the
individual level it demonstrates her determination, talent, hard work.
More importantly, however, we must admire the case of Oprah Winfrey
because at the societal level it 'demonstrates' that the system is open, the

American Dream is alive, and if Oprah can make it from "Hattie Mae's pig farm in Mississippi to the pinnacle of wealth, power, and success," then *anyone* can make it in America – as long as they have the personal motivation and resilience!

But, in practice, it is only highly exceptional individuals with a great deal of luck who break out of poverty, and it is misleading for psychologists to continue to focus on individual motivation and resilience. Leslie Anderson has argued that "Promoting resilience without also working to address societal conditions that often make resilience necessary is only a partial response."[49] Exactly the same is true with respect to motivation: Promoting motivation at the individual level only helps a few exceptionally talented people, the star tokens who then go on to 'prove' the system is open.

We must progress beyond the perspective of mainstream psychology, which treats motivation and resilience as properties of self-contained, mobile individuals. Yes, there are exceptional individuals such as Oprah Winfrey – but she is one in every ten million or so. The vast majority of people are welded to the conditions they are born into, and if they are born lower class they remain enmeshed in interlocking deprivations. Psychological science must make greater efforts to change the interlocking deprivations imposed on the lower class by their material, social, and political conditions. It is not enough to point to intrapersonal characteristics as the solution to poverty and class-based inequalities.

It is ironic that 'self-help' ideology is preached by the middle and upper classes but actually mostly practiced by the poor. Middle- and upper-class members begin life with huge inherited resources, and their 'self-help' is built on enormous advantages relative to the 'self-help' of individuals born into poor families. It is the lower-, rather than middle- and upper-class members, who actually act on the basis of 'self-help' and 'individual responsibility,' because they have extremely scant resources and a relatively weak support system. For example, in educational competition, it is individuals born into upper-class families who enter elite universities through the help of 'legacy' placements and monetary donations made to universities by their families. Individuals born into lower-class families do not have such resources – or money for private schools and tutors. What lower-class individuals do have is the risk of being seen as dangerous and threatening.[50]

In the post-9/11 world, large numbers of the lower class face the additional burden of being seen as serious security threats. The increased security surveillance impacts all society, but the lower class are the primary targets. Lower-class Whites, who remain a neglected group in social and psychological research,[51] are scrutinized for possible involvement in radical right-wing movements, while the non-White lower class are seen as targets for possible involvement in Islamic terrorism. The enormous increase in security comes at a high cost to civil liberties and the open society. Governments have used the excuse of terrorism, crime, and the war on drugs to restrict civil liberties and to violate privacy rights, with the poor across all ethnic groups suffering the most serious detrimental impact (such as closer surveillance and stricter punishments).

Concluding Comment

By researching motivation and resilience as if the characteristics of individuals and their brains determine their success in society and their ability to withstand adversarial conditions, mainstream psychology and reductionist neuroscience, guided by the causal-reductionist ethos, have served the important ideological function of justifying class-based inequalities. Largely absent from mainstream psychology is acknowledgment of the invisibility that poverty brings and the harsh material conditions that characterize the lives of the lower class and that significantly decrease the probability of success independent of individual characteristics.

Of course, a few lucky exceptional lower-class individuals are able to rise up the status hierarchy and succeed 'against all odds.' These individuals, such as Oprah Winfrey, serve as tokens to justify increasing class-based inequalities and further propagate the myth that society is open and meritocratic. In the twenty-first century, reductionist neuroscience has added a veneer of scientific legitimacy to this trend, using 'advanced technology' to pinpoint causal mechanisms in the brain that purportedly explain motivation and resilience. The deeper political impact of these research biases is to further weaken the interests of the lower class and to move the focus of psychological research further away from class-based inequalities. Of course, the children of affluent families also face challenges, and there are 'costs' and 'risks' to affluence – such as substance abuse and anxiety (Luthar 2003). But there are already relatively large resources dedicated to solving the 'costs of affluence.' Psychological science must direct more efforts to understanding the *conditions* suffered by the different social classes, with special focus on changing the conditions of the poor.

CHAPTER 7

Group Life and Diversity

The causal-reductionist nature of mainstream psychology has resulted in a disproportional focus on the behavior of individuals and on brains and brain parts and the relative neglect of group and intergroup behavior. But this situation is slowly changing. One important way in which groups have gained more attention in mainstream psychology, including in standard introductory psychology texts, is through the influence of ethnic minority movements and multiculturalism. 'Multicultural psychology' has now become accepted as an approach to psychological research and practice that gives special attention to ethnic minorities.[1] In multicultural psychology, group differences and cultural variations take on greater importance. Multiculturalism is now a highlighted theme particularly in educational psychology,[2] in counseling and clinical arenas,[3] and in organizational behavior.[4]

Increases in the numbers of ethnic minority members has also resulted in more attention being given to groups, such as minority students in education.[5] A relatively large number of texts examine racism and race relations, with either a focus on all people of color or with particular focus on the African American experience.[6] There are also handbooks that focus on the experiences of all or specific minorities.[7] The feminist movement has also resulted in groups getting more attention in mainstream psychology, with a focus on the psychology of gender and feminism.[8] The greater attention given to group and intergroup psychology has been associated with intersectionality becoming a dominant perspective through which to explore social inequalities related to ethnicity, gender, and groups generally.[9]

The most neglected aspect of group and intergroup psychology remains social class and poverty. Although some researchers have examined inequality and social class,[10] poverty,[11] the experiences of working-class Whites,[12] and the contrasting lives of rich and poor,[13] these topics deserve far more attention in psychological science. While group and intergroup psychology remains relatively neglected in mainstream psychology, within this neglected field the psychology of poverty and social class receives far too little attention.

In this chapter I first argue that group and intergroup psychology should be given greater importance in all of psychology. After all, the collective social world precedes and is the root of our individual experiences. Human beings and human consciousness emerge out of the collective world (as discussed in Chapter 5 of this text), and psychological science should give more attention to our collective lives. Second, I argue that far more attention needs to be given specifically to poverty and social class, particularly because poverty and social class provide strong contexts that shape individual behavior. The norms that regulate the lives of the lower class are largely constructed by, and mostly benefit, the upper class. In the final section, I discuss how the focus on ethnicity, multiculturalism, and the celebration of ethnic group differences has failed to improve the educational performance of ethnic minorities, because the problem of poverty and the plight of the lower class has not been adequately addressed. Celebrating ethnic group differences without addressing the problem of *the poverty suffered by most ethnic minority members* is not an effective solution to their deep material problems.

The Primacy of Collective Processes

Isolation is used as a severe punishment in human societies; solitary confinement is known to have serious detrimental mental and physical consequences.[14] Humans are wedded to, and dependent upon, the collective and, at least since the time of Aristotle, have been described as social beings.[15] At birth we are 'thrown into' the already structured world of our society, with its vast informal and formal moral and legal systems. We can only survive (at least initially) through high levels of conformity and obedience.[16] Our individual survival depends on belonging to, fitting in with, and receiving support from the collective.

This dependency means that infants survive by developing strong social and emotional bonds with caretakers. Infants react negatively when their caretakers fail to interact with them in a harmonious, socially supportive manner, such as when a mother's face becomes 'still' and unresponsive.[17] The implication is that it is not only in a strictly material sense, in matters of functionality and survival, that individual humans are dependent on the others.

Extensive research, pioneered by John Bowlby (1907–1990), demonstrates that the central role of attachment is revealed by looking beyond intrapersonal processes, to relationships *between* people. As Charles Zeanah and colleagues have argued in discussing the clinical applications of attachment theory,

> Assessment of attachment involves a paradigmatic shift in the clinical frame. Following the long tradition of medicine, psychiatric disorders are conceptualized as existing within an individual, even if the disorder has significant interpersonal manifestation ... The quality of the child-caregiver attachment, on the other hand, requires shifting from considering clinical problems as existing within an individual child to conceiving of clinical problems (and strengths) existing between caregiver and child.[18]

Attachment involves emotional bonds between the infant and caretaker, which research suggests can be at least as important as material dependency of the infant to the caretaker. For example, in Harry Harlow's (1905–1981) classic study of infant rhesus monkeys isolated soon after birth and reared with surrogate mothers made of wire or terry cloth, half of the infant monkeys received milk from the wire mother and the other half from the terry cloth mother.[19] The feel of the surrogate mothers differed (the terry cloth mother was much softer and more comforting), but each provided the same amount of food. Both groups of infant monkeys spent far more time with the terry cloth surrogate mother – the cuddly one. Research on attachment pioneered by Bowlby on humans and Harlow on animals both highlight the foundational importance of *social relations* and emotional bonds in development.[20] Thus, psychology must look beyond intraindividual processes, to social relations.

The sources of human consciousness are also social (as discussed in Chapter 5 of this text).[21] As infants develop, they learn language first as a means of communicating with their primary caretakers and others. They learn turn-taking in verbal expressions, first babbling sounds and then words, through public forms of communications.[22] These external forms of communications with others come first and then later are internalized as forms of inner speech, thinking through problems 'by oneself.' But for the first few years of life, children often speak aloud, and adults also sometimes engage in 'talking out aloud.' Thinking is a process with roots 'out there' in collective life.

Human cognition, then, is best understood not as private acts carried out by isolated individuals but as actions rooted in and stemming from the collective and using public symbolic tools – language being the main one. This perspective makes it clear that psychological science can best explain cognitive development through focusing on the integration of the individual in collective processes and group life. But exactly the opposite approach is adopted by mainstream psychology, which is reductionist and gives highest priority to understanding the world from the perspective of the isolated, self-contained individual.[23]

By placing collective processes and group life at the center of psychological science, we necessarily give priority to the world outside and its social characteristics – particularly social class differences, resource inequalities, and poverty. This 'outside-in,' 'societies to cells' approach leads to a direct concern with collectives, differences in the normative systems of groups, and the organization of relations between groups.

Why More Attention to Social Class and Poverty?

Lack of political clout, inadequate or no health insurance, hazardous working and living conditions, failing schools, food insecurity, unsafe childcare, absent fathers, missing role models, lack of political influence … poverty is associated with many disadvantages.[24] Being financially poor and working in low income, unstable, often physically hazardous jobs with little or no stability or benefits is just one dimension. But perhaps an even more important dimension of poverty is the lack of connections, skills, and information – the types that enable members of the middle and upper class to find better educational and employment opportunities for themselves and their families, to further improve their standard of living and life quality. For example, consider the following question, which I call the *'lawyer test.'*

> *How would you get advice about what it is like working as a lawyer and how to become a lawyer?*

Members of the middle and upper class are likely to answer something like, "I would ask my aunt, she is a lawyer," or "I would ask my father's best friend because he is a judge and was a lawyer before that," or "Easy, our next-door neighbor and good family friend is a partner at a law firm."

Whereas members of the middle and upper class know lawyers and judges as either family members or friends, lower-class individuals only know lawyers and judges in their roles as the accused, the incarcerated, and the outcast. They know lawyers and judges because they or their families and friends are ordered to appear in courts and stand before the authorities as 'criminals,' whereas the members of the middle and upper class socialize with lawyers and judges, have drinks and dinners with them on an everyday basis. Just as the relationship between the lower class and lawyers is very different from that of the middle and upper class and lawyers, their broader life experiences are fundamentally different and need to be understood through a different psychology, one that gives more attention to the special experiences of the lower class.

Simply put, the lower class live shorter, more hazardous, precarious lives. This would matter less if the gap between the different social classes was decreasing and if lower-class individuals were benefitting from improved opportunities to move up the social hierarchy. But this is not the case – far from it. In-depth studies have demonstrated that more and more wealth is concentrated in the hands of a smaller and smaller number of individuals, and inequality is increasing: The share of wealth owned by the top 1 percent increased from 45 percent in 2009 to 50 percent in 2017;[25] also, the number of billionaires it takes to equal the wealth of the poorest 50 percent of the global population declined from 380 in 2009 to 42 in 2017,[26] and to 26 in 2019[27]. The wealth of billionaires has been increasing at a faster rate than that of the poor, although there is controversy about the exact differences.[28]

There are also extraordinary signs of how the superrich are amassing and spending their growing fortunes. This matters for psychologists, because it is another sign that the lifestyles and behavior patterns of the different social classes are becoming even more different. For example, astonishingly, the price of the most expensive yachts bought by the superrich has risen above *a billion* dollars each (!) (www.beautifullife.info/automotive-design/worlds-top-10-most-expensive-luxury-yachts/). But while the superrich are buying billion-dollar toys for their amusement, according to the World Bank, 2.7 billion people still live on less than $2 a day.[29] Oxfam estimates that 2,381,034,349 people lived in poverty in 2018.[30] The COVID-19 pandemic is likely to increase the number of people living in poverty by 420–580 million.[31] The plight of the poor in low-income societies is summed up as having no work, no pay, no food.[32]

In major corporations in the United States and other Western societies the poor are falling further behind in relative terms,[33] even though research shows that higher CEO pay can result in the CEO being seen as a less effective leader.[34] This trend is taking us back to the time of the pharaohs. The poor are financially and in terms of life conditions as far below the richest group as the slaves were from the pharaohs five thousand years ago. Inequality in the United States is calculated to be about the same as it was in the Roman Empire.[35] This suggests that despite all our tremendous scientific and technological advances, in terms of resources our societies are as unequal as they were thousands of years ago.

Current research suggests there are limits to how we can simulate wealth inequalities in experiments. For example, consider an experimental study

using brain imaging where participants were given high or low amounts
of money ($80 vs. $30) and asked to evaluate transfers of money to themselves or to the other player.[36] Indicators of both expressed preferences
of participants and brain activation suggest inequality to be less appealing. This led the authors to conclude that "Our results provide direct
neurobiological evidence in support of the existence of inequality-averse
social preferences in the human brain."[37] These kinds of laboratory situations, involving individuals temporarily made 'rich' or 'poor' by being
given small or smaller sums of money, provide stimulating talking points.
However, they are inadequate indicators of what happens in the larger
world, where inequality is increasing on a vast scale, *despite* the avowed
"existence of inequality-averse social preferences in the human brain."

Moreover, social mobility between social classes in the United States
and some other societies has declined or stagnated,[38] in part because success in education is closely tied to family monetary wealth. Michael Kraus
and Jun Won Park have noted that "In the United States ... analysis of
National Educational Survey data finds that only 28.8% of high aptitude
students from lower social class families earn four-year degrees, whereas
that number is 74.1% among high aptitude students from higher social
class families."[39] Moreover, students from higher social class families tend
to target more prestigious universities.[40] This highlights continuity of
inequalities across generations.

The correlation between the earnings of fathers and sons is 0.47 and
0.50 in the United States and the United Kingdom respectively, compared
to 0.15 and 0.17 in Denmark and Norway respectively.[41] The clear implication is that in the United States and the United Kingdom, sons are very
likely to have similar incomes to their fathers, but far less so in Denmark
and Norway. This means that in the context of the United States and the
United Kingdom, there is stagnation or decline in the probability of a
child born into a lower-class family moving up to join the upper classes.
The resulting 'broken social elevator' or 'broken ladder' has been noticed:[42]
50 percent of Americans now understand that parents' education is important to get ahead in life. This understanding in turn shapes the goals and
aspirations of the next generation: Children from upper-class families aim
high and get material and other support to reach high; no matter where
they aim, children from lower-class families get very little support to reach
higher than their parents.

Research on social mobility is revealing that in order to understand the
full impact of family characteristics on children, it is necessary to take a
multigenerational approach. That is, the probability of a child succeeding

is shaped not only by the characteristics of parents but also by grand-parents and other previous generations.[43] This has led to the identification of conditions where there is a hoarding of opportunities, and what Charles Tilly has called "durable inequality,"[44] when unequal stratification becomes entrenched across generations. One reason for this is the increasing cost of higher education, particularly in the United States and the United Kingdom, two countries where the correlation between the income of parents and children is particularly high. For example, in the United States in 1980 it took 26 percent of the median family income to cover college tuition, but this figure had doubled by 2004.[45] Also, the computer and social media revolution, instead of liberating the poor, has disproportionally laid them open to fraud and internet scams[46] – even the Internet favors the rich. In the American context, this has led some important researchers to declare that the American Dream is in serious trouble: Opportunities for 'making it in America' have suffered serious decline.[47]

These changes in the experiences of the poor and of different social classes have resulted in greater focus on inequality in the mass media. A 2017 study of media coverage of inequality found "a compatibility between the rise of inequality on the one hand and an increased coverage in the media on the other."[48] Given this change in media coverage, one would also expect the discipline of psychology to react far more strongly to such changes, so that poverty and the challenge of huge and growing class-based inequalities become the central themes in psychological research.[49]

Poverty As a Strong Context

[P]overty may favor behaviors that make it more difficult to escape poverty.

Johannes Haushofer and Ernst Fehr[50]

In the twenty-first century a series of studies have put the spotlight on various behaviors that are characteristic of poor people and that seem to work against the poor climbing out of poverty (as discussed in Chapter 2 of this text). For example, in a study of Vietnamese villages, people in poorer villages were shown to be more risk averse, so that relative to more affluent people they selected to gain smaller and earlier rewards rather than larger rewards at a later time.[51] That is, the poor displayed more *loss aversion*, where losses loom larger than gains, well known to cognitive scientists.[52] But in explaining how the poor behave differently, we must be careful not to fall into the trap of reductionism. The *source* of the behavioral differences between rich and poor are not intrapersonal differences, such as differences in neural or cognitive processes. Rather, the source lies outside individuals and is to be found in collective processes, relations between groups and the world 'out there.'

Behaviors such as lower tolerance for risk among the poor arise out of the material conditions of their lives. In a study using online surveys administered shortly before or after payday to 3,821 participants in the United States with annual household incomes below $40,000, it was found that the before-payday sample behaved in a more present-biased manner, seeking more immediate rewards.[53] This reflects the difficult material conditions facing the lower class: They have lower or no savings, and less opportunity to take loans at reasonable interest rates when they need access to additional money. Less than half of US households actually have 'emergency savings,' enough money saved to cover expenses for three months.[54] At the country level, the saving rate is positively related to income,[55] reflecting the practical reality that people can save only when they have more money than what is needed to cover basic costs. These social class differences became starkly apparent during the COVID-19 pandemic, when the poor fell further behind in income.[56]

This interpretation of individual behavior through giving priority to social circumstances and collective life broadly is in line with the reconceptualization of findings from the classic *marshmallow test*, a measure of delayed gratification.[57] A preschool child is left alone with two marshmallows or some other tempting treat. If and when the child eats the treat(s), rather than wait for larger rewards at a later time, this indicates her inability to delay gratification. A large body of studies indicate that a child's ability to delay gratification is correlated with later outcomes, such as academic and work performance.[58] The ability to delay gratification is seen to be the 'engine of success' in many different areas, where individuals are more successful if they have the ability to make investments for later rewards. Although some recent studies have questioned the replicability of marshmallow test findings, the general consensus is that the results from this test do correlate (if not causally predict) performance in some key domains in later life.[59]

The mainstream interpretation of findings from the marshmallow test have been individualistic, focusing on individual differences in intrapersonal characteristics such as self-control. The idea is that those individuals who show better self-control as a preschooler will continue to show superior self-control as a teenager and in adulthood and do better over the course of their lives generally[60] – because of their individual characteristics. Laura Michaelson and Yuko Munakata tested an alternative, more socially based explanation: "[A] child's ability to wait might be less important than the social and environmental circumstances influencing their willingness to wait."[61] These researchers tested the influence of both delay of gratification (individual measure) and social support (collective measure) on outcomes, which included academic achievement, problem behaviors, and social skills. The results confirmed the powerful impact of social support: Children who delay gratification might be doing this because they are growing up in a more supportive environment, where they can trust the continued availability of resources and 'backing' in general. If a child is growing up in an environment in which resources are scarce, where there is food insecurity, and less certainty about the future, it seems rational to take the available marshmallow now and not risk waiting for a second marshmallow in the future – the second marshmallow might not be available in the next minute.

This more social interpretation aligns with findings from research on cognition and poverty, showing that poor people are risk averse – preferring to take a smaller reward now rather than wait for a larger reward later (as discussed in Chapter 2 of this text). The poor live in a less stable, more uncertain environment, in which they have less control over their lives. They work in unstable and insecure jobs, often without benefits, and have little or no savings to fall back on. Lower-class families are more likely to suffer food insecurity, and if they fall ill, their health care and support system is weaker. In these circumstances, it is rational to grab at whatever resources are on the table now, because everything could disappear in the next minute. Children as young as five are aware of their level of wealth.[62] Those from lower social classes have future selves that are less vivid and that overlap less with their present selves, which hinders planning and motivation.[63] As I discuss in the next section, the behavior of the lower class is often incorrect from a middle- and upper-class perspective, but it is what works in the less stable environment of the poor.

Lives of the Lower Class Regulated by Norms Established by the Upper Class

We need to understand the behavior of the lower class in a holistic way. Poverty is transformative, in that it encompasses all aspects of the person. Although the poor are not homogeneous, all of them have less power and fewer choices. Their behavior, including their decisions on risk-taking, has to be understood in the context of this powerlessness and limited choice – which arise from their situation in the larger world. This larger world is regulated by normative systems that are largely created by, and for the benefit of, the upper class rather than the lower class. In this section, I explore the power of norms as demonstrated through psychological research on norm formation and conformity to norms. Also relevant to our discussion are *rules*, prescriptions for how individuals in particular role relationships (e.g., loan applicant–lender; employee–employer; tenant–property owner) should behave, whereas norms prescribe correct behavior in given contexts.

Conformity and Obedience to 'Incorrect' Norms

Norms and rules derive their power from their shared, collective nature. They are integral to what Emile Durkheim (1858–1917) and later Serge Moscovici (1925–2014) discussed as *collective* or *social representations*,[64] shared views of the world prevalent in a group. Collective representations already exist and regulate perceptions and actions in a group before an individual member is born, and they continue after the individual member leaves this world. The collective nature of these shared views mean that they do not depend on any one individual; indeed, individuals have limited ability to change shared representations. Continuity in the characteristics of group life is influenced by collective representations and the norms and rules integral to them. In this way, even after a thousand years there are characteristics that mark different religious and national groups so that, for example, Jews, Muslims, and Christians are distinguishable.

From the 1930s, research pioneered by the Turkish-American psychologist Mozafer Sherif (he is briefly mentioned in Chapter 10 of this book) demonstrated that norms can be both arbitrary and powerful.[65] Sherif developed a highly effective laboratory experiment, using the *autokinetic effect*, which was first discovered by astronomers in the nineteenth century and which involves the apparent movement of a star. This optical illusion arises from the nearly imperceptible micromovements of the eye.[66] The same effect can be achieved by presenting a single point of light in a dark background. Different individuals see different amounts of movement, some less and some more – even though the star, or spot of light in a laboratory, never actually moves.

Sherif placed individual participants in a laboratory and asked them to make 100 estimates of the amount of movement of a spot of light over four sessions (400 total personal estimates). He found that each individual eventually established a personal norm. Sherif then brought participants together in small groups and asked them to make estimates in a group setting. He discovered that in the group setting there emerges a 'group norm,' with individuals changing their personal estimates of the amount of perceived movement to conform to the newly created group norm. When Sherif took individuals out of their groups and had them give estimates by themselves, he found that the group norm continued to influence the individuals. The influence of the group was greater on individuals who had made their first estimates as part of a group and weaker on individuals who had first made estimates in isolation and had the opportunity to develop a personal norm before joining a group. Of course, in the world outside the psychology laboratory, a developing child is from the start of life immersed in the group and under the influence of group norms. This implies the enormous power of group norms in everyday life. The influence of the group is even greater when the situation is more ambiguous and less structured, so we have to rely on others to verify our own assessments.[67]

Building on Sherif's Norm Formation Research

A variety of studies conducted after Sherif's pioneering research have shed further light on the power of arbitrary groups norms. In studies conducted by Solomon Asch (1907–1996), the sole naïve participant made judgments of line lengths in small groups. Asch's confederates were the majority in these groups and gave what were clearly incorrect estimates of line lengths, setting up an incorrect norm that put pressure on the lone naïve participant. About one-third of the naïve participants conformed and gave what were 'obviously' incorrect answers. More recent research using functional magnetic resonance imaging suggests that individuals who conform and give incorrect answers in the Asch line-estimation experiment are actually changing their perceptions, without necessarily being consciously aware.[68] Thus, the group is literally shaping the way we see the world.

The power of arbitrary norms was also highlighted by the research of Irving Janis (1918–1990) on *groupthink*, the tendency for people in groups to converge on unwise courses of action they would have avoided if they were making the decision individually.[69] When individual group members imagine the group leader has established particular norms and wants a particular outcome, they often suppress their own critical judgments, go along with what they think the collective norm is, and arrive at destructive group decisions. Examples are the Bay of Pigs invasion, when the US government covertly backed an ill-advised invasion of Cuba in 1961 that utterly failed, and the US-led invasions of Afghanistan in 2001 and Iraq in 2003, which continue to have disastrous consequences in terms of both human lives and material costs.[70]

The power of arbitrary norms is also demonstrated by the minimal group paradigm experiment pioneered by Henri Tajfel (1919–1982) and his associates, in which individuals are placed into groups that differ from one another on the basis of a trivial and arbitrary criterion – such as the number of dots they see on a screen.[71] Simply placing an individual into a category, 'X' or 'Y,' can result in bias shown in favor of the ingroup. Social identity theory postulates that such biases reflect a human need for a positive and distinct identity. This need itself is usefully interpreted as a norm: Through socialization processes individuals learn that the correct way to behave is to show favoritism to their ingroups.

But to what extent do such arbitrary and incorrect norms influence behavior outside the laboratory? I turn to this question in the next section.

Norms in the Larger World

Immersion in the social world from birth tends to blind us to the arbitrariness of the norms to which we learn to conform. We grow our hair long or short depending on whether we are female or male, select clothing 'correct' for our gender, learn to drive automobiles on the right or left side of the street depending on the country we live in, and follow thousands of other norms as if they are all natural and inevitably correct. Consider how we learn about popular sports games, such as soccer, track and field, basketball, and tennis. Why should a soccer team consist of 11 players and not 110 players? Why should the sprint be 100 meters and not 10 meters or 30 meters? The Olympics has long jump and high jump competitions, but why is there not a side jump competition? Why should the basketball court be 94 feet long and not 194 feet long? Why should the tennis net be 3 feet and 6 inches high at the posts and 3 feet high in the center and not 6 feet and 6 inches high at the posts and 6 feet high in the center? The history of ball games such as tennis reveals that they were played according to very different rules in the past, and what we consider to be the 'correct' way of playing today is peculiar to our era. For example, in the Middle Ages tennis was a team game played in an open square or yard in town, in which players used their hands to hit the ball.[72]

Of course, psychological research is also regulated by arbitrary norms that have no objective basis but are adhered to religiously by psychologists. Consider, for example, the norm that a finding is reported as 'significant' if the probability of the findings being arrived at by chance is less than 0.05 and 'highly significant' if the probability is less than 0.01. These are completely arbitrary norms;[73] nevertheless, one still has to play according to the 'accepted' (albeit arbitrary) rules if one is to be accepted as a player in the 'game' of psychological science.[74] The cut-off points for 'significant' and 'highly significant' could have been set at 0.005 and 0.001, or even 0.0005 and 0.0001. There is nothing magical about the probabilities 0.05 and 0.01, but psychology journals and psychologists generally follow this norm as if it is 'natural' and written in stone. If a manuscript is submitted to a mainstream psychology journal and a different set of cut-off points are reported, the authors will come under pressure to conform and adopt the 'correct' cut-off points of 0.05 and 0.01.

There is, then, overwhelming experimental and 'everyday life' evidence demonstrating the power of arbitrary (and sometimes incorrect) norms. But equally important is the source of norms, which tends to be people with greater power and resources. Research traditions in psychology, political science, and related domains support the view that norms are largely shaped by upper-class elites,[75] through ownership of the media and major corporations, as well as through monetary contributions to educational and religious bodies.[76] Consider, for example, how norms regarding fashion are shaped through the media – suddenly short jackets and thin pants become the 'in' fashion through our exposure to images and messages from the media. Of course, universities are not immune: Consider how a large monetary donation from a billionaire can start or change research trends at universities, impacting the careers of thousands of researchers.

The poor conform to norms; they do not get to shape norms. To become 'successful,' individuals from poor families face the challenge of changing themselves to take on middle-class characteristics, learning to talk, dress, and behave in ways that help them 'pass' as middle class. When students from poor families gain entrance to elite educational institutions, their challenge is to learn middle-class norms and conform to their new surroundings. The culture of the elite educational institution is created by others and, at least at first encounter, is for the most part alien to the poor.[77] Similarly, after graduation the 'successful' individual from a poor family will get hired at a law firm or some other institution that also has an 'alien' professional culture.

The norms to which the upwardly rising individual has to conform are not necessarily superior to the norms they left behind in their economically poorer communities of origin. There is no objective basis according to which speaking with a certain accent is better than speaking with another accent or drinking a certain wine is better than drinking beer. However, we know from empirical research that norms can be arbitrary and even incorrect, yet still have a powerful impact on behavior. In the next section, I consider norms associated with diversity.

What Type of Diversity Should We Focus On?

I have argued that mainstream psychology has neglected group and inter-group psychology,[78] and in particular it has given far too little attention to poverty and social class. But mainstream psychology is now giving more attention to ethnic groups and multiculturalism. However, because of the continued neglect of poverty and social class differences, the attention given to ethnicity has failed to yield positive outcomes. This is because of the powerful role of poverty in areas such as ethnic minority performance in education.

An important goal of multiculturalism and the celebration of group differences is to give group members a sense of confidence and pride in their own group heritage. It is assumed that this sense of group confidence and pride will lead people to be accepting and open toward outgroup members. This is referred to as the *multiculturalism hypothesis* and was formally articulated by the Canadian prime minister Pierre Elliot Trudeau (1919–2000) in the Canadian House of Commons on October 8, 1971.[79] It is also assumed that a sense of ethnic pride and distinctiveness, 'we are different and special,' will lead ethnic minority students to feel confident and to become more successful in education.

But it is curious that despite the dominance of multiculturalism in education for about half a century, the plight of most minority students has not improved in the education system. First, ethnic minority students are not performing well in schools and in competition to gain entrance to higher education institutions, particularly the more competitive universities. Research on student participation in competitive school programs that facilitate entrance to higher education institutions (e.g., Advanced Placement, AP, and International Baccalaureate, IB, programs) shows steady gaps across ethnic groups, with Black and Hispanic students participating at much lower rates – as low as approximately one in five Black students and two in five Hispanics students participating compared with one in two White students.[80] Black and Hispanic students continue to score about 200 points lower than Whites on the SAT test, still required for many competitive universities.[81]

Second, many ethnic minority students who do gain entrance to universities are not performing well in higher education.[82] For example, among students who began at any kind of higher-education institution in fall 2010, Black and Hispanic students had the lowest completion rates within six years: only 38.0 percent and 45.8 percent respectively, compared to 62.0 percent for Whites. Also, among students at all four-year public institutions of higher education, Black and Hispanic students had the lowest completion rates within six years: only 45.9 percent and 55.0 percent respectively, compared to 67.2 percent for Whites. Black male students at four-year public institutions had the lowest completion rate (40.0 percent) of any group. Again, Asians performed better than Whites on all these measures, and I return to this topic below.

How do we explain these trends? The prevailing tendency among researchers has been to focus on differences across ethnic and gender groups,[83] ignoring the role of social class. However, the few studies that give a nod to social class provide a glimpse of the extraordinarily important role of poverty and the fact that some students are severely resource deprived (lacking food, money to buy books, computers, and other essential equipment). For example, a review of 771 studies published between 2005 and 2014 showed that resource deprivation is a major factor in low student performance in math and science.[84] A national study of factors leading to educational success among African American, Hispanic, Asian, and White high school students across 1,057 schools clearly demonstrated the importance of resources in outcomes, for both White and minority students: "[T]he strongest overall predictors of educational performance are social class-based (demographic) characteristics ... such that income, parental education, and the availability of educational resources within the home provided the 'best' indicators of subsequent educational performance."[85]

Thus, my claim is that ethnic minority children who are from lower-class families are held back in education by poverty. The majority of African American and Hispanic children do not do well in school because they lack resources (material, social, and otherwise).

In addition to giving priority to social class rather than ethnicity in order to ensure that larger numbers of children from the lower social classes reach universities, we need to question whether our priority should be on the celebration of group differences or the celebration of human commonalities.[86] Human beings have a great deal more in common than they have different. Also, extensive psychological research demonstrates that we humans are attracted to others we see to be similar to ourselves. The implication is that we should socialize children to see themselves as part of one humanity, with characteristics that are in important respects similar to all other humans. Ethnic minority children are far better helped by policies that demonstrate our common humanity and how children from all ethnic groups are able to compete and succeed academically.

Concluding Comment

Instead of starting the task of understanding human cognition and action from micro, intrapersonal processes, we need to start with collective processes and move from the societies to cells, from the collective to the individual. The most powerful macro force shaping individual behavior is social class: The rich and the poor are vastly different from another in areas such as performance in education because of their huge and increasing differences in their material conditions and resources. Despite the enormous impact of social class on cognition and action, social class continues to receive inadequate attention in mainstream psychology. On the other hand, ethnicity does receive attention, particularly through multiculturalism.

Unfortunately, attention to ethnicity, the celebration of group differences, and multiculturalism have not improved the educational performances of most ethnic minority students. This is because the most important factor impacting the lives of these students is poverty, and related challenges such as food insecurity. There is an urgent need for psychologists to make poverty and social class a more central theme in their research, teaching, and practice.

PART II

Rethinking Behavior in the Larger World

Through tattered clothes (small) vices do appear.
Robes and furred gowns hide all.

King Lear (4.6.180–181)

The three chapters in Part II explore the psychology of mental health (Chapter 8), justice (Chapter 9), and life in non-Western societies (Chapter 10), with particular attention to the experiences of different social classes. Those in positions of privilege and authority shape the context in which the lower class must survive. In the following chapters, we discover that the ways in which the context has been shaped is not to the benefit of lower-class individuals – their difficult material conditions and lack of power and status expose and heighten any shortcomings they might have.

In the domain of mental health, life conditions are more stressful and difficult for those with less power, resources, status – and as logic would lead us to expect, the poor suffer graver mental health problems. However, the most recent solution they have been offered is a 'science of happiness.' In line with neoconservative ideology, positive psychology argues that priority be given to 'feeling happy.' This 'solution' captures much of what is wrong with mainstream psychology, as discussed in Chapter 8 of this text. The (in)justice system is discussed in Chapter 9, where we see again that the poor are treated unfairly. The outcomes of justice processes are harsher for the lower class. In the final chapter in Part II, the appropriateness of mainstream psychology is examined for non-Western societies generally and the different social classes in non-Western societies specifically. We see that mainstream psychology is more relevant and beneficial to the lives of the upper class in non-Western societies.

CHAPTER 8

Mental Health and 'Be Happy' Psychology

[T]he diagnosis of kleptomania ... refers to an irresistible compulsion to shoplift or pilfer ... Shoppers of all social classes stole, but authorities used social class to distinguish criminal acts of theft from those purportedly reflecting mental pathology. To put it bluntly, ordinary women were regarded as thieves, but upper-class women's acts of theft were explained as a product of mental illness. The diagnosis of kleptomania excused their behavior, shielded them from criminal prosecution, and allowed the upper-classes to maintain a posture of moral superiority.

Rachel Hare-Mustin and Jeanne Marecek[1]

Growing evidence connects economic inequality and poor mental health ... Experience of socioeconomic disadvantage, including unemployment, low income, poverty, debt and poor housing, is consistently associated with poorer mental health.

Anna Macintyre, Daniel Ferris, Briana
Gonçalves and Neil Quinn[2]

Courses on abnormal psychology and clinical psychology are extremely popular among students at universities around the world. Both the mainstream courses and the mainstream texts on abnormal psychology go through a standard set of topics,[3] including major paradigms, diagnosis and assessment, and varieties of disorders and treatments. The classification of mental disorders in mainstream courses and texts generally follows the *Diagnostic and Statistical Manual of Mental Disorders* (*DSM*), first published by the American Psychiatric Association in 1952 and repeatedly revised since then.[4] The general orientation of mainstream approaches to mental health is still reductionist, giving priority to dispositional factors and neglecting contextual factors – particularly social class and poverty. But the progressive ideas of Laura Smith,[5] William Liu,[6] Catherine Haslam,[7] Keith Payne,[8] among others, is helping to gradually bring more attention to the social context of mental health, as well as poverty and therapy. Related to this is the influence of community psychology, which also gives importance to context in explaining health and undertaking interventions.[9]

The relationship between social class and mental health is complex, as indicated by the two quotations above. On the one hand, as noted by Anna Macintyre and her colleagues, research demonstrates a relationship between poverty and mental health: The poor are more likely to suffer mental health problems. The situation is particularly grave in low-income societies, where most people with serious mental health problems do not receive any treatment.[10] On the other hand, as Rachel Hare-Mustin and Jeanne Marecek (quoted above) observe, mental illness has at times been strategically used to protect affluent individuals, so that their wrongdoing is the result of 'illness' rather than 'criminality.'

The second reason for the complexity of the relationship between social class and mental health is that causation, when present, is not always unidirectional. Research evidence demonstrates that poverty and the harsh conditions of life result in higher rates of mental health among the lower class.[11] However, we must also consider evidence that supports the so-called *downward drift hypothesis*,[12] suggesting that individuals who suffer mental health problems are unable to make progress in their education, careers, and so on and tend to drift down to lower social classes and end up in poverty. The implication is that under some conditions mental health can be a cause of poverty, rather than poverty being a cause of mental health. However, the weight of research evidence supports the view that the difficult conditions of life for the poor are inducive to mental illness.[13] For example, children in lower-class families suffer greater mental health problems, and also have less access to treatments, than do children in upper-class families.[14] The implication is that the dire mental health conditions of these lower-class children is a result of their lives as members of economically strapped families and not their personal 'downward drift.'

This chapter first introduces the main varieties of mainstream conceptualization of mental health disorders and treatments. Having presented the mainstream perspective, critical and alternative perspectives are offered, starting with the highly critical perspective of the so-called anti-psychiatry movement. Next, the relatively new and celebrated 'positive psychology' movement is critically examined, and the cultural and political biases of this movement are highlighted. The positive psychology movement presents us with a simplistic focus on happiness, independent of poverty and other such contextual issues (*happiness* is understood in individualistic terms as a positive subjective experience; *well-being* includes objective states of affairs, including poverty and other social determinants of health).

In the final part, I return to the relationship between social class and mental health, which is of the greatest importance and deserves more attention.

Mental Health Disorders and Treatments

In applied domains such as counseling, where the important role of life conditions in mental health becomes more obvious, there are clear tensions between the work of practicing counselors and the reductionist approach taken by the *DSM*. In an article in *The Professional Counselor*, Victoria Kress and coauthors point out that "The DSM system does not include sufficient emphasis on contextual factors."[15] However, the DSM system does provide the most widely used classification system in the world in the area of mental health. Thus, the discrepancy between the practical need to give importance to context and the reductionist approach of the DSM is cause for concern.

The DSM-5 (2013) includes the following among the categories of psychological disorders: neurodevelopmental disorders (including autism and intellectual disabilities), schizophrenia spectrum (chronic, maladaptive style of thinking, feeling, and acting), bipolar and related disorders (involving major shifts in energy level, mood, concentration), depression disorders (persistent sadness, lack of energy and motivation), anxiety disorders (persistent worry and fear, preventing normal functioning), obsessive-compulsive disorders (reoccurring thoughts, *obsessions*, and actions, *compulsions*), trauma-related disorders (including posttraumatic stress disorder, PTSD), dissociative disorders (involuntary escape from reality, such as through memory loss), somatic symptom disorders (debilitating focus on fatigue, pain, and other physical symptoms), eating disorders (including anorexia nervosa and bulimia nervosa), sleep–wake disorders (conditions resulting in sleep deprivation), substance abuse and addictions (persistent drug use that causes dysfunctionality in life), personality disorders (rigid and unhealthy pattern of cognition, emotion, and action), and paraphilias (disorders of sexual arousal and preference).

The criteria for diagnosing each disorder are also set out in DSM-5. For example, schizophrenia is diagnosed by the presence of two or more of the following symptoms, one of which must be from the first three symptoms listed: delusions (unfounded beliefs), disorganized speech, hallucinations (mistaken perceptions), abnormal emotional and social behavior, and movement disorder. Hundreds of combinations of symptoms are given in DSM-5 for depression. This means that individuals with different symptoms can meet the criteria for the same diagnosis.

MORE EXTREME INTERVENTIONS
            Lobotomy
            Electroconvulsive shock therapy
            Drug therapy
            Psychoanalysis
            Behavior therapy
            Cognitive therapy
            Humanistic therapy
MILDER INTERVENTIONS

Figure 8.1   Hierarchy of treatments for psychological disorders, from the more extreme
to milder interventions

The DSM-5 uses a categorical approach to diagnosis, so that each psychological disorder is distinct from other disorders. The only exception to this is personality disorder: Clinicians have the option of evaluating individuals in a way that involves both multiple categories and personality dimensions, so that a more complex and realistic assessment is reached.[16] Most experts are critical of the categorical approach adopted in DSM-5,[17] in large part because in practice the different psychological disorders are not isolated 'islands,' separate from one another. Patients who suffer one form of mental health problem tend to also suffer other problems; for example, anxiety, depression, and substance abuse are common comorbidities among schizophrenic patients.[18] Thus, the categories of psychological disorders reported in DSM-5 do not map neatly on to the actual patterns of disorders found in the real world.

In terms of the treatment of psychological disorders, I find it useful to conceptualize a hierarchy (see Figure 8.1) from 'extreme intervention' to 'mild intervention,' with lobotomy at one end of the continuum and humanistic therapy at the other end (I am simplifying, because there are an estimated 400 different psychotherapies[19]). This review of treatments sets the context for the critical discussion of treatments that follows in this chapter.

Lobotomy or 'psychosurgery' involves direct intervention (e.g., cutting out parts of the brain, severing links between brain parts) in the brain and has a long history in different parts of the world.[20] However, the exact nature of this intervention and the meaning of lobotomy have changed over the years.[21] Lobotomy has been banned in some countries (e.g., Germany) and legislatively regulated in others (e.g., the United States). Another severe intervention for psychological disorders is *electroconvulsive shock therapy* (ECT), "the application of electricity to the scalp in order to induce seizure activity."[22] ECT is seen as particularly useful in cases of severe depression, when the patient does not respond well to other types of treatments. A related treatment that uses electricity is deep brain stimulation (DBS), which involves implanting electrodes that produce electrical impulses in targeted parts of the brain. ECT and DBS are alike in that the mechanisms of how exactly they help certain patients is not well understood – do they inhibit or excite or disrupt certain neural networks or influence through a combination of all the different effects?[23] Similarly, lobotomy is still a primitive and 'last resort' treatment, because it is often impossible to undo, and it is not clear exactly when and why this treatment brings benefits. However, these extreme treatments tend to be attempted when other treatments have failed and when the patient's life is in danger (typically, from suicide).

Drug therapy is the next most intrusive form of treatment, and for various economic reasons drug therapy is now very widespread. A 2017 publication reported that 16.7 percent of the US population filled in one or more prescriptions for psychiatric drugs over a year, the most common being antidepressants.[24] Drug therapy in particular was attacked by the so-called anti-psychiatry movement from the 1960s and continues to be severely criticized in the twenty-first century. For example, Peter Gøtzsche and his colleagues have argued that "Psychiatric drugs are responsible for the deaths of more than half a million people aged 65 and older each year in the Western world … Their benefits would need to be colossal to justify this, but they are minimal."[25] The various side-effects (e.g., sexual dysfunction[26]) of psychiatric drugs are of particular concern. However, drug therapy has increased in part because it is seen to be a more economic, less labor-intensive form of treatment than other forms of treatments. No doubt big pharma's excessive advertising and lobbying power have also influenced this harmful outcome.[27]

Psychoanalysis, behavioral therapy, and cognitive therapy involve similar levels of direct intervention in the life of the patient. Each of these is associated with a particular school of psychology and one of their main differences is their focus on the past, present, or future of the patient. Psychoanalysis is strongly influenced by Sigmund Freud's (1956–1939) ideas and is heavily focused on the past history of the patient, particularly childhood experiences, as a key to present psychological disorders. A cost of becoming 'civilized' and fitting into society is for individuals to repress thoughts, wishes, motivations, and so on that are considered taboo in society. Repressed psychological phenomena become part of the unconscious and continue to influence behavior, without people being consciously aware of this influence. In this way, irrationality shapes behavior.

Behavioral therapy, arising out of the behaviorist school of psychology and especially the research of B. F. Skinner (1904–1990), assumes that psychological disorders have come about the way all behavior takes shape: through learning.[28] Behavior that can be learned can also be unlearned and reshaped. Thus, behavioral therapy involves using environmental engineering to shape behavior to become functional. For example, phobias are treated by training a patient to replace an anxiety or fear response with a relaxation response.

Instead of focusing on overt actions, cognitive therapy, influenced particularly by Aaron Beck,[29] focuses on styles of thinking, such as attributions, beliefs, and attitudes that result in negative views of the self. Finally, the least intrusive treatment approach is *humanistic therapy*,[30] which gives priority to reaching the authentic and constructive self for the client, through collaboration with the therapist. Humanistic therapy is the least intrusive because the client collaborates with the therapist and helps guide the mutual explorations of the two. Although I have listed humanistic therapy alongside the standard therapy, Carl Rogers and other leading humanistic therapists have been highly critical of other major therapies, particularly those that involve a high level of intervention (I further elaborate on this below).

How effective are the different therapies? A number of reviewers have concluded that over the long term, the common therapies have about the same rate of success.[31] However, supporters of cognitive behavioral therapies have been highly vocal in arguing the superiority of their approach.[32]

But this brief review of therapies would not be complete without also giving attention to positive psychology,[33] which is both an ideology and an approach to psychological disorders. The wider implications of positive psychology are discussed later in this chapter.

Rethinking the Mainstream Approach to Mental Health

I begin by briefly discussing criticisms of mainstream mental health approaches emerging from the 'anti-psychiatry' movement and humanistic psychology from the 1960s. Next, I engage in a more focused critical discussion on positive psychology and the relationship between social class and mental health.

Anti-psychiatry and Humanistic Critics of Mainstream Therapies

The mainstream approach to mental health came under sustained attack particularly from the 1960s, as part of wider criticisms of 'the establishment.' This critical attack brought about concrete changes, for example, in what was considered a mental disorder: "On 15 December 1973 the board of the American Psychiatric Association (APA) voted unanimously (with one abstention) to remove the diagnosis 'homosexuality' from the organization's Diagnostic and Statistical Manual of Mental Disorders."[34]

A first set of critics of mainstream treatments, led by Ronald Laing and Thomas Zsasz, were branded as 'anti-psychiatry'; they rejected mainstream approaches to mental health, including the labels used to categorize patients. For example, Ronald Laing and Aaron Esterson explained, "We do not accept 'schizophrenia' as being a biochemical, neurophysiological, psychological fact … Nor do we assume its existence."[35]

Laing and Zsasz rejected the reductionism of mainstream approaches to mental health and refused to see the 'problem' as being in the individual; rather, they focused on the context. Laing gave high importance to family relationships: The helpless baby is born within a family that has certain fairly stable characteristics, and if family relations are dysfunctional then the child will face grave difficulties. Given the importance of the family for the mental health of children, Laing and Esterson tried to develop a method "that enables us to study at one and the same time (i) each person in the family; (ii) the relations between persons in the family; (iii) the family itself as a system."[36] Their focus was in part on relations within the family, a context in which the developing child has relatively little power.

Zsasz developed an analysis that depicts those labeled as 'mentally ill' as scapegoats, victimized the way witches were centuries ago. In contrast to the victimized, in every society there are also those who are celebrated the way saints were looked up to in medieval times: "The athletes, the beauty queens, and the movie stars are the modern-day 'saints' – and the cosmetics manufacturers, doctors, psychiatrists, and so forth, their assistants. They are honored, admired, and rewarded … who are the people who fall in the class of the witches and sorcerers? Who are the people who are persecuted and victimized in the name of 'health' and 'happiness'? There are many. In their front ranks are the mentally ill, and especially those who are so defined by others rather than by themselves."[37]

This analysis depicts the 'mental health community' as playing an important role in maintaining social order in societies characterized by group-based inequalities: Those who think 'differently' are rejected as 'mentally ill.' This critical 'anti-psychiatry' perspective has deep historical roots and continues to influence twenty-first-century researchers and practitioners. For example, a recent collection of critical discussions argued for "a shift from the predominant biomedical, empirical and pharmacological paradigm toward an integrative, interdisciplinary approach where pharmacological treatments are not the only source of healing, since the object is not a malfunctioning machine."[38]

In addition to the 'anti-psychiatry' critics, humanistic psychologists rejected mainstream treatments and argued for a more accepting, collaborative relationship between the therapist and the client. Humanistic psychologists rejected the label 'patient,' which they replaced with 'client.' What mainstream treatments depicted as 'mental illness,' humanistic psychologists interpreted as explorations of the self; they pointed to a client's need to reorganize the self, through collaboration with the therapist. As Carl Rogers proposed, "Psychotherapy deals primarily with the organization and functioning of the self. There are many elements of experience that a self cannot face, cannot clearly perceive, because to face them or admit them would be inconsistent with and threatening to the current organization of self."[39]

Building on the antireductionist approach adopted by the antipsychiatry and humanistic critics of mainstream mental health treatments, I next turn to assess the relationship between social class and mental health. This discussion uses the example of positive psychology, both because of the dramatic and rapid rise of positive psychology and because it epitomizes reductionism.

The 'Happiness Turn,' Social Class, and Mental Health

Until recently, human history has been a tale of woe: warfare, plague, famine, injustice, poverty, ignorance, and violent death. The last two centuries have witnessed if not the eradication of, but a great reduction in, these ills. When life is a vale of tears, it is natural that politics, religion, science, medicine, and the arts should be about defense and damage. But what happens when life is no longer a vale of tears?"

Martin Seligman[40]

[T]he present system of global governance fails to adequately protect public health. This failure strikes unevenly and is especially disastrous for the world's most vulnerable, marginalized, and poorest populations ... the fact that people's life chances differ so widely is not simply a problem of poverty, but one of socioeconomic inequality. The differences in health manifest themselves in gradients across societies, with physical and mental ills steeply increasing for each step down the social ladder, along with other health-related outcomes such as violence, drug misuse, depression, obesity, and child wellbeing.

The Lancet-University of Oslo Commission
on Global Governance for Health[41]

Positive psychology has presented us with a highly charged reductionist message that fits with a politically right-wing agenda: The world is now a much better place and we should focus on what makes *individuals* happy. As Richard Lazarus points out, the premise of positive psychology "is that if individuals engage in positive thinking and feeling and abandon or minimize their preoccupation with the harsh and tragic – that is, the stressful side of life – they will have found a magic elixir of health and well-being."[42] Happiness can become a cause, rather than a consequence, of improvements at work, in health, education, and other settings. The implication, sometimes made explicit, is that material measures such as *Gross Domestic Product* (GDP), the market value of the goods and services produced in a country, are outdated and should be replaced by a 'happiness index.'[43] Not surprisingly, politically right-leaning governments have jumped at the opportunity to take the spotlight away from group-based economic inequalities, and critics have argued that these governments are, in the words of the father of positive psychology, "trying to distract people with the sop of happiness."[44]

What has been labeled the 'happiness turn' epitomizes the celebration of individualism and the rejection of context, particularly social class and poverty, in mainstream approaches to mental health.[45] This is in contrast to research evidence that demonstrates context to be of the highest importance in individual experiences,[46] and strong arguments from Brock Bastian,[47] Barbara Ehrenreich,[48] Daniel Horowitz,[49] among others, that show happiness is far too narrow and misses out on the full range of human emotions and experiences, as well as their sometimes surprisingly constructive consequences.[50] Despite some key positive psychology researchers actually reporting that happiness does relate to wealth (a point I discuss in more depth later in this chapter), the tacit and (often indirect) implication of the positive psychology movement is that our objective is to make people happy and we can make them happy even if they remain poor. By implication, it really does not matter that wealth concentration is increasing and the poor are being left farther behind; none of this need impact happiness.

The political biases in this message become clearer when it is contrasted with the message of researchers and sources with a different political message, such as the Lancet-University of Oslo Commission on Global Governance for Health (quoted above), with its focus on the political origins of health inequality. The Lancet-University of Oslo Commission report points out the relationship between resource inequality in society and health broadly. Later in this chapter, I discuss further research demonstrating that greater resource inequality has detrimental health consequences for all of society, but particularly for the poor. I begin by discussing the growth of the positive psychology movement, and from this point of departure I broaden the discussion to the relationship between mental health and social class.

Positive Psychology and Happiness

The essence of the positive psychology movement is captured in an influential paper by Shelly Gable and Jonathan Haidt,[51] positive psychology advocates, which begins with a quotation from Robert F. Kennedy arguing that the gross national product does not reflect aspects of life such as the joy of children at play, or the beauty of poetry, or wit or courage. In a similar way, argue Gable and Haidt, the "gross academic product" of psychology misses out on important aspects of the human experience, particularly related to happiness; psychology has been "learning how to bring people up from negative eight to zero but not as good at understanding how people rise from zero to positive eight."[52]

A (mostly implicit) assumption underlying the positive psychology movement is that lower-class people can be trained to be just as happy, or even happier, as upper-class people. This assumption has been highly influential around the world, leading national and international authorities to try to implement measures of happiness as indicators of national progress.[53] The implicit message is: Don't worry about increasing inequality, just look at the happiness index! Even when people are poor, we can help them to be happy; also, their low purchasing power means they will consume less. This way, the world can achieve sustainable development. From this perspective, it makes perfect sense to quote Robert Kennedy to argue that gross national product does not reflect joy or poetry. Of course, this argument is easier to make when one is a member of the more affluent group and when one is not one of the lower class who suffer relative deprivation in a societal context of *enormous and increasing* inequalities.

Psychologists arguing for the priority of happiness and less emphasis on income were supported by (what proved to be misleading) early research suggesting that there is a positive correlation between happiness, life satisfaction, and income within but not across countries, and this correlation disappears above an income that meets basic human needs.[54] But subsequent research has questioned the validity of this so-called *Easterlin Paradox*. Daniel Sacks, Betsey Stevenson, and Justin Wolfers have summarized major findings in this way: "[R]icher people report greater wellbeing than poorer people ... richer countries have higher per capita well-being than poorer countries ... economic growth over time is related to rising well-being ... there is no satiation point beyond which the relationship between income and well-being diminishes."[55] Additional research suggests that the focus on income (the stream of money a person receives from different sources) in the Easterlin Paradox is misleading, because wealth (total market value of a person's assets) has a more important influence on happiness.[56] Research on the relationship between size of inequalities and health further highlights the inadequacy of a focus on happiness independent of material wealth.

Inequality and Health

The British epidemiologist Michael Marmot uses the tragedy of the *Titanic*, the passenger liner that struck an iceberg and sank in the North Atlantic on April 15, 1912, to illustrate the striking findings of his research on health inequalities and social class. Drowning rates among the *Titanic* passengers varied across the social classes of passengers: highest among the third class, lowest among the first class. Marmot's groundbreaking research shattered a myth about the 'stressful' life of the elite with 'crushing responsibilities' and 'heavy burdens,' compared to the lower class who presumably lead less stressful and less burdened lives.[57] Focusing on the long-term health of British civil servants, Marmot demonstrated that those in higher positions actually enjoyed better health. The supposed 'carefree' life of those in the lower positions was associated with poorer physical and mental health.

Considerable research evidence has accumulated to show that economic disadvantage is associated with poor mental health.[58] The key to a healthier society, according to a number of leading researchers,[59] is *a more equal society*. Greater inequality brings poorer health. The United States is the largest economy in the world and has one of the highest per capita incomes, but has *lower* life expectancy compared to other wealthy nations, the *worst record of violence and murder*, and relatively grave mental health problems particularly *among the poor and minorities*.[60]

Research suggests that everyday life stressors have long-term mental health consequences.[61] Rather than endorsing the view that 'what does not kill you, makes you stronger,' research findings actually endorse the view that the wear and tear of daily stressors result in "long-term damage to individuals' mental health."[62] The difficult life conditions of lower-class people create stress, anxiety, and trauma and generally represent environments conducive to poorer mental health. *The greater the resource inequalities in society, the greater the experiences of relative deprivation among the lower class.*[63] These feelings of relative deprivation are magnified by the espoused rhetoric of the American Dream, claiming that the United States is a meritocracy and anyone can make it to the top if they have the necessary talent and hard work. In reality, though, the lower class experience less control over their lives, as well as minimal participation in decision-making generally. The American Dream remains a dream for almost all of them. Nevertheless, the American Dream leads them to feel personally responsible for their poverty and failure to 'make it' in the 'land of opportunity.'

Given the grim reality of lower-class life on the one hand and the 'be happy' message of positive psychology on the other hand, how has this contradiction influenced positive psychology? This contradiction has placed positive psychology in a dilemma. On the one hand, the empirical findings clearly show that poverty is associated with unhappiness, and (as I discuss below) some leading positive psychologists have admitted this. On the other hand, in important respects positive psychology has continued on its merry way, neglectful of its extreme right-wing political leanings, and focused on the reductionist message that individuals can be helped to feel happy by therapists, irrespective of their actual economic conditions. Through the magic of cognitive behavioral therapy, the poor can remain economically poor but be made to feel happy. The entire positive psychology enterprise could be summed up in the phrase 'beyond money,'[64] since those who lack money are magically helped to feel they do not need money.

But the fact that the difficult, stressful, and anxiety-provoking life conditions of the lower class, including inferior health care services,[65] are conducive to worse mental health stubbornly continues to intrude into the rosy picture painted by positive psychology (I need not address the attempts by advocates of positive psychology to position themselves as scientific, for example, by claims about a precise 2.9 positivity ratio that governs our lives, because others have demonstrated this to be nonsense[66]). Consider, for example, these statements from reports authored by leading positive psychologists:

> [A] lack of resources such as health, income, and social support is frequently associated with unhappiness.[67]
>
> [I]n our analysis with 166 countries, we found that under adverse conditions in which both social and material quality of life are bad, most people were not happy.[68]

In a related discussion of the research literature underlying positive psychology, David Myers and Ed Diener asked and also answered two key questions:

> ... first, whether people are happier in rich rather than poor countries. The answer ... is yes (although other variables, such as a stable democracy, safety, and education, ride along with income).
>
> Second, we asked whether, within any country, rich people are happier than not-so-rich people. Are those who drive a Mercedes to work happier than those who ride the bus? The answer is again yes.[69]

In a surprising twist, reflecting the contradiction at the heart of positive psychology, these researchers examined the consequences of wealth inequality and came to the same conclusion as Marmot, "Happy growth is shared growth."[70]

When money is transferred to them, the general result is lower stress and better mental health for the lower class. For example, in a study conducted in Kenya,[71] households were randomly assigned to receive unconditional cash transfers of $1,525 or $404. The larger cash transfer led to more significant improvements in psychological well-being and lower stress. Similar experimental interventions to help the lower class in other countries have also led to positive outcomes for their mental health.[72] In the United States, improvements in mental health were experienced by the poor who were randomly selected to receive health insurance.[73] In a review of twenty-five studies that report changes in psychological well-being as a result of decreased or increased poverty, the general weight of evidence showed that lower poverty leads to improved mental health or stress.[74] Thus, the empirical basis of positive psychology has come to be seriously questioned.[75]

Finally, relative wealth is even more important than absolute wealth. In countries where there are greater wealth inequalities, such as the United States and the United Kingdom, the poorest groups suffer more relative deprivation and the health consequences for them are even more detrimental.[76] The central importance of relative wealth means that psychological science should pay far more attention to wealth and income distributions in societies.

Concluding Comment

The difficult life conditions of the lower class make them more prone to suffer mental illness. The mental and physical health problems of the lower class are even greater in societies where wealth inequalities have been rising faster, such as the United States and the United Kingdom.[77] In more unequal societies, the poor suffer more severe mental and physical health problems (although multiple minority status does not have a simple additive effect on severity of mental health problems[78]). These important trends need to be given more attention in mainstream psychology and particularly by the positive psychology movement, which gives priority to helping individuals 'feel happy' rather than actually improving their life conditions.

Because the United States continues as the First World of psychology,[79] the causal-reductionist model underlying American psychology continues to dominate psychological research and practice around the world. Consequently, movements such as positive psychology, with their cultural and political biases against the interests of the lower class, gain traction internationally – when they should be treated with much more skepticism. This is part of the ideological bias in mainstream psychology, which continues to give inadequate attention to social class and the interests of the poor.

CHAPTER 9

Looking through the Wrong Side of Prison Bars: The Psychology of Injustice

[T]he prison has emerged as a powerful and often invisible institution that drives and shapes social inequality.

Sara Wakefield and Christopher Uggen[1]

I am discussing prisons and jails because lower-class people are enormously overrepresented there.[2] (Prisons are places where individuals convicted of a crime are held; jails hold individuals awaiting trial or convicted of minor crimes – see note on terminology.[3]) While ethnicity, gender, and social class clearly intersect in victimhood associated with incarceration,[4] my main focus remains on giving priority to a contextual explanation to the plight of the poor. As Bruce Western and Becky Pettit have explained, "Class inequalities in incarceration are reflected in the very low education level of those in prison and jail ... prisoners ... are drawn overwhelmingly from the least educated."[5] There are certain characteristics of the (in)justice system, such as the role and nature of bail,[6] that victimized poor people across ethnicities and genders and that enable superrich criminals such as the sex-offender Jeffrey Epstein to get luxury treatment while supposedly serving time in prison.[7]

But the causal-reductionist explanations of incarceration continue to have a lot of sway and fits with popular media depictions of prisons. Consider, for example, the riot that took place in the prison in Attica, New York, in 1971 and ended with ten correctional officers and thirty-three inmates being killed or the 2016 prison riot at Roraima, Brazil, that resulted in inmates being damaged so badly that they could only be identified by their body parts.[8] How can we explain such violent prison riots?[9] Mainstream psychology directs us to focus on the personality of inmates and prison guards. Surely prison guards and prisoners are 'special' and different from us; surely there are features of their personalities, such as high aggression, that cause violence in prisons? This causal-reductionist approach assumes that individual prison guards and prisoners are abnormal in terms of their personality traits, neurocognitive characteristics, or some other individual-level feature. The assumption is that we, who are psychologically normal, would not behave with that kind of violence, irrespective of whether we are in the role of prisoner or prison guard. But research demonstrating the power of context forces us to reject this comfortable assumption, by suggesting that it is the *context* of the prison and not the personality characteristics of prison inmates and guards, that leads to dehumanizing behavior in prisons.[10]

As Wakefield and Uggen (quoted above) argue, prisons reinforce and magnify inequalities in society: Prisons are filled with lower-class people, and their poverty is perpetuated by the experience of 'serving time' in prison. Those who serve time in prison become disadvantaged in finding employment and housing, as well as being civically engaged, among other ways. The path to prison often begins with failing schools in poverty-stricken neighborhoods, contributing to the school-to-prison pipeline.[11] From this perspective, the psychology of the criminal justice system is the psychology of how the poor of all ethnic groups and genders are victimized by the 'justice system' to serve time in prisons, and their time in prison serves to increase the probability that they continue being poor and politically disenfranchised after leaving prison. The rate of incarceration in the United States is six times that of the typical Organisation for Economic Co-operation and Development (OECD) countries (these are the advanced Western countries, including Germany, France, and the United Kingdom).[12] In critically exploring the significance of this trend, I address four basic questions: (1) Who goes to prison? (2) What happens to them in prison? (3) What happens to the families of those who go to prison? (4) What is the wider psychological purpose of incarceration? My discussion focuses largely on the situation in the United States, but many of the trends identified are also relevant to other parts of the world. Prisons everywhere are predominantly occupied by the poor.

There are many important topics I will not have space to cover related to how the prison system ensnares the poor. For example, the bail system in the United States also 'punishes poverty'; the lower ability of the poor to pay bail results in more pretrial jail time for them.[13] The poor do less well as crime-victims: Juries give harsher punishments when the victim of a crime is middle class compared to lower class.[14] Accused individuals with higher educational attainments are seen as less dangerous and less blameworthy.[15] *Crimmigration*, the merging of criminal law and immigration law,[16] has victimized poorer immigrants in particular. In general, poorer people are more likely to be sentenced to prison for violating the law.[17] These are all important topics, but in this chapter I focus on a narrower set of issues within the broader topic of social class and prisons.

Who Goes to Prison?

The most direct and accurate answer to this question is that the poor go to prison.[18] As Sara Heller, Brian Jacob, and Jens Ludwig state in their review of family income, neighborhood poverty, and crime, "criminal offending and victimization rates tend to be disproportionally concentrated among low-income people living in high-poverty communities."[19] The Columbia University researcher Amanda Geller and her colleagues have assessed the situation in this way: "The high level of parental incarceration is of particular concern for low-income children because incarceration rates are highest among the most disadvantaged."[20] In the years 1978–2009, there was a 430 percent increase in the number of prisoners held in state and federal prisons in the United States,[21] and the most common characteristic of the inmates was being poor.

The relationship between poverty and prison became a research focus early in the twentieth century, with now classic studies exploring how life in poor neighborhoods leads to major disadvantages and a higher likelihood of poor individuals both committing and being victims of crime.[22] Economic recessions, such as the huge recession of 2008, provide researchers an opportunity to test the impact of economic hardship: Findings show that economic downturns not only lead to higher crime,[23] but they also increased suicides and worse health.[24] Thus, the housing crisis and widespread foreclosures around 2008 resulted in not only individual-level health decline but also community-level malaise in terms of rising family dysfunction and crime levels. The indications are that the COVID-19 pandemic will detrimentally impact the poor even more severely than the middle and upper classes.

In an extensive review of research on urban poverty and neighborhood effects on crime, Corina Graif, Andrew Gladfelter, and Stephen Mathews found that in 2012 alone there were more than 250 articles on this topic.[25] On the basis of this robust research literature, these authors report that poverty and related characteristics of neighborhoods "continue to predict multiple crime-related outcomes, including: individual's exposure to violence … risk of victimization … adolescent violent crime … aggression … arrests for violent behavior … domestic violence … incarceration … and recidivism."[26] But some studies suggest that family poverty is even more predictive of adult crime than is neighborhood poverty. For example,

Valentina Kikulina, Cathy Widom, and Sally Czaja examined the experiences of children with a history of neglect, gathering detailed information on both their family and neighborhood poverty.[27] They discovered that family poverty, but not neighborhood poverty, played a distinct and significant role in predicting whether those children end up getting arrested as adults.

For the purposes of research, a 'stand in' for wealth differences is educational differences: The poor are characterized by low educational attainment. A strong negative correlation has been demonstrated between crime and education: The higher the years of schooling, the lower the different indices of crime.[28] This begins with the earliest years of education: Attending preschool programs is associated with lower crime.[29] A one-year increase in average education levels was found to reduce state-level arrests by 11 percent.[30] There is evidence that the impact of education on crime is consistent across cultures.[31] For example, a study in Sweden concluded that "one additional year of schooling decreases the likelihood of conviction by 6.7% and incarceration by 15.5%." One interpretation of this research trend is that those families who have the monetary and other resources to invest in the education of their young, from preschool onward, are also ensuring a lower likelihood of their better educated young ending up in prison.

While I have highlighted the victimization of the poor in the (in)justice system, it is also important to acknowledge the role of other factors, as reflected by intersectionality research. First, the vast majority of prison inmates are male; for example, in 2016 males made up 93 percent of the total prison population in the United States; the imprisonment rate per 100,000 US residents for male adults was 1,109 and for female adults it was only 82.[32] A variety of factors influence this difference, including higher aggressive behavior among males,[33] and biological and sociocultural differences.[34]

A second huge disparity is based on ethnicity: A disproportionally high number of African Americans serve prison time in the United States.[35] In 2016 the imprisonment rate for Whites was relatively low (only 274 per 100,000 US residents) but for African Americans it was 1,609 – almost six times as high.[36] In a study of life after leaving school among American men, JooHee Han found that relative to Whites, Black men have an 84 percent higher risk of experiencing incarceration.[37] Although crime rates in the United States have been falling since the 1990s,[38] the incarceration rate of poor African American men has increased. In 2014 Ronnie Tucker predicted that "if these trends continue in America, one in three African

American men born today can expect to spend time in prison during their lifetime."[39] The school-to-prison pipeline is particularly destructive for African American men.[40] But underlying these trends are harsh economic disparities, captured by a 2017 Washington Post headline "White families have nearly 10 times the net worth of black families and the gap is growing."[41] The African Americans ensnared by the prison system are almost exclusively poor, as are the White Americans in prison.

What Happens to Them in Prison?

There was a quadrupling of expenditures on corrections between 1980 and 2010.[42] Given this increase in costs, we would expect prisons to have become much better at educating and reforming prisoners – particularly given the positive impact of education on crime, as we reviewed early in this chapter.

The most obvious group to focus on to assess the impact of incarceration is young people: They can be more readily influenced by educational programs and have more time to reap the benefits of educational and reform opportunities over the course of their lives. Anna Aizer and Joseph Doyle conducted a very well designed study that examined outcomes for two groups of youths charged with a similar crime, those who were and those who were not sent to a juvenile detention center.[43] The results clearly demonstrate the detrimental impact of incarceration in the United States, which imprisons young people at a rate seven to eight times higher than other comparable countries.[44] Those who were sent to a detention center were 22 percent more likely to be incarcerated as an adult and 13 percent less likely to graduate from high school. Rather than 'reforming' juveniles, incarceration negatively impacted their lives and lowered their beneficial contributions to society.

The reasons why incarceration has a detrimental impact on youth are not difficult to discover. Detailed documentation of violence and other abuses against incarcerated youth reveals a sustained pattern of mistreatment in juvenile detention centers.[45] Major national reports of the experiences of incarcerated youth reveal at least half of the youth suffered solitary confinement of more than twenty-four hours,[46] solitary confinement being a practice with well-documented detrimental outcomes.[47] At least one in ten incarcerated youth suffer sexual abuse at the hands of a staff member,[48] but some studies report higher levels of abuse. For example, one study of incarcerated youth reported that almost all of them experience some type of abuse.[49] Both for incarcerated youth and adults, the reported levels of abuse in prison probably underestimate the problem, because in many detention centers, there are inadequate systems for incarcerated individuals to report abuse.[50]

Research studies focused on both incarcerated juveniles and adults in different juvenile detention centers and prisons show that incarceration is a time of continued criminal behavior,[51] in part because the environment of detention centers and prisons are conducive to criminality. In their current form detention centers and prisons fail to educate and reform incarcerated juveniles and adults.

What Happens to the Families of Those Who Go to Prison?

> Broadly conceptualized, the prospective link between early life exposure to violence and victimization and subsequent antisocial behaviors is known as the cycle of violence.
>
> Matt DeLisi et al. (2010)

In considering the question of what happens to the families of the incarcerated, it is useful to adopt a 'cycle of violence' perspective. This is because in many cases the individuals who are incarcerated have experienced personal abuse, belong to families with a history of abuse, and help to shape a next generation that suffers abuse. The juvenile detention center and/or prison is just another component of the 'cycle of violence,' which could only be broken by an intervention that involves serious educational and reform alternatives and opportunities. As they exist today, juvenile detention centers and prisons are not intended to, nor do, provide these. They simply perpetuate cycles of violence.

Collateral Consequences of Incarceration

An extensive research literature demonstrates that incarceration detrimentally impacts the families of incarcerated individuals.[52] Researchers have described this impact as "collateral consequences,"[53] involving a wide range of processes, from perceptions of greater injustice and unfairness at the individual level to damaged ability to participate in civic and community life. The key factor causing damage to family life is the removal of a central member, typically the father, rather than the type of institution (e.g., federal, state, or local facility) in which the individual is incarcerated.[54] A direct and perhaps the most important consequence of a father's removal is the increased likelihood of the union dissolving and the mother moving on to a new partner.[55] Of course, this does not mean that the dissolutions of unions is always bad. But the emotional impact on children is often detrimental.[56]

Following Sara Wakefield and her colleagues,[57] it is useful to conceptualize the 'collateral consequences' of incarceration as consisting of two categories: informal and formal. In addition to breaking up romantic partnerships and marriages, "For the children of incarcerated parents, parental incarceration increases mental health and behavioral problems, infant mortality, homelessness, grade retention, body mass index, harsh parenting, and material hardship, among many other social problems."[58] But incarceration also has wide formal consequences for the families of prisoners. Formerly incarcerated persons are not able to hold certain jobs and are in highly important ways excluded from participating in civic life, such as voting in elections and serving on juries. These exclusions have important wider political and social consequences, because convicted formerly incarcerated persons are disproportionally poor, male, and African American and their disenfranchisement results in further weakening of political influence among African Americans.

Moreover, research has demonstrated that the boys of incarcerated fathers are significantly lower on measures of noncognitive school readiness (i.e., aggression, anxiety, concentration, depression, disobedience, hyperactivity, social withdrawal),[59] and they also have more behavioral problems.[60] The children of incarcerated, paroled, and recently released parents are estimated to number about 3.2 million in the United States.[61] Consequently, incarceration is having a detrimental impact on the educational performance and overall behavior of large numbers of children, particularly lower-class males.

Despite progress in some areas of civil rights since the 1960s, the incarcerated population in the United States is pushed to the side and given less importance in politics and policy decision-making. For example, conventional data on educational attainment excludes the incarcerated population, and it consequently seriously underestimates the level of inequality in educational attainment across social classes and ethnic groups. Stephanie Ewert and her colleagues estimate that by excluding the incarcerated population, high school dropout rates are underestimated by about 40 percent for young African Americans.[62]

What Is the Wider Psychological Purpose of Incarceration?

What are we to make of the so-called 'prison boom' in the United States and the widespread use of prisons in many different countries around the world? By the second decade of the twenty-first century there were about 1,700 correction facilities in the United States, housing a population of about 2.3 million prisoners.[63] From our discussion of the research literature so far in this chapter, it is clear that the incarcerated are predominantly lower class and the families of the incarcerated suffer severe consequences – particularly when the prisoner has a child who is a minor, which is in about half the cases. As part of a 'cycle of violence and deprivation,' the children of incarcerated parents are transformed into victims, becoming less likely to succeed in education and more likely to commit crimes.

Increased presence of police at schools is worsening the situation for students with behavioral problems. Police presence has been increasing because of school shootings, such as the tragic events that took place at Sandy Hook Elementary School in Newtown, Connecticut, in 2012, when twenty-six people were shot and killed. However, empirical evidence suggests that increased police presence at schools also increases the probability that a child will be referred to a police officer even for a minor offense, which previously would have been dealt with by teachers and other school staff.[64] Consequently, the effort to place police officers in schools as a way to make students and school staff safer has had the unintended consequence of making schools an even less supportive place for students who have more behavioral problems – the children of incarcerated parents tending to disproportionally be among these.

The evidence clearly shows that education serves as insurance against a person going to prison, but as things stand, incarceration does not serve to reform or educate the majority of the incarcerated. Studies of recidivism in the United States,[65] as well as the available international evidence,[66] show a pattern of repeat offenders, studies showing between 50 percent and 80 percent of offenders being rearrested within five years of their release and nearly 50 percent returning to prison within three years of their release.[67] The empirical facts clearly demonstrate that prisons as they function today do not reduce recidivism; as Francis Cullen and colleagues demonstrate, it is factually incorrect to argue that prisons teach criminals that crime does not pay.[68] Given the enormous investment authorities in the United States and other nations have made in the so-called prison industrial complex, and given that clearly education and reform are not the prime effects of incarceration, prisons must be serving a different purpose.

The Wider Function of Prisons

It is probably more accurate to claim that twenty-first-century prisons have taken shape through multiple factors and motivations, rather than one or a few. At the broadest level, as argued by Michel Foucault (1926–1984), the prison serves a wider function of discipline, similar to schools and other institutions, that help shape the cognitions and actions of modern citizens, particularly the lower class.[69] The discipline and control function of the prison is closely tied to its punishment function: Prisons not only consist of extremely difficult conditions for inmates during the period of incarceration but also lead to intense stress and hardship *after* release. Studies of the experiences of prisoners after their release demonstrate that reintegration into society is extremely difficult, often involving long periods of unemployment, financial stress, reliance on others for food and shelter, poor housing or homelessness, and psychological isolation.[70] Bruce Western and his colleagues have noted in their study of life after release from prison that "In the larger context of the poor neighborhoods and poor families to which former prisoners return, leaving prison is a challenging transition that strains surrounding sources of assistance."[71] Of course, most prisoners are unable to reintegrate successfully and return to prison.

Financial motives also directly and indirectly influence the growth and shaping of modern prisons. Private companies have far more extensive influence in the lives of the incarcerated population than is suggested by the percentage of the prison population that is managed by private companies (private companies manage 8.4 percent of the US prison population and 5.4 percent of the jail population[72]). At the organizational level, the hierarchical and disciplinary organization of prisons and factories are similar.[73] In this sense, it is a 'natural' move for private corporations to play an increasingly important role in government operated prisons and jails, such as by 'providing employment opportunities' for prisoners, for which prisoners receive very little or no pay. There is some variation across states in how much money prisoners receive for their work, with some extremes where they receive almost nothing. For example, "Although ninety percent of prisoners in Florida work, most of the prisoners are unpaid. One study estimates the average hourly wage at $.02 an hour."[74] On average across states in the United States, prisoners who are 'employed' retain only about 20 percent of their wages,[75] although international surveys show a lot of variation across nations.[76]

Private corporations also treat prisons and jails, as well as the entire incarcerated population and the prison guards and other staff, as a huge opportunity for profit making. Prisoners do not profit from prison, but the American private sector does. The market for a wide range of goods and services to the incarcerated population of over two million provides enormous business opportunities and profits. These goods and services include food, clothing, medication, and health services, as well as specialized equipment and technologies for prison guards. The profit motive explains why the prison population remains stubbornly high, despite the decline in crime rates since the 1990s. A number of popular books have examined the role of the profit motive in shaping the prison system,[77] but unfortunately the political clout of the incarcerated population and their families remains too insignificant to reform the prison system.

Concluding Comment

[N]othing could be made of it by anybody.
Charles Dickens, *Bleak House*[78]

Although the prison features prominently in *Great Expectations* and a number of his other novels,[79] it is in *Bleak House* and the infamous case of Jarndyce and Jarndyce that Dickens attacks the justice system most comprehensively and directly. People are pulled into the 'justice system' as if they have entered a thick fog, quickly losing their way, unable to make any sense of what is happening to them. The twenty-first-century reader might imagine that the justice system of the nineteenth century as explored by Dickens is far removed from our twenty-first-century justice system – and this is true for middle- and upper-class people. But for the lower class, things have really not changed much since Dickens wrote about prisons, the justice system, and unfairness in society.

When looked at from the perspective of the lower class, there is little that is fair about the justice system in the United States and most other major societies – it is designed to ensnare the poor of all ethnic groups and genders. Psychologists are giving more attention to the plight of the poor, entrapped by a prison system that punishes them for profits. As Chris Surprenant points out, "Incarceration is big business in the U.S.A."[80] Businesses that provide food, clothing, and services to the approximately 2.3 million prisoners in the US prison system make large, sometimes gigantic, profits. In exchange, these prisoners often provide labor either without pay or for a pittance and receive no education or training of value. Prisons and the injustice system as experienced by the lower class need to become a more important focus in psychological science. The psychological research that does examine social class differences in ethical behavior suggests that higher-class individuals are more likely to behave unethically when such behavior benefits themselves.[81] What keeps the rich from ending up in prison is their greater wealth, not their more ethical behavior.

CHAPTER 10

Psychology for the Masses in Non-Western Societies

I am writing these words in a hotel room overlooking the Nile River, in the Egyptian capital, Cairo. Egypt is a multilayered society, a fusion of one complex civilization rolling through another over thousands of years. In the outskirts of Cairo are the monumental pyramids of ancient Egypt, dating back 5,000 years to the age of the pharaohs. In Old Cairo there are buildings from classical Roman times, when Julius Caesar and Mark Anthony, the 'new boys on the block,' passed through a mere 2,000 years ago. There are also ancient Christian sites, dedicated to St. George and other early Christian martyrs, as well as synagogues giving witness to the long history of Jewish communities in Egypt. Then there are countless architectural and cultural signs of the more recent arrival of Islam in Egypt only 1,400 years ago, as well as Egypt becoming a part of the Ottoman Empire in the sixteenth century and coming under Western influence in more recent times, until gaining its independence from Great Britain in 1922. It seems every great power has rolled through and left its marks on Egyptian society.

Egypt provides an appropriate launching pad from which to assess the global relevance and appropriateness of mainstream Western psychology. While class-based inequalities and the poor in the US and other Western societies have not received adequate attention in mainstream psychology, the needs of non-Western societies have also been largely overlooked. There are some exceptions, such as William Ascher's excellent social psychological analysis of poverty alleviation programs in developing countries.[1] Also, the field of cross-cultural psychology has expanded considerably since the late twentieth century, exploring how behavior varies across cultures.[2] But as I have discussed in earlier chapters in this book, cross-cultural psychology shares the same fatally incorrect causal-reductionist assumptions as mainstream Western psychology and has not resulted in serious attention being given to the needs of lower-class masses in non-Western societies.[3] Most cross-cultural psychology research has compared the expressed attitudes, values, beliefs, and so on *of students* (!) across different societies,[4] telling us very little about the psychological experiences of the lower-class masses, particularly in non-Western societies.

Psychological research designed to address needs of the majority of people in non-Western societies must go beyond one-hour surveys and laboratory studies and come to grips with the complexity of long-term continuity and change.

Understanding Change and Continuity in Non-Western Societies

The twenty-first century has provided some harsh illustrations of how Western authorities fail to understand behavior in non-Western societies. This failure has led to some tragic Western government policy mistakes, extremely costly in terms of both human lives and material resources (of course, some non-Western leaders, such as President Saddam Hussein [1937–2006] of Iraq, have misunderstood Western societies). For example, consider the invasions of Afghanistan (in 2001) and Iraq (in 2003) by US-led forces, which resulted in decades of destructive violence, costing hundreds of thousands of lives and trillions of dollars, with benefits only for arms manufacturers and military contractors. In launching the invasions, President George W. Bush of the United States, Prime Minister Tony Blair of the United Kingdom, and some other Western leaders gravely misunderstood Afghan and Iraqi societies, with dire consequences particularly for the Near and Middle East region. The US-led war in Afghanistan ended in 2021, with President Joe Biden and some other Western leaders utterly misunderstanding the supposed 300,000 strong US-trained Afghan military, which evaporated as soon as they faced Taliban forces without the US-led military to back them. The Biden administration completely failed to differentiate between the surface and deeper characteristics of Afghan society. On the surface, in 2021 there existed a 300,000 Afghan military ready to fight the Taliban, but at a deeper level this force did not exist; it was a mirage. Unfortunately, the exportation of mainstream psychology to non-Western societies also involves tragic misunderstandings and outcomes, discussed throughout this chapter.

The danger of misperceiving non-Western societies is particularly acute in the domain of change: recognizing and distinguishing between surface change as opposed to deeper continuities. For example, throughout thousands of years, there have been a variety of changes in Egyptian society, but there are also foundational psychological continuities. We need to be extremely diligent and observant to distinguish between psychological changes and continuities in this ancient civilization. For example, take the issue of the relationship between leaders and followers, which is influenced by the psychological characteristics of leaders, followers, and also their interactions.

Earlier today I visited Al-Rafa'i Mosque, where many of the Egyptian royalty are buried, including King Farouk (1920–1965), the last king of Egypt. The last Shah of Iran, Mohammad Reza Pahlavi (1919–1980), is also buried in this colossal mosque – he fled Iran and died abroad after the 1979 anti-Shah revolution in Iran. On the surface, at least, it seems that leader–follower relationships in contemporary Egypt and Iran have fundamentally changed, moving from monarchy to a form of representative government, in which the people participate in elections to select their leaders. However, in this as in other aspects of life in low-income societies such as Egypt and Iran, surface changes and rhetoric can be highly misleading.

At a deeper level, there are important continuities in the political systems of Egypt and Iran, as well as in the political behavior of leaders and followers in these ancient lands. Even though 'elections' are now held regularly and large sections of the populations participate by voting, at present, the president of Egypt and the supreme leader of Iran are both all-powerful males and in their dictatorship positions for life. In essence, they are continuing a style of 'strongman' leadership, represented by pharaohs and shahs, that has been dominant in their societies for thousands of years, even though on the surface they have adopted the rhetoric and façade of modern societies with representative governments.

The behavior of leaders and followers in Egypt and Iran continue long-established traditions of the masses being forced to obey an all-powerful male leader. This deep continuity underlying surface-level changes, such as a change of title from pharaoh to 'president' in Egypt and from shah to 'supreme leader' in Iran, reflects a broad challenge that confronts psychologists in their quest to understand low-income, non-Western societies. We must begin by accepting that it is necessary to dig beneath the level of leaders' expressed attitudes and rhetoric in order to appreciate the deeper characteristics and continuities in these societies.

It is essential to keep in mind the foundational differences that continue to exist between Western and (particularly low-income) non-Western countries. Mainstream psychological science has so far asked research questions predominantly from the perspective of middle and upper classes in high-income Western societies. We need to know more about the

psychological experiences of the lower class. We have a vast research literature on leadership and management and people who give orders, but
we know less about those who are only experienced in taking orders. The
research literature on children in affluent and relatively peaceful Western
societies is enormous and growing, but there is too little psychological
research on the 420 million children, almost one-fifth of all children worldwide, who are living in a conflict zone.[5] Michael Wessells, an expert on
children and armed conflict at Columbia University, has noted, "Armed
conflict exacts a heavy toll of suffering on children ... who comprise
approximately half of the population of most war-torn countries and ...
half of the world's refugee population."[6] War-torn countries and refugee
populations have received far too little attention in mainstream psychological research. Wessells also warns that Western models and practices often
fail to bring positive outcomes when they are exported to non-Western
societies to solve the problems of children in armed conflict, because they
do not fit the needs of local populations and circumstances.[7]

The problems facing Western and non-Western societies are very different in so many ways. For example, as Paul Moreland describes, the demographic transitions experienced by Western and non-Western societies are
different.[8] Most Western societies, as well as Japan and Russia, are experiencing low birth rates and declining indigenous populations. This is the
opposite of most non-Western societies, particularly those in Africa, where
population growth is still disproportionate to available resources and where
education, health, and other essential services are not able to cope with the
roughly 60 percent of the population that is below the age of twenty-five.[9]

Whereas Western societies have a 'senior bulge,' with rapidly increasing numbers of people over sixty years of age, many non-Western societies (particularly in Africa) have a 'youth bulge,' with most people still
below twenty-five years of age. Cognition and aging, Alzheimer's disease, social relations with younger generations, weight disorders (obesity,
anorexia nervosa, bulimia), loneliness – there are a host of research issues
that should be the priority of at least the more affluent sector of Western
societies, but there are a host of others – such as cognition and action in
children growing up in extreme deprivation, overcrowding, impoverished
health care, illiteracy and very limited educational opportunities, dicta-
torial leadership, lack of opportunities for political participation – that
should be more of a priority for non-Western societies, *as well as the poor
in Western societies.*

Many other differences between Western and non-Western societies are
relevant to psychological functioning. For example, populations in Western

societies are now about 80 percent urban-dwelling, whereas low-income non-Western societies are still only about 50 percent urban-dwelling.[10] Moreover, urbanization is associated with rise in poverty in low-income non-Western societies, with urban poverty reaching about 40 percent in Africa.[11] Most of the 1.2 billion people who live below the World Bank's poverty line of $1.25 a day live in low-income non-Western societies;[12] over half of the 710 million population of sub-Saharan Africa live in dire conditions below this poverty line. Life expectancy is about twenty years lower in Africa, and thirty years lower in some African countries, than it is in Europe and North America.[13] Poor life conditions in low-income non-Western societies in part arose because of their extraordinarily high population growth: "From 1950 to 1970 the population of Third World countries increased by 56%, more than twice as much as that of First World countries."[14] Also, life conditions in low-income non-Western societies have been made worse by enormous volumes of hazardous waste being dumped in low-income countries by multinational corporations, mainly based in the United States and the European Union.[15] Of course, the COVID-19 pandemic has worsened living conditions for lower-class masses in low-income non-Western societies because of their dire poverty and less developed health-care systems.

The Modern and Traditional Sectors of Non-Western Societies

The low-income societies of Asia, Africa, and South America are character-ized by huge rifts between a modern sector (which is relatively more afflu-ent, urban, educated, fluent in English and other Western languages, and generally Westernized) and a traditional sector (which is relatively poor, rural, low in education, and unfamiliar with English and other Western languages). The governing elite in low-income non-Western societies are part of the modern sector and adopt lifestyles that are similar to middle- and upper-class lifestyles in high-income (mostly Western) societies. The goods and services they use tend to be similar to goods and services used in the West. They send their children to schools and universities that are either in Western countries or are very close copies of Western schools – including their language of instruction being English.

Enormous inequality persists between the ruling upper class, part of the modern sector, and the lower-class masses, who constitute the core of the traditional sector. In 2016 the top 10 percent income earners accounted for 61 percent of the national income in the Middle East, and 55 percent in Sub-Saharan Africa, Brazil, and India (the figures for Russia,

46 percent, and China, 41 percent, are closer to Europe, 37 percent, and the United States and Canada, 47 percent).[16] The plight of the masses has been exacerbated by dramatic increases in population size; for example, Cairo is now an enormous city of almost 20 million inhabitants within a nation of about 100 million people. Although free education is promised in the Egyptian constitution, the low level of government investment in schools means that in practice families have to pay even for basic elementary education.[17] As a consequence, many children (particularly girls) from lower-class families miss out on basic education.

Walking around Cairo brings one face to face with the challenges confronting most low-income non-Western societies: young and fast-growing populations, overcrowding, decrepit housing, poor health, education, and public transportation services, and extreme pollution. The terrible air quality is visible on the buildings, which are mostly corroded and covered in layers of soot and dust. The canals and irrigation channels fanning out from the Nile River to feed farms and orchards are choking with plastic bottles and bags and garbage of various kinds. Environmental pollution is even more visible in Egypt and other low-income societies than it is in the affluent societies of the West.

These special characteristics of low-income societies create extraordinary opportunities for the application of psychological science to improve life conditions for people in these societies. About fifteen million people are killed each year in low-income societies from malaria, diarrhea, AIDS, and other preventable diseases.[18] In many cases, health challenges faced by low-income societies are different. For example, in low-income societies, both men and women with high income are more likely to be obese, whereas in high-income societies the association between obesity and income is mixed for men and negative for women (i.e., high-income women are less likely to be obese).[19] Also, solutions to societal problems available in low- and high-income societies tend to be different, in part because of the higher level of corruption in low-income societies – as measured by both perceptions of corruption and direct measures of bribe giving.[20] In low-income societies, a higher percentage of resources is wasted through corruption, and there is greater need for research on psychological processes underlying the behavior of corrupt officials. Available research shows that corruption in low-income societies is substantial in magnitude and has a negative impact on economic activity.

Challenges such as high levels of illiteracy, poverty, unfamiliarity with technology, crowding, overpopulation, environmental pollution, political repression, corruption, and the like require special applied and research attention from psychological science. Special training is needed for psychologists to work effectively in the very different conditions of low-income societies.[21] Most importantly, psychologists working in low-income societies must develop their research questions from *the local context* and not copy research programs that deal with the issues faced by people in California, New York, and other centers of research in high-income societies. But this issue is almost completely ignored in both mainstream psychology and cross-cultural psychology.

Next, I discuss the global context of mainstream psychology becoming active in non-Western societies, such as Egypt and Iran. This is important to examine, because of the harm done by mainstream psychology to the poorest sector in low-income non-Western societies.

Western Psychology Is Exported to Non-Western Societies

Modern psychological science was developed in Western societies, first with Germany and other European countries taking the lead in the nineteenth century and then the United States taking the lead from the early twentieth century.[22] The very few non-Western researchers who contributed to the development of scientific psychology, such as Muzafer Sherif (1906–1988), did so by moving to work in Western countries (Sherif left Turkey to work in the United States[23]). The dominance of the United States in psychological science has been overwhelming over the last century: For example, it leads in standard measures such as *PsychLIT* entries (a database of abstracts of research in the field of psychology) and has a far greater research impact than even all of Europe combined.[24]

The United States established itself as the First World of psychology, even before the final collapse of the Soviet Union in 1991.[25] As the sole superpower of psychology, the United States exports psychological methods, theories, findings, and know-how in general to the Second World of psychology, consisting of the other industrialized nations, including Europe and Russia, and to the Third World of psychology, consisting of countries in Asia, Africa, and South America.[26] The most significant change in this order that has taken place over the last few decades is that China has moved from being part of the Third World of psychology to joining the Second World of psychology.[27]

The influence of Britain, France, and other former colonial powers is to some degree still evident in the psychological science of their former colonies. For example, Britain has some influence in psychological science in Australia, India, and Pakistan, just as France has influence in psychological science in its former colonies of Algeria and Morocco. This explains, for example, the strength of social identity research in Australia and social representations research in Algeria.[28] However, the First World of US psychology is far more important in shaping psychology in both ex-colonial powers, including in the United Kingdom and France, and other countries' ex-colonies, including Australia and Algeria.

Since the late twentieth century there have been serious attempts to develop 'indigenized psychologies,' defined "as the scientific study of human behaviour (or the mind) that is native, that is not transported from other regions, and that is designed for its people."[29] However, indigenized psychologies have made little progress in meeting the needs of lower-class masses in non-Western societies. More progress has been made toward this goal by liberation psychology,[30] which has developed in Latin America through the research of Maritza Montero and others.[31] Liberation psychology has been concerned particularly with community empowerment and the need for psychologists to intervene to lower inequalities and injustices. But despite the promise of a distinct non-Western psychology, which would reflect the needs and priorities of non-Western societies, the vast body of psychology in non-Western societies continues to be a copy of US psychology. This includes psychology in China, Iran, and other societies with expressed ideologies that are very different from Western capitalist democracies.

Exportation of Mainstream Causal-Reductionist Psychology to Non-Western Societies

Why is it that the mainstream reductionist psychology of the United States has been transferred 'wholesale' to non-Western societies? The explanation for this situation is in the relationship between the modern sector of low-income societies and Western high-income societies. The 'psychology industry' in non-Western societies is part of the modern sector. People in the modern sector, and particularly students in Westernized universities of non-Western societies, have styles of cognition and action that are more in line with individualism than their counties' collectivism. This has important implications for cross-cultural research, because (as I discuss below) the vast majority of 'cross-cultural' studies use student samples.

The elite of non-Western societies, even in the largest societies such as India and China, tend to be educated either in Western universities or local universities modeled after Western universities. Similarly, psychology departments, psychology curricula, psychology journals, psychology conferences, and just about everything concerning psychological teaching, research, and practice in non-Western universities are modeled on the US and other Western societies.

The spread of mainstream US psychology around the world has been characterized by a process of *double-reification*, "involving the exportation and propagation of cultural phenomena from one nation to another, and the later harvesting of the outcomes of this exportation through so-called international research, as validation for universalization."[32] For example, modern ideas about human rights have been spread around the world through the mass media and education systems at least in the modern sector of non-Western societies. Then, international surveys have shown the sharing of the same basic ideas about human rights particularly among young people, and this has been taken as evidence of the universal nature of 'universal human rights.'[33] This process of double-reification is strengthened through a high reliance on student samples; a study of major social and cross-cultural journals revealed that the percentage of published articles using student samples actually increased from 1980 to 2004, to reach 87 percent in the flagship cross-cultural journal. In almost all cases when the study involved non-Western societies, the students sampled in surveys were part of the modern sector.[34]

Finally, psychological research tells us that people in such positions of high power and status (i.e., Western and Western-trained psychologists) come to believe they deserve their lofty positions and feel confident about their abilities and knowledge.[35] There is no reason to believe that Western and Western-trained psychologists are immune from such biased, self-serving perceptions: believing they are justified to export psychology from high- to low-income societies.

Critically Rethinking Western Psychology in Non-Western Societies

By focusing on the domain of mental health, we can more specifically identify the kinds of problems that arise when psychology is exported wholesale from high-income to low-income societies. Even if we disregard the issue of culture and context, and assume that we should export mental health services and know-how 'wholesale' from high-income to low- and middle-income societies (which is an incorrect assumption!), we encounter major obstacles. First, mental health is a relatively low priority for political leaders in low- and middle-income societies. Surveys show mental health policies in low- and middle-income countries to be weak (often in draft form or unpublished) and that leadership in these countries lacks awareness of the significance of mental health in the larger society.[36] Second, there is a severe shortage of trained mental health professionals outside high-income societies.[37] This shortage is so great that even if all the trained mental health professionals in low-income societies worked full-time, they would only be able to provide services to less than 10 percent of those needing help in a major and relatively advanced low-income society such as India. In practice, mental health professionals in low-income societies tend to only operate in the modern sector of their societies, limiting themselves to the urban rich. This is detrimental, because the poor have more mental health problems.

It is only the relatively affluent Westernized people in the modern sector of low-income societies, including some students, administrators, and faculty in universities, who have access to psychological counselling and therapy. But serious problems arise even when the exported psychology operates within this very limited modern sector, because the assumptions and orientation of Western approaches are questionable. As Pittu Laungani has explained, "Until recently ... Counselling and psychotherapy were seen as western enterprises. And given the belief of many therapists that their own models had universal applicability, few serious attempts were made to examine the role of any cultural factors in their therapeutic practices. Over the years the western models of therapy acquired 'world supremacy' and were used in virtually all parts of the world. To a large extent they still are."[38] Laungani goes on to point out that the hegemony of Western psychological models is now being questioned, in large part because the needs of most people in low-income societies from psychological science are in major ways different (a topic I discuss in greater depth later in this chapter).

The critical reassessment of exporting psychological research and practices 'wholesale' from high-income to low- and medium-income societies led Judith Bass and colleagues to ask, "Does this mean that instruments and concepts developed in industrialised countries are irrelevant for studying mental illness in other contexts? Not necessarily. Rather, their appropriateness will vary across cultures and by illness, and therefore needs to be explored."[39]

Special Mental Health Needs: The Case of the Forcibly Displaced

Low-income societies have populations with special mental health needs. For example, in 2018 there were almost 71 million forcibly displaced persons in the world, up from about 43 million in 2009.[40] Every day in 2018, 37,000 people were forced to flee their homes – mostly from violence in low-income societies, and they ended up seeking shelter in other low-income societies. Even when high-income countries are involved in wars, the persons displaced by the wars tend to be from low-income countries – examples being the invasion of Afghanistan and Iraq by US-led forces in 2001 and 2003, resulting in millions of displaced Afghanis and Iraqis but *not* displaced Americans, Europeans, and other high-income invaders. About half of the refugee population in 2018 were children under the age of eighteen, up 41 percent from 2009. While the mass media and Western politicians give a lot of attention to the arrival of displaced persons in Western countries, such as Donald Trump's focus on displaced persons from South America and the 'need to build a wall' to keep them out of the United States, the vast majority of displaced persons both escape from and find refuge in low-income societies.[41]

The experiences of displaced persons in low-income societies need a great deal more research attention from psychologists. Studies of refugee camps demonstrate a wide and persistent pattern of mental health problems, particularly among youth in these camps.[42] A study of refugee camps in Bangladesh, Kenya, Nepal, Tanzania, Thailand, and Uganda revealed harsh conditions that harmed the psychological health of refugees.[43] Lack of control over even mundane aspects of their lives, such as lack of privacy and distance from local citizens and major cities, put pressure on even the most resilient refugees. In line with this, a study of refugees in the Democratic Republic of Congo showed refugees developing an identity centered on collective helplessness: They came to believe they were part of a group with little control over their own lives.[44] The implication is that psychological interventions are needed to better arrange the living conditions of refugees, so as to improve their mental health.

Need for Psychological Research on Displaced Persons

As the number of forcibly displaced persons around the world and particularly in low-income societies increases, research and practicing psychologists need to focus on psychological factors that impact the lives of the forcibly displaced – such as the millions displaced from Ukraine after the Russian invasion (2022). Some of these factors are unexpected. For example, one obvious policy solution is to return displaced people to where they fled from. However, a study of refugees who returned to Burundi after prolonged exile (they had left to escape violence) revealed a pattern of exclusion and discrimination against them on the part of those who had never fled and a feeling of alienation among some returnees.[45] Another important outcome is the enormous role of psychological factors in well-being. We are used to thinking about the material impact of war and displacement, but Michael Wessells points out, "Attention is often given to the physical attacks on children and their families, and the enormous damage inflicted by bullets, bombs, shrapnel, landmines, and unexploded remnants of war. However, the full impact of war on children becomes apparent when one considers the enormity of the psychological harm caused to children, the shattering and toxification (rendering them sites of high, unrelieved levels of stress) of their social environments, the lack of access to basic necessities and security, and the loss of important sources of social support for their well-being."[46]

A focus on children and conflict highlights the special features of low-income societies and the reasons why psychological science in low-income societies should not be a copy of that in high-income societies. Simply put, there are problems to be tackled in low-income societies that do not exist in the same way in high-income societies. For example, child soldiers have been extensively recruited and used in armed conflicts in low-income societies,[47] as illustrated by the case of the Lord's Resistance Army in Uganda, which forcibly recruited 60,000–80,000 mostly male children to serve as soldiers. But in many cases, the extremely difficult life conditions in low-income societies experiencing violent conflict result in children 'voluntarily' joining armed groups as a means of gaining access to life-saving resources, such as food and shelter; this was the case during the 'civil war' in Sri Lanka.[48] Girls are also often pushed to become child soldiers to avoid domestic abuse, forced marriage, and various forms of gender-based exploitation.[49] A study of 258 former child soldiers in Nepal revealed that difficulties in everyday life, including very poor economic and educational prospects, were major factors pushing children to join armed groups.[50] These 'push' factors are particularly powerful in conflict situations where caretakers have been killed or have disappeared, leaving children to seek alternative forms of protection and means of survival.

Just as the power of context in low-income societies helps to explain why young people 'volunteer' to become child soldiers, the power of context can lead individuals in these societies to radicalization and terrorism, for example, as is reflected by the dangerous rise of Islamic State in Africa during the third decade of the twenty-first century.[51] This issue is addressed by the 'staircase to terrorism,'[52] a context-based model that has proved influential in explaining the rise of terrorism, including the 9/11 attacks. Imagine a staircase in the middle of a building, with all the people starting on the ground floor. Each of the floors is characterized by particular psychological processes; the people on the ground floor are motivated mainly by fairness and assessment of the justice of their living conditions and treatment. Some individuals feel they are treated unfairly and they move to the first floor to improve their lives. Those who find options to improve their situation remain on the ground floor, but a small group remain highly dissatisfied and move to the second floor where the main psychological process is *displacement of aggression*. This is the diversion of hostility away from an immediate target to an alternative target – such as diverting aggression away from one's local government to the United States.

Until the third floor of this model, people on the staircase see terrorism as immoral. However, those individuals who reach the third floor experience a major change: They come to see terrorism as justified. They are not yet ready to undertake terrorist acts themselves. However, because other measures have not helped them, they adopt a 'the ends justify the means' mentality and are willing to support terrorist organizations through funding, networking, and other means. Some of the individuals who reach the third floor move up to the fourth floor, where they experience a cognitive transformation, coming to see the world as 'us versus them,' 'we are good, they are evil,' 'the good are justified to destroy the evil.' It is on the fourth floor that individuals become more isolated and detached from a mainstream universal morality that condemns killing. A few of these individuals move to the fifth floor, where they commit terrorist acts intended to kill.[53]

Of course, terrorist attacks are also carried out by right-wing extremists from high-income countries, such as the attack by a White nationalist Australian on two Muslim mosques in New Zealand on March 15, 2019, killing fifty people.[54] But the popular media in the United States and some other Western countries tend to avoid labelling radicalized White nationalists as terrorists. As Jessica Johnson has described, radicalization tends to be rendered invisible by Whiteness.[55]

Finally, I have argued that the needs of low-income versus high-income societies from psychological science are in some major ways different. For example, civil wars, forced displacement, the rise to power of violent Jihadi Islamic groups such as Islamic State, and child soldiers are to some degree unique to low-income societies and do not exist in the same way in high-income societies. These distinct problems create special needs from psychological science. However, we must keep in mind that the poor in high-income societies do have some experiences that are in important ways similar to that of the poor in low-income societies. For example, the experiences of powerlessness, invisibility, relative deprivation, and criminalization are common to the poor in both low-income and high-income societies.

Concluding Comment

The needs of low-income and high-income societies from psychological science are in important respects different. The populations of low-income societies have special characteristics not shared by most people in high-income societies. For example, extreme hardships arising from dire economic conditions, wars (including invasions of low-income societies by the militaries of high-income societies), widespread gang violence, the rise in power of Islamic State and other violent religious groups, and extreme and widespread poverty lead to consequences such as mass forced migration and mental health difficulties.

The special conditions of low-income societies should result in psychological research questions and applied projects appropriate for these societies. But with a relatively small number of exceptions, this has not been the case. So far, psychological knowledge has been exported 'wholesale' from high-income to low-income societies, with the result that the impact of psychological science has remained limited to the modern sector of low-income societies. The exported psychological science has addressed the needs of only the upper class in low-income societies. There is an urgent need for more attention to be given to the needs of lower-class masses in non-Western societies from psychological science.

But this focus on the needs of the masses must arise from genuine and free inquiry on the part of psychologists, and not from dogmatic politically motivated programs driven by dictators. Experience has clearly demonstrated that authorities in dictatorships (such as Iran, North Korea, and Syria) are not capable of generating a progressive program of psychological research that would benefit the masses of their societies. Such an alternative program would require the freedom to explore the psychology of politically sensitive behaviors such as corruption, misuse of power, and gender inequality.

PART III

Looking Ahead

The two chapters and the Afterword in Part III of this text look ahead to future developments. Research methods in psychology are critically examined in Chapter 11. I argue that a major shortcoming in mainstream psychology is the interpretation of research results through a causal-reductionist model. Irrespective of whether quantitative or qualitative, or laboratory or field, or other types of methods are adopted, a causal-reductionist interpretation of results is misleading. We must adopt broader interpretations, beyond causal-reductionism. A second major theme in the chapter is the reductionist and misleading interpretation of 'research ethics' in mainstream psychology. Focus is placed on bureaucratic procedures and individual rights, ignoring important issues such as collective rights and duties, and the ethics of ignoring research questions concerning poverty, class-based inequalities, and increasing wealth concentration in fewer and fewer hands.

Rising inequality and increasing wealth concentration, as well as increased relative deprivation, characterize our twenty-first century world. These trends are being exaggerated by the COVID-19 pandemic. How can psychological science contribute to improving the *plight of the poor* across the world? There is a range of possible solutions, from minor reforms to radical violent revolutions. Psychological research can help explore the viability and outcomes of these different solutions. But this potential will only be achieved if there is a change of focus toward psychological research that avoids reductionism and mechanistic causal models. Our research focus needs to move to plasticity and hard-wiring both inside and *outside* the individual: in what ways and how fast can collective behavioral changes take place, and what are the limitations to changes? This shift in focus will help psychologists to more directly address the plight of the poor internationally.

The most obvious and historically prominent solution to the plight of the lower-class has been revolution, a topic very seldom touched on by psychologists.[1] In France, Russia, Cuba, Egypt, Iran, and many other countries, the revolutionary path to change has been attempted. Governments have been violently overthrown, dictators cast aside, and new 'revolutionary' regimes have been put into place. However, I argue that psychological factors, particularly limits on political plasticity and hard-wiring both inside and outside individuals, mean that radical revolutions only have limited, short-term success. By helping us better understand the limitations of revolutions, psychologists can pave the way for more foundational changes that benefit the lower-class masses and all of society in the longer term.

In the brief Afterword, I argue that having gained global presence, psychological science has a duty to meet the needs of the majority of people in the world, this majority being relatively poor and low in power and influence.

CHAPTER II

Rethinking Research Methods

It is in the domain of research methods that, despite criticisms from quali-tative researchers,[1] feminists,[2] critical race theorists,[3] and various others,[4] the causal-reductionist model has had the greatest impact. Mainstream psychological methods are positioned as 'scientific,' and anyone who opposes them becomes 'anti-science.'[5] It becomes an 'anti-science' posi-tion to point out that not all human behavior is causally determined. Also, that the object of study in psychology is human beings, who have unique collective and individual characteristics, such as implicitly and explicitly self-reflecting and showing reactions to being studied – characteristics not shared by chemicals, atoms, and other such phenomena studied by biolo-gists, geologists, chemists, physicists, or any other scientists.

Mainstream psychology claims that mainstream research methods are 'neutral and ethical.' They are supposedly neutral, in the sense that they are not shaped by political positions and values. They are supposedly ethical, in the sense that they follow the rules of ethics outlined by professional psychology associations (by far the most globally influential being the American Psychological Association, founded in 1892). But these claims are misleading. First, because they ignore the deeper political biases in mainstream psychology – biases that I shall discuss later in this chapter. Second, because although considerable attention is given in mainstream psychology to the issue of ethics, it is a reductionist, naively narrow, and even deceptive interpretation of ethics.

Focus is placed almost exclusively on the rights of individuals and on nar-row methodological topics that completely ignore what is by far the most important ethical issue: the research questions explored by psychologists and the collective rights and duties they neglect (topics I elaborate on later in this chapter). This is epitomized by the functions of the Internal Review Board (IRB) now active on every major university campus. IRBs give detailed atten-tion to the ethics of how individual participants are treated in the narrow confines of studies, but they ignore the broader ethics of research questions examined by psychologists and the broader influence of psychology in support of the status quo, with its huge and growing wealth inequalities.

Using Science As a 'Neutral' Cover: The Background

[Y]ou have scientists who work for pharmaceutical companies trying to discover new medications for the diseases that afflict humans. You have scientists who brave the bitter cold of the Arctic to take ice samples that they can use to track the course of global climate change. You have scientists who sit in observatories with their telescopes pointed to the heavens, searching for and classifying celestial bodies. You have scientists who work at universities and do science to acquire knowledge in their chosen fields (e.g., psychology, biology, or physics)."

Bordens and Abbot[6]

From the latter part of the nineteenth century, a concerted effort was made to position mainstream psychology as a *bona fide* science and this effort continues today, as reflected by the quote above where the authors classify psychology with biology and physics. A study of fifteen widely used introductory psychology texts revealed that psychology is routinely positioned in this way.[7] For example, Feist and Rosenberg argue that "not only is psychology a science, but it is also considered a core science, along with medicine, earth science, chemistry, physics, and math."[8] Sdorow and Rickabaugh assert that "Physics, chemistry, biology, and psychology differ in what they study, yet each uses the scientific method."[9] As I show below, it is in the interpretation of the 'scientific method' that mainstream psychology takes the wrong path.

The presentation of psychology 'as a science' in the latter half of the nineteenth century was marked by a deep dilemma. This dilemma is most clearly reflected in the research of Wilhelm Wundt (1832–1920), routinely described in major introductory psychology texts as the father of scientific psychology, largely because he established the first psychology research laboratory in 1889.[10] The experimental tradition initiated by Wundt involves the manipulation of independent variables (assumed causes) to test their effect on dependent variables (assumed effects). This approach has been wholeheartedly adopted in twenty-first-century mainstream psychology texts, so that every experiment "is designed to answer essentially the same question: Does the independent variable (IV) cause the predicted change in the independent variable (IV)?"[11]

The experimental tradition in mainstream psychology assumes that all human behavior is causally determined, in the sense that each time 'cause

X' is present then 'effect Y' necessarily follows.[12] This 'causal tradition' is routinely and simplistically described as being rooted in research by Wundt. But this is only part of the story of Wundt's research, because in addition to the laboratory method and causal psychology, Wundt also completed ten volumes of what is best described as 'cultural psychology,' focused on values, traditions, language, and other features of culture that he believed are less suitable for study using the laboratory method and the causal model.

Cultural psychology assumes that important parts of human behavior are not causally determined but regulated by normative systems – customs, norms, rules, values, and other important features of culture.[13] The 'regulation' of behavior is different from deterministic causation, because it assumes that human beings have some measure of choice and intentionality in how they behave (as discussed in Chapter 5 of this text). Most of the time most people follow the *norms* that act as guides for correct behavior in a given context, rather than behave 'incorrectly.' For example, the arrangement of the furniture in my university office is such that year after year visitors shown to my office sit in the chair opposite my desk, and I sit in the chair behind my desk. However, a visitor could decide to enter my office and sit in 'my chair' rather than the chair normally occupied by visitors. The only thing preventing visitors from doing this are the norms and rules for correct behavior in that particular context. A student or some other visitor might decide to behave 'incorrectly,' but this has not happened over the last three decades.

Does the position of furniture in my office cause visitors to sit in a particular chair? Not in the same way that gravity causes a book thrown in the air to drop to the floor. The book could not 'decide' to fail to drop to the floor, but a visitor to my office could decide to sit in 'my chair' rather than the chair that is more obviously positioned for the use of visitors. Alternatively, a visitor might decide to sit on the floor, or to stand. The fact that visitors to my office follow a normative pattern of behavior in where they choose to sit means that in that setting their interpretation of correct behavior guides their actions and makes where they sit predictable.[14]

Mainstream psychology adopted and built on Wundt's causal model and laboratory method but completely neglected his cultural psychology and the 'normative model.' The main reason is that mainstream psychologists adopted a deterministic model of science on the assumption that this is what the 'real' sciences such as chemistry and physics have done. But of course, even if this were the case (which it is not), the subjects of study in psychology and sciences such as chemistry and physics are profoundly

different. The subject of psychological study is human beings, who explicitly and implicitly self-reflect and show reactions to being studied.[15] This
is unlike the various chemicals and other phenomena studied in chemistry, physics, and other sciences. This difference matters because it neces-
sitates methods and explanations that assume that *in addition to behavior
determined by causes, there is also intentional behavior guided by normative
systems*.

Of course, some human behavior is causally determined. For example,
imagine I am in a car accident and receive a head injury, which causes me
to temporarily lose memory. The physical impact to my head caused neuronal damage and the subsequent memory loss. This is *efficient causation*, a
single temporarily preceding cause that fully explains the effect. However,
this kind of causation actually concerns a small amount of human behavior; most of human behavior is not causally determined but normatively
regulated and is best understood by examining normative systems and
how they are used by people as guides to behavior in different contexts.

All of the major schools of psychology, including psychoanalysis,
behaviorism, cognitive psychology, and now neuroscience, have adopted
an overly simplistic and misleading causal model of behavior. For Freud
and the psychoanalytic movements, the causes of behavior are assumed
to be in the unconscious; these causes tend to remain hidden to individuals themselves because they are repressed through various defense
mechanisms (such as displacement, projection, and reaction formation).
For behaviorists, the causes of behavior are stimuli, and cause–effect relations are studied through stimuli–response associations. B. F. Skinner
(1904–1990) argued that free will is an illusion and in order to organize the
world in a more rational way, we must progress beyond our outdated ideas
on 'freedom and dignity.'[16] By reengineering the environment according to behaviorist principles, we can shape human behavior to create a
more peaceful and just world. Cognitive psychology gradually overtook
behaviorism as the most influential school of psychology from the 1960s,
bringing the mind back into mainstream psychology but continuing the
causal tradition by assuming cognitive mechanisms as causes of behavior.
Neuroscience dominates psychology in the twenty-first century and, with
some exceptions,[17] follows a narrowly causal-reductionist line of research.

The emergence and dominance of reductionist neuroscience in the
twenty-first century have in important ways taken psychology back to
behaviorism.[18] Both behaviorists and reductionist neuroscientists assume
behavior is causally determined – whereas behaviorists assume behavior to be causally determined by environmental stimuli, reductionist

neuroscientists see the causes of behavior to be in the brain. As George Graham explains: "Neuroscience describes inside-the-box mechanisms that permit today's reinforcing stimulus to affect tomorrow's behavior. The neural box ... cannot exercise independent or non-environmentally countervailing authority over behavior."[19] The deterministic model of behavior adopted by behaviorism and reductionist neuroscience leads to a rejection of free will, a topic I return to later in this chapter.

Causal and Normative Accounts of Behavior

[P]sychologists are committed to studying mental life and behaviour by using what is known as the scientific method.

Haslam and McGarty[20]

Scientific knowledge ... is based on studies conducted by researchers. In a nutshell, scientific knowledge is knowledge we can trust.

Pajo[21]

One hallmark of scientific thinking is the assumption of determinism. This is the doctrine that the universe is orderly – the idea that all events have meaningful, systematic causes.

Pelham and Blanton[22]

Mainstream psychologists have invested heavily in developing research methods that achieve a high level of control over variables, so that the relationship between (assumed) cause and effect, independent variable(s) and dependent variable(s), can be identified. In practice, the assumption of *psychological universalism*, that all human beings are basically the same in terms of fundamental psychological characteristics, has led mainstream psychologists to give little serious attention to the issue of sampling in their actual research studies (this is very different from the drilling psychology students receive on sampling in their research methods classes). Psychological universalism implies that it does not make any difference if the participants in research are White undergraduates in an expensive and exclusive American university, or impoverished adult villagers from northern Pakistan, or taxi drivers in Nairobi, Kenya, or even poor African Americans in Alabama, United States. The uniformity of psychological characteristics in all these different groups means that any human being could 'stand in' for any other(s). The practical outcome of this assumption underlying mainstream psychology is that psychological research is conducted mostly with undergraduate students serving as participants (the issue of samples in psychological research being WEIRD was discussed in Chapter 5 of this book).[23]

Because of the psychological universalism assumption, in practice the issue of sampling is given far less attention in psychological research than the topic of control. Indeed, the highest priority is given to research methods that (are assumed to) allow the highest level of control over variables. The explicit goal of this control is to identify causation.

The laboratory method is assumed to provide the tightest control over variables, and the vast majority of psychological studies have involved one-hour laboratory experiments. Of course, the controlled experiment has a constructive role to play in research. For example, tightly controlled experiments can highlight particular issues and bring to public attention major challenges, as Stanley Milgram did in his seminal experiments demonstrating that even individuals with normal personality profiles can under certain conditions follow orders to do grievous harm to others.[24] However, it is more accurate to apply a normative rather than causal interpretation to the results of such experimental laboratory research.

A normative account of behavior in psychology experiments assumes that participants behave as most people behave in most situations, that is, in the manner they see to be 'correct' for the context. Participants in laboratory experiments ask themselves questions such as 'what is this experiment about?' 'How am I supposed to behave?' But participants do not all arrive at the same answers. As a result, although many people do behave similarly, there tends to be some variation in how participants behave in the experimental situation. Consequently, even in tightly controlled experimental studies such as those conducted by Milgram, there is variation in how participants behave. When Milgram conducted his research with US samples, about 65 percent of the participants followed orders to give lethal levels of shock to a stranger. In replications of Milgram's experiments in other societies, the level of obedience varied, from as low as 40 percent to as high as 90 percent.[25] Very importantly, this means that between 60 percent and 10 percent of participants (never 0 percent) in these studies refused to obey the orders of the authority figure.

The normative account gives primacy to the meaning-making that participants engage in, leaving room for variations across individuals and groups. Irrespective of whether the research is conducted in a laboratory or in the field, or whether it is quantitative or qualitative, or whether it involves fMRI or other instruments, the main focus of a normative interpretation is the human being (research participant) engaged in the construction of meaning and decision-making. In this regard, meaning construction and decision-making are achieved by a whole human being embedded in social, cultural, and political contexts, not by parts of the brain.

Reductionism Enabling Authoritarianism

> Only of a living human being and what resembles (behaves like) a liv-
> ing human being can one say: it has sensations; it sees; is blind; hears;
> is deaf; is conscious and unconscious.
>
> Wittgenstein[26]

> [I]f someone has a pain in his hand … one does not comfort the
> hand, but the sufferer.
>
> Wittgenstein[27]

In behaviorist accounts of behavior, stimuli serve as causes; in reductionist neuroscience accounts of behavior, the brain and more often parts of
the brain are assumed to be causes of behavior.[28] But both behaviorism
and reductionist neuroscience are committing what Maxwell Bennett
and Peter Hacker call the *mereological fallacy*, the attribution of the
properties of wholes to parts.[29] As Ludwig Wittgenstein (1889–1951)
(quoted above) points out, it is the person and not parts of a person
or bits of a brain that senses or does not sense, sees or does not see,
hears or does not hear, has pain or does not have pain, is conscious or
unconscious.

Reductionist neuroscience research has amassed a large body of evidence
indicating that particular parts of the brain are necessary for certain types
of behavior. New research studies are refining the picture of relationships
between particular brain parts and particular behaviors, such as emotions.[30]
For example, research has shown that emotion regulation can be associated
with long-lasting changes on amygdala responses.[31] While such research
demonstrates that the amygdala needs to be functional in order for an individual to experience and regulate emotions in a healthy way, it is not the
amygdala that 'feels fear,' 'becomes jealous,' or experiences other emotions.
Individual human beings experience emotions. Following Wittgenstein, it
is a person who feels sad because of a death in her family, and it is to the
person we express sympathy and condolences, not to a body part.[32]

Reductionist neuroscience leads to a position where parts of the body,
not the person, are considered as causal agents. Even more important than
that, 'causes' are conceived as outside the realm of agency and human
intentionality. The brain or parts of the brain as causal agent means that
behavioral outcomes are 'part of the natural order.' For example, research
on the genetic roots of intelligence treats genes as determinants, and as if
they operate in a vacuum (see Chapter 3 of this text).

From this perspective, 'causes' in the brain are assumed to be an outcome
of human evolution, relatively static and continuous. They are the outcome

of long-term natural development. By implication, 'causes' have not been put into place by humans; they are integral to 'nature' and they take a long time to change. Consequently, social structure, class-based inequalities, problems such as poverty, and the socio-political system broadly stem from the stable 'causal agents' found in the brain. 'The cause' becomes the brain or brain parts, and not intentional political actions or political systems or other features of the world 'out there' intentionally built by humans with political goals – such as exploitative economic and social policies intentionally implemented by governments. Intentional persons and intentionally created social structures are replaced by brain parts.

This reductionism is justified as 'science,' with heavy reliance on fMRI and other 'advanced' brain imaging technology. Just as the Skinner Box and other technologies were used to position behaviorism as 'scientific psychology' in the early twentieth century, fMRI and other means of monitoring the brain are now being used to position reductionist neuroscience as the 'real science' of psychology. In the next section I discuss another key component of this reductionist movement in psychology: a narrow and misleading interpretation of ethics in psychology, which is highly unethical in that it tramples on the collective rights of the poor and ignores the duties of the rich.

Reductionism and Misleading Ethics

No matter what type of claim researchers are investigating, they are obligated – by law, by morality, and by today's social norms – to treat the participants in their research with kindness, respect, and fairness.
Morling[33]

[W]e use a set of rules and regulations that are primarily concerned with protecting the rights of people who participate in research studies. These rules are called research ethics.
Pajo[34]

[R]esearchers have ethical standards, both formal and informal. Formal codes of practice are explicitly designed to limit harm to participants.
Haslam and McGarty[35]

Anyone engaged in research in twenty-first century universities, either as a researcher or research participant, will come across (apparently) extensive and detailed rules for ethical behavior in research. Students taking courses on research methods in psychology will also study research methods texts that cover ethics; the above quotations are from representative texts commonly used in such courses. Most texts focus on the American Psychological Association's five general principles for guiding research with human participants:[36] IRB, informed consent, deception, debriefing, and research misconduct (e.g., data fabrication/falsification, plagiarism).

However, a first objection to the interpretation of ethics adopted in mainstream psychology is that major bodies of research that fit the criteria of psychological science have involved unethical behavior by researchers. As Laura Brown has argued,[37] the underlying assumption that science per se is necessarily good, politically neutral, and ethical is problematic. She insightfully lists some of the ways in which the norms of psychological science have been oppressive:

> One of the founding fathers of American psychology, G. Stanley Hall, was infamous for promulgating the "scientific" belief that higher education would make women infertile and that women were intellectually inferior to men. At various times, psychological science has taught as received wisdom the "facts" that people of color or Jews were genetically inferior in intelligence; that lesbians and gay men were psychologically deviant; and that women who worked outside the home were suffering from various disruptions of normal female development.[38]

In earlier chapters, I critically discussed the limitations of ethics in mainstream psychology, particularly in domains such as intelligence and mental health (Chapters 3 and 8, respectively). The major problem is that in the history of modern psychology, there have been numerous instances in which 'scientific research' that meets the narrow requirements of 'ethics in psychology' has produced evidence that actually work to harm particular disadvantaged groups. For now, my concern is specifically to highlight the inadequacy, in terms of rising class-based inequalities and the interests of the poor, of the very limited interpretation of ethics adopted in mainstream psychology.

Ethics Reduced to the Micro Level

> Formal codes continue to focus narrowly on risks to the individual research participant, in the specific context of the experiment or study, but neglect questions about risks to the group to which the participant belongs. Even more rare are questions about whether or not certain types of research, no matter how ethically conducted, harm the culture because they directly or inadvertently perpetuate reactionary or oppressive norms.
>
> Laura Brown[39]

A foundational shortcoming of mainstream psychology is the reductionist interpretation of ethics. All the focus has been on how *individual participants* are treated in the research process, for example, the level of deception and anxiety experienced by individual participants in studies and experiments. Reductionism has meant that 'ethical concerns' in mainstream psychology have been utterly misguided and misdirected. IRB committees at universities have devoted enormous amounts of time and resources to ensure that individual participants experience minimal anxiety and stress as a result of research procedures. In the meantime, in the course of their everyday lives the poor (including poor Whites and poor ethnic minorities) routinely and continually face enormous anxiety, stress, and exploitation.

Most importantly, IRB committees do not question the ethics of mainstream psychology devoting most if its resources to research questions that are of little or no benefit to the lower-class masses in Western and non-Western societies. The IRB has become an integral part of the university bureaucracy, and 'official research ethics' means that there are a set of boxes that have to be 'ticked' in the correct order, as if this makes psychological research ethical – irrespective of the questions being addressed by the research.

Concluding Comment

The causal-reductionist model has resulted in psychological research that is for the most part designed to discover the 'causes' of behavior, typically within individual persons and increasingly within brains and brain parts. But most human behavior is normatively regulated rather causally determined, and the sources of normative systems regulating behavior are 'out there' in social, cultural, and political systems. Besides, the most important part of research are the questions beings asked, and this key issue is neglected as being outside the domain of ethics in research methods.

Clearly, we need to expand our conception of 'ethics' and research methods in psychological science. First, by going beyond causal-reductionist explanations of research results, we explicitly include intentionality as part of our explanations of behavior – including how society is organized, how wealth concentration and class-based inequalities are increasing, and how the lower-class masses have special needs and interests that are different from the rich. Second, mainstream psychology must also focus on the urgent questions arising from the needs of the lower-class masses. These include issues such as powerlessness, 'invisibility,' polluted home and work environments, abysmal educational opportunities and health services, and the relative deprivation associated with the enormous and increasing wealth gap that characterizes major societies in the twenty-first century.

Far more limiting than the research methods used by mainstream psychologists are the research questions they have (and have not) addressed. Basic questions about the impact of poverty on social and cognitive processes are starting to be addressed by a relatively small number of researchers.[40] For example, we now know that Zip code influences SAT scores,[41] as well as basic brain development.[42] Even less often addressed are questions about the social and cognitive processes that characterize the rich and the superrich. These group and intergroup issues are of the highest ethical importance, but they are ignored in mainstream psychology. Instead, mainstream psychology trivializes ethics by limiting it to the individual level, completely ignoring the supremely ethical issue of research questions asked and not asked.

Different 'crises' experienced in psychology, such as the replication crisis of the early twenty-first century (which involves a failure to replicate many published studies, as discussed in Chapter 6 of this text), have resulted in a slight broadening of research methods. For example, there is now more interest in field research in psychology.[43] However, a wider range of research methods will not lead to a more worthwhile psychology, if research results continue to be interpreted through the incorrect causal-reductionist lens that currently dominates mainstream psychology.

CHAPTER 12

Revolution and Psychology

Because mainstream psychology is founded on causal-reductionism, certain topics are not given adequate attention in mainstream teaching and research. In earlier chapters I have discussed the examples of psychology and poverty as well as psychology and social class. In this chapter I turn to the topic of psychology and revolution, as another example of a topic that becomes far more relevant and significant in psychology when we abandon causal-reductionism and ask questions from a lower- rather than upper-class perspective.

There has evolved, outside mainstream psychology and mainly through European influence,[1] a growing body of psychological research on collective action and intergroup relations.[2] However, this research fails to address certain puzzling aspects of revolutions, in Western and non-Western societies.[3] For example, why do so many revolutions fail to improve the conditions of the poor and result in the continuity of class-based inequalities?

In the twenty-first century, the appeal of revolution has reemerged in both Western and non-Western societies, from both politically left-wing and right-wing perspectives. The rise of authoritarian strongmen, such as Donald Trump, has meant that right-wing populist movements across the world also envisage revolution as a path to political dominance. But from the perspective of the poor, the key psychological issue is not whether a revolution is being attempted by the radical left-wing or the radical right-wing, but why even *after* major revolutions class-based power and resource disparities persist and why leader–follower relations continue as before?

Put bluntly, it makes little difference to the poor if after a revolution the new dictator is representing the political left or right, if it is Stalin or Hitler, or representing religion, as in the case of Khomeini – the key question is why the same authoritarian leader–follower relationship persists after revolutions. In order to dig deeper into such questions, we need to examine different types of change associated with revolutions. For example, we need to also consider the possibility of progressive change without revolutions.

Societal change toward greater justice and freedoms, equality of opportunity, and a more open system broadly can come about *through gradual social evolution rather than violent revolution.* For example, such an evolutionary process seems to underlie the progress made by Scandinavian societies, which are in many respects world leaders in justice, openness, and democracy.

Change and Revolution

The intense passion of crowds attacking the hated Bastille Prison in Paris in 1789, the fury of colonists invading British ships and hurling chests of tea into Boston harbor in 1773, the deadly extremism of Red Army forces executing Tsar Nicholas II and all his family in 1918, the deep hatred of Iraqis taunting Saddam Hussein before hanging him in 2006, the ruthlessness of Libyan revolutionaries exterminating Muammar Gaddafi like a cornered rat in 2011 – such images are part of the fire and fury of *revolution*, which *at the minimum* involves the overthrow and replacement of the governing power in society, be it an individual (e.g., a monarch), a group (e.g., religious fundamentalists), or a social class (e.g., the aristocracy, the superrich). On the surface, revolutions seem to bring change 'from the bottom-up' and represent serious attempts to meet the needs of the poor. But deeper examination reveals that so far we have achieved only *system 1 revolutions*, which involve change of regime, but we have failed to achieve *system 2 revolutions*, which also transform cultural systems and everyday behavior of both leaders and followers.

System 1 revolutions bring changes in regimes without improving the relative deprivation of the poor. Thus, hundreds of years after the American and French revolutions, the poor in the United States and in France are relatively extremely deprived.[4] The rage and energies of the masses can lead to System 1 revolutions but are not enough to achieve system 2 revolutions. I witnessed the enormous rage of revolution in Iran, when the intense explosion of hatred against the shah shared by tens of millions of people toppled his regime. But the outcome after the 1979 revolution was an even harsher dictatorship in Iran, this time with an 'Islamic' front and with even worse economic and political consequences for the poor.

Perhaps the most depressing experience I have had in my life was to visit Iran decades after the 1979 Revolution, remembering the bright dreams and idealistic slogans of the revolutionary period. We talked of freedom and justice but ended up with dictatorship, corruption, and injustice in a hated Islamic Republic where the poor continue to experience severe economic hardship under a corrupt regime.[5]

But it is not only the 1979 Revolution in Iran that resulted in disappointing outcomes for the poor, women, and minorities. Women and minorities in America, where the Revolution of 1776 promised so much, had to wait until the twentieth century before they could at least on paper attain equality and the right to vote in political elections. In practice, even today voter suppression and the disenfranchisement of the poor and disadvantaged have become routine in the United States.[6] Why has progress been so slow despite dramatic regime changes following the American, French, Russian, Chinese, Cuban, and other revolutions?

Although psychological science has not attempted to address the kinds of questions that arise about revolutions from the point of view of the poor, psychological science has given some attention to collective mobilization. The conditions under which people take nonnormative collective action have been explored by social identity theory,[7] relative deprivation theory,[8] contact theory,[9] and other major psychological theories.[10] Social identity theory and system justification theory have provided more comprehensive examinations of not just collective action but also psychological mechanisms that enable the continuation of injustices.[11] For example, research shows that people tend to adopt ways of thinking that justifies their own disadvantaged position and interprets their poverty as fair.[12]

The same focus on the question of "why collective action takes place?" is evident in discussions of revolution by social and political scientists outside of psychology. This includes such classic sociological works as "Toward a Theory of Revolution" by James Davies,[13] as well as more recent research arising out of the social movements tradition,[14] the Marxist tradition,[15] and emerging traditions linked to new digital communications.[16]

The main research question arising from all these traditions in psychological, social, and political sciences is captured by the title of Ted Gurr's influential book: *Why Men Rebel*.[17] But particularly from the perspective of the poor, there is a great deal more to revolutions than 'Why men rebel.' Following Christopher Hill's groundbreaking analysis of the English Revolution,[18] we must ask not just *what* took place but what did *not* take place and *why*. After revolutions succeeded to topple governments, why did the ideal society envisaged by the revolutionaries not come about?

Revolution, Change, and Continuity

'The more things change, the more they stay the same' – this phrase seems perfectly applicable to political revolutions. Revolutionaries attack the injustices of current policies, but after coming to power, typically the new 'revolutionary government' simply takes over the privileges of the former elite, and the poor continue to suffer inequalities and injustices. Firebrand revolutionary leaders mobilize the lower class and promise to turn the establishment upside down, but then they become staunch members of the establishment after gaining power. Again and again in history, we find the old phrase rings true – plus ça change, plus c'est la meme chose. To use the imagery of the poet William Butler Yeats, the "lash goes on" even though there has been a revolution and those riding high on horses, whip in hand, have exchanged places with those on foot being whipped.[19]

Yet, some things do change. Slavery has been outlawed, and women and minorities have gained (at least on paper) the vote and at last enjoy improved conditions in many countries. We now have a United Nations Declaration of Human Rights ratified (1948) by every major nation. In the previous two centuries, many countries broke out of absolute dictatorship and made some progress toward democracy. Life expectancy, infant mortality, and health in general have improved for people in most parts of the world. Even in some of the worst dictatorships, there is an acknowledgment that ideally the government should reflect the will of the people – that is why they go through the trouble of holding so-called 'democratic elections' in dictatorships such as Russia and Iran.

Although things seem to stay the same, then, some progress does come about in political behavior and political systems, and revolutions seem to play a role in bringing about this change. However, puzzling questions persist about the role of revolution in this dance of change and continuity across time: Why do so many revolutions that topple dictatorships result in the continuation of dictatorship with a new face?[20] Recently, the Chinese Revolution resulted in 'Emperor for Life' Xi Ping, the Iranian Revolution exchanged The Turban for the Crown,[21] and the Arab Spring also replaced one set of dictators with another. The American Revolution might be argued to have had different outcomes, but the coming to power of Donald Trump has once again raised serious questions about the health of American democracy.

Questions Arising from Psychology about Revolution

Psychology is at the heart of questions about political revolutions, but its potential contributions remain neglected in mainstream psychology. The last book with the title of *The Psychology of Revolution* was by Gustave Le Bon (1841–1931), over a century ago. Revolutionaries attempt to change society from one political system to another, and in order to succeed, there must be accompanying change in the cognitions and actions of people, both the leaders and followers. Revolutionaries often implement policies designed to change behavior; for example, the Russian revolutionaries explicitly attempted to use the psychological research of behaviorists to bring about behavioral change toward their political goals, which avowedly included a classless society.[22] This project failed, in part because of the shortcomings of behaviorism.[23]

From a psychological perspective, important questions arise about the possible potentials and limitations of what revolutions can achieve to advance the interests of the poor. What can revolutions change and how fast? Are there certain limitations to the kinds of behavioral change that can come about? Are there parts of political behavior that can't be changed – at least, in a matter of a few years or decades or even centuries? What important features of political behavior can we change in the short term? Given human psychological characteristics, is fully developed or 'actualized democracy' possible?[24] Is political change always toward better developed democracy? Always from less open to more open societies, from less to more freedom, less to more justice, less to more equality? Can societies move from democracy back to dictatorship? Is dictatorship or democracy more closely matched with our 'hardwired' psychological characteristics? These questions concern what I have termed *political plasticity*, the malleability of political behavior, or how much change in political behavior is possible and how fast.[25]

The challenge of understanding change is central to all of psychology.[26] This includes understanding neurological and cognitive changes during human development[27], as well as changes in interpersonal relations, group dynamics, intergroup relations, and organizational behavior.[28] The understanding of behavioral change is both a foundational goal for research psychologists and a necessary starting point for interventions by practicing psychologists, in areas such as mental health and education. This shared interest between researchers and practitioners comes together in some projects. For example, Mrazek and colleagues tested a multifaceted intervention designed to bring about wide-ranging behavioral change.[29] They demonstrated improvements in a number of areas, including standardized test performance, working memory, life satisfaction, and physical health. The optimistic tenor of this and many other recent studies match the optimism of numerous popular books highlighting the view that we have underestimated our capacity to change human behavior.[30]

However, despite change being central to important areas of applied psychology, plasticity has been a major focus of research only in brain science.[31] The vast body of mainstream psychological research on social and political behavior has neglected the ways in which we can change and how fast. More specifically, psychologists need to address the question of how behavioral change can take place in a way that improves the life conditions of the poor. As part of this effort, we must better understand the psychology of revolution and why the consequences of revolutions have not (so far) solved the problem of enormous class-based inequalities – even given the optimism associated with the 'Rose uprising' in Georgia, the 'Orange uprising' in Ukraine, and the 'Tulip uprising' in Kyrgyzstan in 2003–2005, which lessened the stranglehold of Russia on these societies.

Psychology and Change after Revolutions

We think of revolutions as involving political change, the collapse of ruling regimes and the rise of new governments. But we must ask questions not just about such transfers of power but also about the changes in cognition and action necessary to achieve and sustain more open and just societies. We must ask questions about what happens *after* revolutions in the behavior of both leadership and the masses.

The term 'revolution' implies far more than just a transfer of power, because revolutions also include the goal of individual and collective progress toward an ideal society. Revolutionaries do not claim to want political power for the sake of having power. Rather, revolutionaries propose new ideologies, such as universal freedom, justice, and egalitarianism, or Communism or radical Islam. The ideals put forward by revolutionaries require tangible changes and improvements in the lives of the lower class, as well as associated psychological transformations, in how people think and act, individually and collectively.

A More Comprehensive Role for Psychology in Understanding Revolutions

> Changing the name of a government does not transform the mentality of a people.
>
> Le Bon[32]

In *The Psychology of Revolution*, Le Bon (quoted above) provides a groundbreaking insight about the psychology of change that unfortunately has remained neglected by mainstream psychologists for well over a century: Change of government does not necessarily bring about a change of how its citizens think and act. In another major work, *The Anatomy of Revolution* (1938), Crane Brinton (1898–1968) provided a complementary

insight concerning the slow pace of behavioral change even in times of
revolution:

> [I]n general ... many human habits, sentiments, dispositions, cannot be
> changed at all rapidly ... the attempt made by extremists to change them
> by law, terror, and exhortation fails ... the convalescence brings them back
> not greatly altered.[33]

These insights from Le Bon and Brinton point to key features of revolution that require psychological study. First, the speed of behavioral change
is different for different stages and activities during revolution. Second, a
change of government can come about relatively quickly, but change in the
behavior of people is relatively slow. However, when we turn to psychological science for explanations, we find that psychologists have neglected
both the study of revolution and the study of change. The reasons for this
neglect have to do with the conceptual and methodological development
of mainstream psychology.

The vast majority of psychological studies are completed in less than an
hour, often in a laboratory setting, with a very restricted (WEIRD) participant pool (discussed in Chapter 5 of this text).[34] Even so-called 'cross-
cultural' studies have increasingly involved only (Western or Westernized)
students as participants.[35] But to study change before, during, and after
revolutions, it is necessary to focus on long-term psychological processes
experienced by ordinary people in interactions. Such dynamic, collective
processes are not suitable for study in one-hour laboratory experiments.
They require new, alternative psychological approaches.[36]

I now turn to examine political plasticity through the case of the Soviet
Revolution and attempts by revolutionaries to change mass behavior. This
is the most important attempt by revolutionaries to utilize psychological
research to manage behavioral change.

The Example of Soviet Attempts at Behavioral Change

> Socialism does not aim at creating a socialist psychology as a
> pre-requisite to socialism but at creating socialist conditions of life as
> a pre-requisite to socialist psychology.
>
> Trotsky[37]

The Communist revolutionaries who came to power in Russia in 1917 and
established the USSR (in 1921) attempted to use psychological science, and
behaviorist principles in particular, to change the behavior of the Soviet
people toward achieving Communist ideals. Communists such as Leon

Trotsky (1879–1940) (quoted above) shared with behaviorists a number of fundamental assumptions about the nature of human behavior,[38] including the Lockean dictum that humans enter the world as 'blank slates' (*tabula rasa*) and become shaped by experiences over the course of their lives. In essence, both the Soviet Communists and the behaviorist school of psychology assumed that human behavior is shaped by environmental conditions. As Trotsky put it, creating socialist conditions of life would lead to socialist psychology.

The rise of the behaviorist school of psychology in the United States coincided with the Russian Revolution and Communist programs attempting to change the behavior of ordinary citizens in Russia. By the beginning of the twentieth century the method of introspection that had come to dominate psychological research in Western societies in the late nineteenth century had confronted a seemingly insurmountable road-block on the issue of 'imageless thought.'[39] The American researcher John Watson (1878–1958) and other radical behaviorists used the opportunity to reject both introspection as a research method and cognition as a topic of research. They insisted that psychology can become a science only if the subject of study is observable behavior (and not invisible thoughts, the mind, subjectivity, and the like). This new school of behaviorism was launched in large part on the basis of research by the Russian researchers Vladimir Bekhterev (1857–1927) and Ivan Pavlov (1849–1936). At the same time, Pavlov's research on classical conditioning was admired by Bolshevik leaders; Lenin declared this research to be "hugely significant for our revolution."[40]

In launching the so-called 'behaviorist manifesto' in 1913,[41] Watson highlighted the idea that by shaping the environment we can shape behavior. The Bolsheviks used behaviorism as a platform to argue that the behaviors accepted as 'natural' in capitalist societies are actually creations of the conditions of those societies; they are neither natural nor inevitable. By changing environmental conditions, we can change the behaviors that become 'normative.' As Stephen Smith put it, Communist radicals aimed to achieve a cultural revolution to bring about "nothing less than the creation of a 'new Soviet person' through the total transformation of daily life."[42] This basic principle was applied to implement a program of collectivization.

The general approach in Soviet collectivization was to achieve a society in which people behave according to the dictum "From each according to his abilities, to each according to his needs."[43] In this collective society, private property and individual incentives were excluded, because it was assumed that they are not necessary for motivating people to work hard. Whereas the environmental conditions of capitalism shaped behavior to pursue individual profits and the amassment of personal wealth, the environmental conditions of the Soviet Union were intended to motivate people to work for collective rewards and the collective good.

Two Illustrative Examples

But how exactly were the Soviet environmental conditions different from capitalist ones? Let us consider two illustrative examples. The first is the reorganization of the use of space in the built environment. The elimination of private property meant that not only were the grand aristocratic palaces now belonging to the state 'on behalf of the people' but ordinary middle-class and even lower-class homes and apartments became national property as well. Existing living spaces were to be used in a collective manner, so that hundreds of families were moved into 'shared' grand palaces and several families were moved into large homes and apartments. Andy Willimott explains that radical Soviet architects "sought to extend from constructivist architectural theory the idea of the 'social condenser' – the notion that all Soviet buildings would act to influence social behaviour and forge new communities through the design of new, socially equitable spaces."[44] As Orlando Figes insightfully points out, "By forcing people to share communal flats, the Bolsheviks believed that they could make them communistic in their basic thinking and behaviour. Private space and property would disappear, the patriarchal ('bourgeois') family would be replaced by communist fraternity and organization, and the life of the individual would become immersed in the community."[45] In essence, Soviet architecture shunned private space and moved people into shared space and communal living.[46] The experience of living collectively in shared space would, supposedly, change how people think and act, so that the collective good rather than 'selfish' individual needs would become people's priority.

A response from capitalist critics to this plan would be that humans have a need for privacy and their motivation to meet personal needs is far stronger than the motivation to meet collective needs. I return to this point after considering a second example of how collectivization was to be achieved, this time in the domain of work. Ironically, in this domain the Bolsheviks also turned to innovations in the United States – which was at the time the emerging capitalist superpower. The Bolsheviks were highly influenced by the ideas of the American industrial engineer Frederick

Taylor (1856–1915), the founder of the movement that became known as 'Taylorism.'[47] For the Bolsheviks, the appeal of Taylorism was that it seemed to provide a scientific approach to organizing the life of workers, standardizing both workers and the tasks they carry out.[48] This resulted in America's organization of work through mass production, such as in the car manufacturing plants of Henry Ford. But whereas in the United States the workers were incentivized through individual rewards, in the Soviet Union, the Communists planned to use standardization and mass production as the basis for incentives through collective ownership and collective profit sharing.

At the heart of collectivization is the psychological puzzle of motivation. The Soviets assumed that the motivation to work for individual incentives and personal property is a product of the capitalist life environment, including schooling, housing, and work and family relations. The motivation of individuals would change from individual to collective when the conditions of life were changed from capitalist to socialist. As a result, Soviet people working in collective farms and factories, living in collective homes, and receiving rewards based on collective efforts would be motivated to work just as hard (or even harder) than individuals living and working in capitalist societies, where people are incentivized by personal rewards for individual performance.

Psychological Research, Collectivization, and Motivation

Are human beings 'naturally' inclined to work harder when they are given the opportunity to gain personal rewards for their work? A line of research that sheds light on this question explores *social loafing*, the tendency for individuals to work less hard in a group than when they work on their own.[49] In support of the capitalist system, one could interpret social loafing as the 'natural' human tendency to work harder when work leads to personal (rather than collective) rewards. But critics point out that people brought up in socialist cultures such as China do not show the same social loafing tendencies as found in participants from the United States.[50] Also, even in Western capitalist societies, under some conditions, behavior moves away from social loafing.

The term *social laboring* refers to the increased effort that arises from a motivation to improve collective outcome.[51] For example, consider a rowing team performing in competition against other teams. To some degree it is possible for individual rowing team members to 'loaf,' but this is extremely unlikely. Each individual team member identifies with the entire group and often individual efforts are *even greater* when part of a team effort. Thus, rather than seeing social loafing as a natural and inevitable human tendency, the more accurate approach is to consider social loafing and social laboring as varieties of behaviors that arise under different contextual conditions.[52]

The conditions created by researchers in the typical social loafing experiments are conducive to social loafing and not social laboring behavior. Think back to the example of the rowing team: The rowing crew are a tightly knit group who identify strongly with their group. They have come to know one another very well over many grueling races, they depend on each other, and they are loyal to group goals. The successful rowing crew has 'team spirit' and each rower sacrifices for the team. It is not surprising that this tightly knit group shows social laboring. In contrast, the typical social loafing research study involves participants who are strangers, gathered for an hour or so in a research laboratory setting, with very little opportunity to develop social ties and loyalties. Why would we expect these strangers to show social laboring?

But if social loafing and social laboring can be created by the appropriate social conditions, why is it that revolutionaries in the Soviet Union, China, Cuba, and other Communist societies have not managed to achieve highly productive societies through collectivism? In a well-researched reinterpretation of the Soviet industrial revolution, Robert Allen has argued that the Soviet Union actually performed well when compared to other Third World countries.[53] Related to this, Gale Johnson and Karen Brooks present evidence suggesting that the conventional interpretation of collectivization as the main cause of Soviet agricultural inefficiency is incorrect.[54] Instead, they point to poor management systems and inefficient pricing as other major factors.

Despite these more positive interpretations of Soviet economic and agricultural performance, the fact remains that the Soviet experiment collapsed and the avowed goals of the Russian revolutionaries were not reached. My argument is that political plasticity played a very important part in this failure: The Russian revolutionaries wanted to bring about enormous changes in Russian society, and to do so, they needed to change the style of cognition and action of both elite leaders and ordinary citizens. Such changes did not come about in the 'planned' way; as Guinevere Nell points out, "The problem of self and other did not dissolve when common property replaced private property: the struggle of the common will and the common good clashing with individual desires, differences between individuals in the society, selfishness, and independence all caused endless problems when a single plan was guiding all production and distribution in the economy."[55] Because of limitations in behavioral plasticity, they were not able to achieve this change – at least not fast enough.

Political Plasticity and Hardwiring outside Individuals

> Without an ideal, the energies of revolutionary groups will be dissipated with a minimal effect on the social and political order ... This is not to imply that an ideal will ever be fully realized.
>
> Blackey and Paynton[56]

All revolutions come with promises of a changed, better world; invariably the idealized promised world is radically different from what people experience today. This ideal society, which revolutionary rhetoric contrasts dramatically with current societal conditions, is used to justify the sacrifices necessary for forcing regime change. Such sacrifices often involve great risk and even loss of life for those who join the revolution, so the revolutionary ideal has to be extraordinarily appealing. But why is it that Blackey and Paynton (quoted above) claim "This is not to imply that an ideal will ever be fully realized"? What prevents revolutionary ideals from being realized?

For sure, in many cases at least some of the revolutionaries are not sincere in putting forward ideals; they do so only as a means to attain positions of power and influence. I came across many examples of this in post-revolution Iran, where opportunistic people, both mullahs and others, used religion as a weapon to enable them to grab power and make personal profit. But even revolutionaries who are sincere when they come to power may eventually succumb to the temptations that power inevitably brings.

Both historical examples and experimental evidence demonstrate that power tends to corrupt.[57] For the vast majority of individuals, power corrupts and absolute power corrupts absolutely. Very, very few people have the moral fortitude of Nelson Mandela (1918–2013), the South African leader who was imprisoned for twenty-seven years during the period of Apartheid in South Africa but who followed a path of peace and reconciliation when he was freed and came to power after the collapse of the cruel Apartheid regime. The vast majority of leaders who come to power after revolutions are like Stalin, Gaddafi, Saddam Hussein, and Khomeini, who suffocate their opponents in blood and cling to absolute power until their last breath.

After coming to power, there is a tendency for many revolutionaries to become more interested in monopolizing power, enriching themselves and their group. Research on motivated cognition demonstrates how people can rely on biased perceptions and evaluations to justify their self-rewarding actions and all-powerful positions, dressed up as 'a service to my people.'[58] There is a great deal of psychological research showing that we are ready to admit to mistakes being made, 'but not by me!'[59] We even position ourselves to feel morally righteous while we are behaving wrongly.[60] Those with greater power and resources are even more likely to show these self-justification biases, because others dare not correct nor stand up to them. Speaking truth to power often has detrimental consequences – in some countries, it results in imprisonment or even death.

But corruption, manipulation and self-deception of leaders are only part of the explanation as to why the ideals of revolutions are not achieved. Another highly important factor is that in order to achieve the ideal society, behavioral changes are required in both collective and individual behavior. Styles of thinking and action need to change in order to achieve the ideal society espoused by revolutionaries, but such changes – essential for system 2 revolutions – are arduously slow and extremely difficult to bring about.

Hardwiring and Plasticity: Inside and outside the Individual

In exploring the limitations and potentials of change, it is useful to conceptualize hardwiring both in the mainstream way of being concerned with the characteristics of brain structures and neural networks but also processes *external* to individuals. Some features of human societies external to individuals are 'hardwired' in the sense that they are deeply embedded, strongly interconnected and thus resilient and extremely difficult to change. For example, consider the phenomenon of leadership: Every major society has leaders. These leaders tend to be predominantly older, male, and strongly motivated to monopolize and concentrate power in themselves and their immediate supporters.

Revolutions often begin with ideals that include a different kind of leadership, greater power distribution and sharing, with slogans such as 'power to the people,' or even no leadership at all – an egalitarian society where there is no elite, central government. Despite such revolutionary ideals, centralized leadership continues to be common in post-revolution societies. Also, there tends to be continuity in the style of leadership. For example, in Iran I experienced change from the shah ruling as an absolute dictator before the 1979 revolution to Khomeini ruling as an absolute dictator after the revolution. Whatever shah/Khomeini uttered was instantly treated as sacred law. Anyone critical of this 'sacred law' was in mortal danger. This continuity from one dictator to the next, using a similar leadership style, has been a familiar theme in revolutions against dictatorship.

Leadership style is an example of a behavior that is extremely resistant to change; such behaviors are embedded in networks of vertically and horizontally organized power relations. Individuals who attempt to change their followership or leadership behavior will be successful only if they can change the relationships they have with others who are situated in their vertical and horizontal networks. Because of the interconnectedness of the behavior of an individual with the many others in networks of leader–follower relations, extreme measures are necessary to change leadership and followership style.

For example, consider what it took to change the leadership role of the Japanese Emperor and his relationship with the Japanese people in the mid-twentieth century. This change in leader–follower relations only came about after (1) Japan was utterly defeated in the Second World War after the dropping of two atom bombs on Hiroshima and Nagasaki, (2) Allied Forces took absolute control of Japanese society, 1945–1952, and (3) General Douglas MacArthur (1880–1964) spearheaded political, educational, and social change programs *forced on Japan*.[61] American intervention imposed widespread reforms on Japanese society. Even with these three tremendously powerful forces at play, leader–follower relations in Japan continue to retain some of their authoritarian, male- and age-dominated, hierarchical nature.

Thus, there is need for psychological research on the role of hardwiring *external* to individuals that results in resilience to change and limits the ways and extent to which revolutions can transform individual and collective behavior.

Future Research on the Psychology of Revolution

A first point is that we can make considerable progress toward actualized (fully developed) democracy through social evolution rather than radical revolution.[62] For example, the progress made in Norway, Sweden, and Denmark, generally regarded as relatively advanced democracies, has been largely through social evolution. Psychological studies of change in these and other relatively advanced democracies (e.g., Switzerland) will help illuminate the psychological processes that are central to peaceful democratic change. Such research can feed back into programs in other societies, including the United States, to help better understand and manage prodemocracy changes.

With respect to psychological research on revolutions, I began by noting that the scant psychological research relevant to revolutions has focused on collective mobilization. This research is valuable but does not cover a key psychological feature of revolution: It is far easier to achieve collective mobilization and bring about regime change (System 1 revolution) than it is to bring about the microlevel changes in cognitions and actions needed to sustain the move from one type of political system to another (System 2 revolution). Revolutionaries have typically toppled one form of dictatorship, only to replace it with another form of dictatorship – they have not succeeded in achieving System 2 revolution.

Psychological science can contribute in important ways to a fuller and deeper understanding of revolutions, as a way to improve the possibility of achieving change toward more democratic and just societies that reduce class-based inequalities and benefit everyone. Below are two ideas about research paths psychologists could take in order to achieve a better understanding of the psychology of revolution.

Micro–Macro Rule of Change: Psychological research is urgently needed on change, particularly the relationship between change at macro (societal), meso (group), and micro (individual) levels. Experience suggests that the maximum speed of change at the macrolevel of formal political and economic systems is faster than the maximum speed of change at the microlevel of psychological processes. Change at the macrolevel can be swift; a government can be toppled in a matter of months, weeks, or even days or hours. Also, after coming to power, the new 'revolutionary' government could rapidly bring about other macrolevel changes. With the stroke of a pen, a government could abolish institutions (such as a parliament), change laws, alter economic policies, and more. For example, the post-revolution changes in leadership in Russia from the tsar to Lenin led to a rapid change in the system of ownership, from most property and wealth being privately owned by powerful aristocrats to all important resources being owned by the state on behalf of the Russian people.

While macrolevel changes, such as those concerned with ownership and collectivization, can take place quickly, the psychological changes needed in order for people to function effectively within a new collectivized system are far slower. Despite being slow, microlevel changes are possible. For example, people are not hardwired to become either 'social loafers' (to make less effort when working in a group) or 'social laborers' (to make greater effort when working in a group). The same individual could become a social loafer or a social laborer, depending on the context. For example, Joan acts as a social loafer when she works with seven other university students to complete a class project but as a social laborer when she is rowing with her seven team members on the university crew team.

Individuals who have been socialized to function in an economic system based on individual responsibility, individual rewards, and private property have developed certain cognitive and social skills for success in this economic system. For example, they are trained to be influenced by reinforcements to individual behavior. From childhood and the earliest years of training in the home, in kindergarten, in schools and universities, and at work, their behavior has been shaped by learning and they have been rewarded based on individual effort. Changing the behavior of such individuals needs systematic social programming over long time periods.

Moreover, in the case of the Russian, Chinese, Cuban, and other Communist revolutions, the entire pre-revolution structure of society was designed based on personal property and individual reinforcements. The motivations, aspirations, and other psychological characteristics of individuals had been shaped within the pre-revolution conditions over thousands of years. Microlevel changes in such behavior need to be programmed and implemented carefully over many generations. Such changes in microlevel behavior can be facilitated through leadership, the next topic we consider.

Leader–Follower Relations: Psychological research is needed to better understand why it is extremely difficult to change style of leadership and leader–follower relations. For example, despite impressive advances in science and technology, despite mass education, and despite being the largest economy in the world, the United States still has not had a female president. Moreover, as the 2016 election of Donald Trump to the White House demonstrated, authoritarian strongman leadership still has popular appeal in America. What are the psychological factors at play here?

It would be a mistake to research the question of leadership through a causal-reductionist approach of focusing on the personality of the leader or of individual citizens. Instead, the focus has to be on the conditions that enable authoritarian leaders to emerge and on the leader–follower relations that are successful in maintaining such conditions. Also, what are the psychological characteristics of the context that result in females' inability to become successful presidential candidates? These questions reflect back on the broader issue of political plasticity, which needs to become a far more prioritized topic so that psychology can better reflect the interests of the lower class.

Political Plasticity: Political plasticity needs urgent research attention, particularly because empirical data shows that the gap between the richest and the rest is increasing.[63] In a devastating analysis, the Stanford

University scholar Walter Scheidel argues that wealth inequality will only be reduced by major wars:[64] It is only when societies face possible defeat and total collapse that the powerful superrich agree to make 'sacrifices' and share more resources with the rest of society. However, I believe that with a more in-depth understanding of political plasticity, psychologists will be able to help shape peaceful change toward a more equal and just society. To use Scheidel's terminology, war need not be the only 'great leveler' – psychologists can replace this function of war with peaceful public policies. But to do so we need to arrive at a far better understanding of political plasticity. This is an essential component of psychology from the perspective of the poor.

Concluding Comment

From the perspective of the lower class, change must become a central topic in psychological science. But not change in the reductionist sense, involving intrapersonal and interindividual processes. Rather, the focus should be on the relationship between macro and micro processes, to better understand why change toward actualized democracy has been so difficult to achieve and how it can be better facilitated in the future.

A focus on change necessarily leads to the study of political plasticity and the question of how fast and how much behavior can be changed in the political sphere. We now have the technological capacity to implement mass participation in decision-making but, in practice, in the early decades of the twenty-first century we have turned more to decision-making by authoritarian strongmen.[65] At the same time, we are experiencing greater concentration of wealth in fewer and fewer hands, and the lower social classes are falling further behind in wealth. The price of this greater inequality includes a less robust democracy and a marketplace that is skewed by political forces to unfairly benefit the upper class.[66] Psychological science must step out of its causal-reductionist shell and engage with these difficult topics in the larger world to enable progress toward actualized democracy.

Afterword
The Path Ahead for Psychology

> Capitalism has suffered a series of mighty blows to its reputation over the past decade. The sense of a system rigged to benefit the owners of capital at the expense of workers is profound. In 2016 a survey found that more than half of young Americans no longer support capitalism.
>
> *The Economist*[1]

> Capitalists Worry About Capitalism's Future.
>
> *The Wall Street Journal*[2]

The above quotations, the first from a lead editorial in the *The Economist* and the second from an article in *The Wall Street Journal,* both politically right-of-center business publications, reflect a seismic shift in political thinking in the first few decades of the twenty-first century. The article in *The Wall Street Journal* describes how some successful leading capitalists are openly expressing serious worries about the future of capitalism. Many people, in both capitalist democracies and in the rest of the world, detrimentally impacted by enormous and increasing wealth concentration and resource disparities, have come to critically question both capitalism and democracy as solutions to the dire problems they face in their daily lives.[3] This is reflected in the global wave of populist, antidemocratic movements, spreading in countries as diverse as the United States, Brazil, Turkey, Poland, India, the United Kingdom, and the Philippines. In a frantic search for alternative paths to meet their urgent needs, many lower-class people have snatched at desperate and illusionary 'solutions,' such as authoritarian leaders like Donald Trump.

The growing gap between the superrich and the rest, and the falling further behind of the poorest group, is creating opportunities for would-be dictators to present themselves as 'saviors,' as the only hope of improving our conditions and even making us 'great again.'[4] Some critics have argued that only a massive world war could put an end to the increasing concentration of wealth and the further falling behind of the poorest group (see the discussion of Scheidel's analysis in Chapter 12 of this text). In this difficult global context where people are desperate to find solutions, there are new opportunities for psychological science to make seminal contributions.

Two major factors mean that psychology is perfectly positioned to address the needs of the lower class and to serve as part of the solution to increasing class-based inequalities. First, psychology is the science of human thinking and action, and as such could focus on the huge and urgent challenges humanity faces, particularly the needs of the poor around the world.[5] Second, psychology has achieved global presence. Since the mid-twentieth century there has been a rapid expansion of psychology around the world, so that in most non-Western societies (which are in general lower-income) a network has developed of universities teaching psychology and training new generations of psychologists. There are now extensive Asian, African, and South American associations of psychologists, with regular conferences, journals, books, and other activities, mirroring the activities of psychologists in North American and Western European societies.[6]

However, the spread of psychology around the world has been based on the causal-reductionist mainstream Western model of psychology. Even in countries such as India, where there is a desperate need for psychological research on poverty, the general tendency is to mimic mainstream US psychology.[7] As demonstrated in this book, the causal-reductionist nature of mainstream psychology has severely restricted the development of psychological science. The search for causes, typically inside isolated individuals and now increasingly inside brains and brain parts, has resulted in a neglect of collective processes and important topics associated with poverty and class-based inequalities. Looking ahead, psychological science must progress beyond the causal-reductionist model in two specific ways.

First, the approach adopted by mainstream psychology can be summed up as 'from cells to societies.' Reductionism influences researchers to begin with, and give priority to, the smallest units and then extrapolate to larger units. The assumption is that it is only through reductionism that psychology can achieve the status of a science. But reductionism has proven to be an invalid approach to studying and understanding human behavior. Human beings emerge from, and take shape through, active participation in the collective social world; many of their most important characteristics are dependent on and emerge from society. The psychological approach to studying human behavior must be turned on its head to become 'from societies to cells.'

Second, psychological science must progress beyond the invalid assumption that *all* human behavior is causally determined. Of course (as discussed in the earlier chapters of this text), some human behavior is causally determined and can be correctly interpreted using cause–effect language. However, much of human behavior is regulated by local normative systems – ideas about correct behavior in the local setting. For example, consider a group of guests who arrive to participate in a wedding ceremony. The way the guests are dressed, what (if anything) they bring with them, how long they remain at the wedding ceremony, and how they behave – all these for the most part take place according to local rules and norms about correct behavior. At the same time, some guests might behave 'incorrectly.' Behavior in such contexts is not causally determined, in the way gravity would cause me to fall to the ground when I lose balance on my bicycle. On my way down to hit the ground, I am not able to 'change my mind' and decide to rise back up onto my bicycle. Gravity makes my fall to the ground inevitable. However, as a wedding guest I could intentionally choose to avoid eating meat – even though this will be seen as 'incorrect behavior' by locals and my host will be offended that I have chosen not to sample and praise the meat dishes on offer.

By breaking out of the causal-reductionist framework, psychological science necessarily gives more importance to collective processes and the power of context. As one of the most powerful contexts, poverty becomes a far more important focus of psychological research.

The Poor and Social Class As Priority

As part of a movement to redirect mainstream psychology to a path that is more beneficial for all social classes, this book presents psychology with greater emphasis on social class and the experiences of the poor. Of course, we should not rely solely on material definitions of poverty; first, because material estimates can differ depending on methodologies and criteria used;[8] second, because poverty, as Amartya Sen has pointed out, is far broader and more complex than a lack of money. Sen sees poverty as a lack of capability, which is influenced by a great deal more than just lack of money: "[I]ncome is only one input among many (our capabilities also depend, for example, on social and political opportunities), and furthermore, given the level of income, our capability prospects depend also on personal factors (such as proneness to inherited disease) and on the environment (including the epidemiological environment) in which people live. The connection between income and capability is also made more complex by the relevance of relative deprivation."[9]

Poverty also refers to a lack of social connections, knowledge, and communications skills, particularly of the kind that enables members of the upper class to maneuver effectively through competitive worlds of top-tier education and employment. As Robert Putnam has described so insightfully,[10] lower-class people inherit far less material wealth, but they also inherit a much weaker set of social connections, networks, know-how, and knowledge about how to 'get on' in the world. Family, friendship, and other informal networks can be a highly valuable inheritance for achieving upward social class mobility.

Mainstream psychology is now giving greater attention to ethnicity, and this is reflected in the contents of standard introductory psychology texts and in the contents of mainstream journals. This focus on ethnicity is laudable and justified,[11] but it is not enough because poverty and the plight of the lower class is a far more extensive and global challenge to take up. Poverty crosses ethnic groups; poor Whites, African Americans, Hispanics – their behavior is all shaped by the strong context of poverty. The increasing concentration of wealth and power in fewer and fewer hands, the material and political impoverishment of the lower class – these are powerful pervasive forces that detrimentally impact the lives of all poor people, of all ethnicities, genders, religions, and so on, across the world. By progressing beyond the causal-reductionist model and interpreting the world from 'societies to cells,' psychological science inevitably gives priority to collective processes, social class, and poverty.

Notes

Preface

1 In the twenty-first century, in both mainstream psychological research and the mass media, priority tends to be given to ethnicity, gender, sexual orientation, and group characteristics *other than* social class. For example, this is reflected in the relatively greater coverage given to ethnicity, gender, and sexual orientation relative to social class in introductory psychology texts. However, research shows that social class is a very powerful factor in shaping behavior in areas such as education (Anyon 2017). For a more detailed discussion of social class in everyday life in the context of the United States see Kraus, Park, and Tan (2017) and in the context of the United Kingdom see Manstead (2018).

2 The lower class are poor relative to the middle and the upper classes. In this sense, I use the terms 'the poor' and 'lower class' synonymously. My use of the term the poor is relative. Of course, I am aware that not all members of the lower class live below the poverty line as typically defined by governments.

3 Examples of edited collections are Fox and Ptillettensky (1997) and Harré and Moghaddam (2012). An example of a book focused on social theory is Elliott (2003).

1 Why We Must Rethink Psychology

1 Hoarding behavior during the 2020 pandemic is discussed in Chen et al. (2020).

2 Kalat (2017, p. 4), emphasis original.

3 Dunstan and Moghaddam (2016).

4 For a more in-depth discussion of causation, see Harré and Moghaddam (2016).

5 Wegner (2002).

6 Harris (2012).

7 For example, Lutz and Thompson (2003).

8 Grossi (2017).

9 For example, see Blair and Raver (2012), Bullock (2019), Lott (2012), Williams (2019).

10 For example, Duncan, Magnuson and Votruba-Drzal (2015).

11 An example is found here, www.psychologicalscience.org/publications/observer/obsonline/brain-behavior-and-the-economy.html

12 See www.apa.org/about/governance/president/deep-poverty-initiative

13 See Lamiell (2003) for a rethinking of psychology in terms of the measurement of individual differences.

14 See the discussions on personalized medicine, e.g., Jain (2021).

15 Notten and de Neubourg (2011) argue that absolute and relative poverty criteria should be used in tandem.

16 Morgan (2019).

17 See the highly insightful study of Booth's work by the historian Asa Briggs (1961).

18 See the report by Burkhauser et al. (2019).

19 This is opposite to the mainstream trend of going from cells to societies or 'neurons to neighborhoods' (Shonkoff and Phillips 2000).

20 I am here following the work of Lex Vygotsky, Jerome Bruner, and Rom Harré.

21 Herrnstein and Murray (1994) present the neoconservative view very well.

22 For example, see Korn (2017).

23 See Oxfam (Jan 2021).

24 Piketty (2014).

25 For example, Melvin J. Lerner founded the journal *Social Justice Research* and edited the *Critical Issues in Social Justice* (Plenum Press).

26 See Pettit and Western (2004).

27 Moghaddam (1987).

28 Moghaddam and Lee (2006).

29 Criticisms of traditional research methods are reflected in the growing number of researchers advocating the addition of qualitative and mixed-methods approaches (e.g., Mertens 2020).

30 Sampson (1981).

31 See Moghaddam and Lee (2006) for a more in-depth discussion of mainstream psychological research methods in a global context.

32 Francis (2012).

33 A number of books review the crisis in twenty-first-century psychology; see Lilienfeld and Waldman (2017) and Hughes (2018).

34 Moghaddam (2013, 2016).

35 Moghaddam (2018).

36 Markus and Fiske (2012, p. 8).

37 Moghaddam (2018).

Part I Psychological Processes

1 Markus and Fiske (2012, p. 8).

2   Cognition and Decision-Making in Societal Context

1 Dickens (1957, pp. 13–14).
2 Edin and Shaefer (2015) provide a moving account of life on $2.00 a day in the United States.
3 Webb (2018).
4 Shafir (2017, p. 131).
5 Bruner and Goodman (1947).
6 Keys, Brozek, Henschel, Mickelson and Taylor (1950).
7 Dorling (2014); Holton (2014); Piketty (2014).
8 See Paas and Van Merriënboer (1994) and the earlier discussion of cognitive processing load by Sweller (1988).
9 Rosen et al. (2018).
10 Lawson and Farah (2017).
11 Schilbach, Schofield and Mullainathan (2016).
12 See readings in Murnane and Duncan (2011).
13 Piketty (2014).
14 The Economist (2021, June 26, p. 12).
15 Carroll (2010) provides one of the best assessments of the rise of global capitalism.
16 Moazed and Johnson (2016).
17 See Wallerstein and Western (2000).
18 Gandini (2018).
19 Bullock, Wyche and Williams (2001, p. 234).
20 An interesting read on this is Seccombe (1999).
21 Bullock, Wyche and Williams (2001, p. 230).
22 Hancock (2004).
23 Williams (2009, p. 40).
24 For empirical evidence, for example see Hall, Zhao, and Shafir (2014).
25 Shafir (2017, p. 133).
26 See Lott and Bullock (2007) for a review.
27 Williams (2009).
28 Appadurai (2004).
29 Dalton, Ghosal and Mani (2014, p. 179).
30 Steele (2007).
31 Steele (2011).
32 Spencer, Steele and Quinn (1999).
33 Aronson et al. (1999).
34 Croizet and Claire (1998, p. 588).
35 Sirin (2005).
36 Krapohl and Plomin (2016).
37 Gorski (2012).
38 See Putnam (2016) for an excellent discussion of inheritance and social class.
39 Croizet and Claire (1998).
40 Bowen and Bok (1998).
41 Jack (2019, p. 22).
42 Jack (2019, p. 185).

43 See Rubin, Evans and McGuffog (2019) and Easterbrook, Hadden and Nieuwenhuis (2019).
44 Kraus et al. (2012, p. 549).
45 Kraus et al. (2012, p. 551–552).
46 For example, see Kraus and Keltner (2009).
47 Aarts, Dijksterhuis and De Vries (2001); Radel and Clément-Guillotin (2012).
48 Cafiero, Viviani and Nord (2018, see Table 3).
49 Martinez et al. (2018).
50 In families experiencing food insecurity, parents suffer greater stress and their behavior toward children becomes less supportive (Cook et al. 2006).
51 Johnson and Markowitz (2018a).
52 Johnson and Markowitz (2018b).
53 Haushofer (2014, p. 862).
54 Bertrand, Mullainathan and Shaffir (2004).
55 Bertrand and Morse (2011).
56 Mullainathan and Shafir (2013).
57 Mani et al. (2013).
58 Shah, Mullainathan and Shafir (2012).
59 Deck and Jahedi (2015).
60 Shah et al. (2018, p. 5).
61 Niemann (2016, p. 451).
62 Grifflin (2019).
63 Lamont and Small (2010).
64 For example, see Lewis (1969).
65 Quoted in Greenbaum (2015, p. 1).
66 For a critical conservative perspective on the culture of poverty debate, see Phillips (2018).
67 See Greenbaum (2015); Small, Harding and Lamont (2010). This is similar to what Jindra and Jindra (2018) refer to in their discussions of poverty as the distinction between discursive and practical consciousness.
68 Barber, Yarger and Gatny (2015).
69 Kim and Raley (2015).
70 Johnson and Loscocco (2015, p. 148).
71 Individual resilience is well known; for a discussion of collective resilience, see Elcheroth and Drury (2020).
72 Shafir (2017, p. 134).
73 See *The Economist* (2021a).

3 Mis-measuring Intelligence and Justifying Educational Inequalities

1 See Cohen (2016) for a lively discussion of eugenics in the United States and Herrnstein and Murray (1994) for a sweeping description of the idea that society is meritocratic based on IQ.
2 Moghaddam (2019).

3 Moore (2003).
4 Lickliter and Witherington (2017, p. 125).
5 Croizet and Millet (2011, p. 188).
6 Frey and Detterman (2004).
7 Croizet and Millet (2011, p. 189).
8 Carnevale and Rose (2003).
9 Sirin (2005).
10 For example, see Goriounova and Mansvelder (2019) and Trzaskowski et al. (2014).
11 For example, see Calvin et al. (2012), Plomin and von Stumm (2018), and Strenze (2007).
12 Haier (2016) provides an overview of this research on the neuroscience of intelligence.
13 Hayden (2013).
14 Plomin and Deary (2015, p. 104).
15 Plomin and von Stumm (2018, p. 148).
16 Herrnstein and Murray (1994, p. 509).
17 Sternberg (2015, p. 78).
18 Carnevale and Strohl (2013, pp. 7–8).
19 For example, see Archer, Hutchings, and Ross (2003), Putnam (2016), Rauscher (2016), and Sacks (2007).
20 Fitzgerald (1925, p. 65).
21 Jaffrelot (2019).
22 Battalora (2013).
23 Thornton (2018).
24 See Yu and Suen (2005) on the *Keju* (Civil Service) exam system.
25 For an overview of the intelligence testing field and its historical background, see discussions in Flanagan and McDonough (2018).
26 Franco (1985) and McPherson (1985).
27 Galton (1869).
28 Many discussions of Galton's life and supposed genius also contain deep flaws; see Fancher (1983).
29 Engelhardt et al. (2016) and Plomin and Deary (2015).
30 Okbay et al. (2016) and Rietveld et al. (2013).
31 Trzaskowski et al. (2014).
32 Trampush et al. (2017).
33 Savage et al. (2018).
34 Goriounova and Mansvelder (2019).
35 Vein and Maat-Schieman (2008).
36 Witelson, Kigar, and Harvey (1999).
37 See Pietschnig et al. (2015) for brain volume and Karama et al. (2012) for cortical thickness. See Hopkins, Li, and Roberts (2018) for a study on chimpanzees.
38 In particular, 'nodal efficiency' is important – this is the effectiveness of a node to communicate information with other nodes (a node being a predefined collection of brain tissue, Stanley et al. 2013). Also see Hilger et al. (2017).

39 Neuroimaging studies show that general intelligence cannot be attributed to one specific region (Goriounova & Mansvelder 2019).

40 For example, Kaminski et al. (2018).

41 Menger (2017).

42 González-Pardo and Pérez-Álvarez (2013).

43 These include three laws. (1) *Law of Dominance*, dominant alleles are expressed in phenotype; only when recessive alleles are inherited from both parents are they seen. (2) *Law of Independent Assortment*, traits are passed on from parents to offspring independent of other traits. (3) *Law of Segregation*, dominant and recessive traits are passed on randomly from parents to offspring.

44 The psychology historian Hearnshaw (1974) has written the definitive biography of Cyril Burt, detailing data falsification.

45 Among those who have defended the twins method in this controversy, see Barnes et al. (2014).

46 Scarr and Carter-Saltzman (1979). Also, see chapter 3 in Moore (2003).

47 Ainslie (1997) and Joseph (2004).

48 Flynn (2007, 2013).

49 Bjorklund (2018).

50 González-Pardo and Pérez-Álvarez (2013, p. 4).

51 Jones, Moore, and Kobor (2018) and Masterpasqua (2009).

52 In the Preface to the second edition of *Inquiries into Human Faculty and Its Development* (1982), Galton refers to the national eugenics movement in Britain, having its home in University College, University of London. Cohen (2016) provides an excellent account of eugenics in the United States.

53 Cohen (2016, p. 114).

54 Reilly (2015).

55 Herrnstein and Murray (1994, p. 364).

56 Flynn (2013, p. 6).

57 Spearman (1904).

58 Cattell (1963).

59 Sternberg (2015)

60 Gardner (2004).

61 For an example, see Bücker, Furrer, and Lin (2015); for general background, see Kent (2017).

62 Parker (2015, p. 4).

63 Buchmann and DiPrete (2006).

64 Nollenberger et al. (2016).

65 Spearman (1904, p. 285).

66 See, for example, Orr (2003) and Yeung and Conley (2008).

67 Bastedo and Jaquette (2011), Conley (2001), Duncan, Kalil, and Ziol-Guest (2017), Goldrick-Rab and Pfeffer (2009), Lopoo and London (2016), Lovenheim (2011), Owens, Reardon, and Jencks (2016), Pfeffer (2018), and Rauscher (2016).

68 For example, see Hertz et al. (2007) and Sacks (2007).

69 Kornrich and Furstenberg (2013).
70 Spencer and Castano (2007).
71 Spencer and Castano (2007, p. 422).
72 Quoted in Cep (2019, p. 76).
73 Kraus and Tan (2015).
74 Kell, Lubinski, and Benbow (2013).

4 Personality and the Power of Context

 1 Funder (2019, p. 5).
 2 Research on self-stereotyping has linked to structural features of sociopolitical systems but typically in relation to gender groups rather than social class (e.g., Laurin, Kay, & Shepherd 2011).
 3 Biernat, Fuegen, and Kobrynowicz (2010).
 4 Biernat (2012, p. 41).
 5 Sheldon and Stevens (1942).
 6 Friedman and Rosenman (1959).
 7 For examples, see chapter 2 in these standard texts: Shiraev (2017), Funder (2019), and Mischel, Shoda, and Ayduk (2008).
 8 For example, Votanopoulos et al. (2020).
 9 The origins of this distinction go back to a speech delivered in 1894 by the German philosopher Wilhelm Windelband (1848–1915), which through psychologists William Stern (1871–1938) and Gordon Allport (1897–1967) became influential among some contemporary researchers (see Lamiell 2003).
10 Funder (2019, p. 25).
11 Funder (2019, p. 25).
12 Funder (2019, chapter 2).
13 Fishbein and Ajzen (1975).
14 Kroesen, Handy, and Chorus (2017).
15 See Moghaddam (1998, ch. 4).
16 Balcetis (2008).
17 Allport (1961).
18 For a review of 'big data' analysis in the twenty-first century, see Dey et al. (2018).
19 Barrett et al. (1998).
20 Norman (1963).
21 McCrae and Costa (2003).
22 Revelle (2009).
23 Both cognitive dissonance theory and self-perception theory would support such interpretations.
24 Derringer (2018).
25 Fischer, Lee, and Verzijden (2018).
26 Balestri et al. (2014).

27 Kohn (1969, p. 189).

28 Ostrove and Cole (2003, p. 679).

29 For one indication, see the enormous literature on personality assessment (Weiner & Greene 2017).

30 For example, Argyle (1994), Auld (1952), Grey (1969), Lafitte (1958), and Sewell (1961).

31 For example, see Fiske (2019), Fiske et al. (2018), Fiske and Markus (2012), Kraus, Piff, and Keltner (2011), and Kraus, Piff, and Keltner (2019).

32 For example, system justification theory, social dominance theory, and materialist theories (Vargas-Salfate et al. 2018).

33 Durante, Tablante, and Fiske (2017, p. 139).

34 Piketty (2014) and Piketty and Saez (2014).

35 Jack (2019).

36 For example, Le Roux, Vallée, and Commenges (2017).

37 Ellis (2017, p. 21).

38 Wolfe (2011–2012).

39 Case and Deaton (2015) and Chetty et al. (2016).

40 Auerbach et al. (2017).

41 Of course, this means that poorer people have less opportunity to benefit from social security, Medicare and other 'rewards' of reaching retirement, because they do not live long enough to enjoy such retirement benefits.

42 Jarjoura, Triplett, and Brinker (2002) and Yoshikawa, Aber, and Beardslee (2012)

43 Barling and Weatherhead (2016).

44 Cusick and Georgieff (2016).

45 Ehrenreich (2011).

46 Kraus et al. (2012), Kraus, Piff, and Keltner (2011), and Piff, Kraus, and Keltner (2018)

47 Gillath et al. (2012).

48 Bjornsdottir and Rule (2017).

49 Labov (2006).

50 Durante and Fiske (2017), Fiske (2019), and Heberle and Carter (2015).

51 Durante, Tablante, and Fiske (2017).

52 Gorski (2012).

53 Horwitz, Shutts, and Olson (2014) and Seligman (2012).

54 For example, see Harrison et al. (2006) and the review by Heberle and Carter (2015).

55 Kraus and Mendes (2014).

56 Mehta, Jones, and Josephs (2008)

57 Kraus and Keltner (2013).

58 Keller (2005).

59 Keller (2005) and Kraus and Keltner (2013).

60 Brown-Iannuzzi et al. (2015).

61 Moghaddam (2008a).

5 Consciousness: Decontextualized and Contextualized Approaches

1 Stoppard (2015).
2 Chalmers (1995).
3 For example, Henrich, Heine, and Norenzayan (2010).
4 Baumeister et al. (2018) provide one of the more critical and insightful discussions of consciousness but insist on treating it as a cause of behavior.
5 There is some push back against reductionism in applied domains, such as therapy; see Borsboom, Cramer, and Kalis (2019).
6 Kraus et al. (2012, p. 549).
7 Vygotsky (1962, 1978).
8 Baumeister, Masicampo, and Vohs (2011, P. 354).
9 James (1981, p. 142).
10 Frith (2019, p. 5).
11 For a test of awareness in patients in a vegetative state, see Owen et al. (2016).
12 Brown and McNeill (1966, p. 325).
13 See Hacker (2012) and Bennett and Hacker (2003).
14 The literature on the neural correlates of consciousness is enormous, but the following give a good indication of current issues: Bayne, Hohwy, and Owen (2018), Dehaene, Lau, and Koulder (2017), Doerig et al. (2019), Frith (2019), Koch, Massimini, and Toinini (2016), Knotts, Odegaard, and Lau (2018), and Tononi and Koch (2015).
15 Koch et al. (2016, p. 317).
16 Hacker (2012, p. 71).
17 For example, Harris (2012) presents a very readable account of this perspective.
18 Wegner (2002).
19 See particularly chapters 1 and 2 in Moghaddam (2005a).
20 Skinner (1948).
21 Kalat (2017).
22 Libet et al. (1983).
23 The formal definition of the readiness potential is "a scalp-recorded slow negative potential shift that begins up to a second or more before a self-paced act" (Libet et al. 1983, p. 624).
24 Libet et al. (1983, p. 625).
25 Pockett and Miller (2007).
26 Libet et al. (1983, p. 640).
27 Schurger, Sitt, and Dehaene (2012).
28 Schurger (2012, p. E2910).
29 For example, Kaufman et al. (2015).
30 Braun, Wessler, and Friese (2021).
31 Braun, Wessler, and Friese (2021, p. 195).
32 Searle (2013, p. 55).

33 Kihlstrom (2017, p. 324).
34 See Kozol (1991). Moreover, entrance to Harvard has become even more skewed in favor of affluent and 'connected' applicants in the twenty-first century; see Arcidiacono, Kinsler, and Ransom (2019).
35 Fox, Levitt, and Nelson (2010, p. 31).
36 Jäkel et al. (2016).
37 Chomsky (1959).
38 See Lightfoot (2020).
39 Chomsky (1959, p. 57).
40 The psychologist Douglas Candland (1993) has provided a lively account of the history of human efforts to communicate with both feral children and animals.
41 Lane (1976).
42 Of course, the case of feral children is ambiguous, because we are not sure if the wild boy of Aveyron and other such individuals began as healthy infants, if they were mistreated and suffered brain injuries early in their lives, and in general what is the cause of their poor psychological functioning in later years. However, these cases add to the broad spectrum of evidence showing how healthy adult functioning requires supportive socialization in childhood. Consciousness and free will are only acquired through becoming enmeshed within, and actively participating in, the narratives of human societies.
43 Jost (2017) is one of the few psychologists who has examined social class.
44 Bellah et al. (1985, p. 145).
45 Fitzgerald (1925).
46 The pioneering individualism–collectivism research by Geert Hofstede (2001) in the 1980s has been followed up and refined by recent research, e.g., Minkov et al. (2017).
47 Putnam (2000).
48 Putnam (2016).
49 Putnam (2016, p. 31).
50 The title of Putnam's (2016) book is *The American Dream in Crises*.
51 Davidai and Gilovich (2018).
52 See Sampson (1977, 1981), Gergen (1974), and Billig (1976).
53 Moghaddam (2010).
54 Sampson (1981, p. 730).
55 Chokshi (2019).
56 Keefer, Goode, and Van Berkel (2015, p. 255).
57 Kraus and Stephens (2012, p. 644).
58 For example, Tomalski et al. (2013).
59 Cusick and Georgieff (2016, p. 17).
60 Brito et al. (2016), Brito and Noble (2018), and Brito, Piccolo, and Noble (2017). See also Noble et al. (2015).
61 Kirkland, Jetten, and Nielsen (2019).
62 Brown-Iannuzzi and McKee (2019).
63 Ashok (2021).
64 Raphael (2011).
65 Stephens, Townsend, and Dittmann (2019).

66 Roy et al. (2019).
67 Chaplin, Hill, and John (2014).
68 For evidence on this relationship, see Bjerk (2007).
69 Shweder and Bourne (1984).

6 Motivation and Resilience: Self-Help Myths and the Reality of Invisibility

1 Latham (2012).
2 Jovchelovitch and Glaveanu (2012, p. 169).
3 For an example of the motivation–resilience link, see Resnick (2011).
4 For example, Drury et al. (2019).
5 Wang et al. (2016).
6 For example, see Howard et al. (2016), Locke and Latham (2004), and Mayo (2019).
7 See the review on social loafing research by Karau and Williams (1993).
8 Critics have particularly been in applied areas such as social work (Collins 2017), where the weaknesses of the 'blame the individual' approach to success and failure become most clearly visible.
9 Apple (2019, p. xix).
10 Moghaddam (2010).
11 In addition to philosophical critiques of neuroscience (Bennett & Hacker 2003; Manzotti & Moderato 2010), there has been occasional but narrow attention to the ideology of neuroscience (e.g., Altermark 2014).
12 O'Connor, Rees, and Joffe (2012).
13 O'Connor, Rees, and Joffe (2012, p. 224).
14 See Blair and Raver (2016) for a brief review of this research literature.
15 See Waugh et al. (2017a) highly critical assessment of research on the neuroscience of poverty.
16 For a related critical discussion, see Prilleltensky (1994).
17 Kohn et al. (1990).
18 Open Science Collaboration (2015).
19 Moghaddam (1987).
20 For example, for the former see Shrout and Rodgers (2018) and the latter see Bishop (2020).
21 Sampson (1981).
22 Jost, Gaucher, and Stern (2015) and Osborne, Sengupta, and Sibley (2018).
23 Jost, Gaucher, and Stern (2015, p. 320).
24 Putnam (2016, p. 32–33).
25 Chetty et al. (2017, p. 405).
26 Long (2020).
27 For example, see Scott Winship's (2018) report, disseminated by the Archbridge Institute, part of whose mission is to rekindle the American Dream.
28 For empirical research, see Day and Fiske (2017); for theoretical support of this argument, see Moghaddam (2008a), particularly discussions of the Five-Stage Model on pp. 81–83).

29 Houle and Miller (2019).

30 Li, Deng, and Zhou (in press).

31 As noted by Revilla, Martin, and de Castro (2017, p. 4), "In the psychology literature on resilience there is a particular interest in the reaction of individuals to stressful circumstances, such as the loss of a loved one or being the victim of a terrorist attack."

32 Goldstein and Brooks (2013a, p. 3).

33 See chapter 28 in Goldstein and Brooks (2013b).

34 For examples, see Garrett (2016) and Mohaupt (2009).

35 Seligman (2011).

36 For example, see Kong et al. (2018) and Wang et al. (2016).

37 Cicchetti and Blender (2006, p. 251).

38 See Carr and Sloan (2003), Cozzarelli, Wilkinson, and Tagler (2001), and Tripathi (2010)

39 For example, Bobbio, Canova, and Manganelli (2010), de Costa and Dias (2014), Godfrey and Wolf (2016), Mickelson and Hazlett (2014), Osborne and Weiner (2015), Vazquez, Panadero, and Zuniga (2018), and Weiner, Osborne, and Rudolph (2011).

40 Weiner, Osborne, and Rudolph (2011).

41 Narayan et al. (2000) and Narayan et al. (1999).

42 Narayan et al. (2000, p. 134).

43 See Johnson, Sears, and McConahay (1971) on Black invisibility.

44 See Agarwal's (2011) discussion of 'The Invisible Poor.'

45 Mumtaz et al. (2014).

46 Narayan et al. (2000, p. 260).

47 Grant (2017, p. 836).

48 Quoted in Grant (2017, p. 836).

49 Anderson (2019).

50 Morris (2002).

51 For an example of insightful research on poor Whites, see Kimmel (2017).

7 Group Life and Diversity

1 For example, see the introductory text by Hall (2018).

2 Nastasi (2014).

3 There are numerous basic texts in this area, for example, Abdullah (2018).

4 See Stevens, Plaut, and Sanchez-Burks (2008).

5 For example, Hutchison (2009) and Tatum (2017).

6 For people of color, see Alvarez, Liang, and Neville (2016). For the African American experience, see Bonilla-Silva (2017), Kendi (2017), and Taylor (2016).

7 Bernal et al. (2002). For specific minorities, see Leong et al. (2006).

8 For gender, see, for example, Helgeson (2016). For feminism, see Hurtado (2003).

9 Collins and Bilge (2016).

10 Jetten and Peters (2019) and Fiske and Markus (2012).
11 For example, Ehrenreich (2011).
12 For example, Gest (2016).
13 For example, Reiman and Leighton (2016).
14 Haney (2018).
15 Aronson and Aronson (2018).
16 See chapter 2 in Moghaddam (2013).
17 Tronick et al. (1978).
18 Zeanah, Berlin, and Boris (2011, p. 823).
19 Harlow and Harlow (1969).
20 Bowlby and Harlow influenced one another in important ways (Van der Horst, LeRoy, & Van der Veer 2008).
21 In this discussion in particular, I am influenced by Vygotsky (1962, 1978).
22 For a more detailed discussion of the significance of turn-taking, see Moghaddam and Riley (2005).
23 Despite the efforts of Henri Tajfel and a small group of European psychologists, mainstream psychology is notoriously neglectful of group and intergroup processes. The struggle to get group and intergroup psychology into the 'mainstream' of American psychology gained momentum in the 1970s and is discussed in Taylor and Moghaddam (1994).
24 'Poverty' is defined in different ways (see chapter 1 in Paterson and Gregory 2019). As will become clear in the following chapters, my approach is to highlight the relative nature of poverty in each particular society.
25 Oxfam (2018).
26 Oxfam (2018, Chart 4).
27 Oxfam (2019). Of the 2,043 billionaires, only 11 percent were female (Oxfam 2018, Table 3 and Chart 3).
28 The rate of wealth increases reported by Oxfam (2019) among billionaires and the poor has faced criticism www.vox.com/future-perfect/2019/1/22/18192774/oxfam-inequality-report-2019-davos-wealth.
   Also, there is pushback from some economists against the narrative of increasing wealth concentration; see *The Economist* (2020a).
29 Clemens and Kremer (2016).
30 Oxfam (2018, Table 9).
31 Sumner, Hoy, and Ortiz-Juarez (2020).
32 *The Economist* (2020b)
33 See Amis et al. (2018) and Katz and Autor (1999).
34 Peters et al. (2019).
35 Holton (2014, p. 53).
36 Tricomi et al. (2010).
37 Tricomi et al. (2010, p. 1090).
38 Major and Machine (2018).
39 Kraus and Park (2017, p. 56).
40 See Mullen's (2009) research on students attending Yale.

41 Gould (2012).

42 Payne (2017) uses the phrase 'broken ladder.'

43 See Mare (2014) and Pfeffer (2014).

44 Tilly (1998).

45 Social Mobility Index (2018).

46 See reports by the Consultative Group to Assist the Poor (CGAP), www.cgap
.org/research/infographic/how-make-data-work-poor.

47 Major and Machine (2018) and OECD (2018).

48 Grisold and Theine (2017, p. 4274).

49 Some more attention is being given to inequality by psychologists (Fiske &
Markus 2012; Jetten & Peters 2019; Manstead 2018), but this valiant research
effort is tiny in the context of the total volume of psychological research
around the world.

50 Haushofer and Fehr (2014, p. 862).

51 Tanaka, Camerer, and Nguyen (2010).

52 See Kahneman (2011).

53 Carvalho, Meier, and Wang (2016).

54 Roll, Grinstein-Weiss, and Despard (2019).

55 Ogaki, Ostry, and Reinhart (1996).

56 Cohen and Casselman (2020).

57 Mischel, Shoda, and Peake (1988).

58 See Mischel (2014).

59 For an alternative perspective on the marshmallow test, see Watts, Duncan,
and Quan (2018). Mischel (2014) provides the conventional wisdom on the
test.

60 Moffit et al. (2011).

61 Michaelson and Munakata (2020, p. 194).

62 Rauscher, Friedline, and Banerjee (2017).

63 Antonopolis and Chen (2020).

64 See discussions of individual and collective representations, chapter 1 in
Durkheim (1953); see Moscovici (1981).

65 Sherif (1936).

66 For a broader discussion, see Howard and Templeton (1966).

67 MacNeil and Sherif (1976).

68 Berns et al. (2005).

69 Janis (1982).

70 See Moghaddam (2013, p. 127).

71 Tajfel et al. (1971).

72 See Gillmeister's (2017) masterly and entertaining cultural history of tennis.

73 See Yaddanapudi (2016).

74 Bakker, van Dijk, and Wicherts (2012).

75 See discussions of elites, system justification, and false consciousness in
Moghaddam (2008a).

76 Although there are local elites in each nation, the global elite tends to be
concentrated in Western countries; see Noam (2016) for media ownership in
different countries around the world.

77 Jack (2019).
78 Taylor and Moghaddam (1994).
79 Trudeau (1971/1992).
80 See Jaschik (2014); see also Kettler and Hurst (2017).
81 Jaschik (2018).
82 For example, see Shapiro et al. (2017).
83 For example, see Sutton et al. (2018).
84 Banerjee (2016).
85 Blair, Blair, and Madamba (1999, p. 552).
86 Moghaddam (2012).

8 Mental Health and 'Be Happy' Psychology

1 Hare-Mustin and Marecek (1997, p. 108).
2 Macintyre et al. (2018, p. 2).
3 For examples of popular texts, see Comer and Comer (2019), Barlow, Durand, and Hoffmann (2017), and Hooley et al. (2016).
4 The DSM was revised for the fifth time (DSM-5) in 2013.
5 Smith (2010).
6 Liu. (2011).
7 See Haslam et al. (2018).
8 Payne (2017).
9 The field of community psychology is robust and in many respects progressive; for example, see the text by Kagan et al. (2020) and Prilleltensky (2020).
10 Becker and Kleinman (2013).
11 For examples, see Funk, Drew, and Knapp (2012), Ljungqvist et al. (2016), Muntaner, Borrell, and Chung (2007), Murali and Oyebode (2004), Nikulina and Widom (2011), Pickett and Wilkinson (2010, 2015), Santiago (2012), Sverdlik (2011), and Sylvestre et al. (2018).
12 The downward drift hypothesis has a long history. For example, see Goldberg and Morrison (1963).
13 For a discussion of mental health with a focus on the social–economic conditions, see Muntaner et al. (2012).
14 Nguyen et al. (2017).
15 Kress et al. (2014, p. 192).
16 Waugh et al. (2017a).
17 Morey and Hopwood (2019).
18 Buckley et al. (2009).
19 Dattilio and Norcross (2006).
20 Byard (2013).
21 Johnson (2014).
22 Lisanby (2007, p. 1940)
23 Chiken et al. (2016).
24 Agmon et al. (2017).
25 Gøtzsche, Young, and Grace (2015).
26 Montejo, Montejo, and Navarro-Cremades (2015).

27 Hoffer (2019).
28 In recent years cognitive behavioral therapy, rather than the 'old fashioned' strictly behavioral therapy, has become influential (Dobson and Dobson 2017).
29 Beck (1976).
30 Cain (2002).
31 Marcus et al. (2014).
32 Derubeis and Lorenzo-Luaces (2017).
33 Seligman (2019).
34 Lewis (2016, p. 83).
35 Laing and Esterson (1970, p. 12).
36 Laing and Esterson (1970, p. 23).
37 Szasz (1961, p. 219)
38 Pereira, Gonçalves, and Bizzari (2019, p. 5)
39 Rogers (1965, p. 40).
40 Seligman (2019, p. 21).
41 Ottersen et al. (2014, p. 631).
42 Lazarus (2003, p. 93).
43 There is an enormous literature on the Happiness Index (Frey & Gallus 2013); also see Stewart (2014) for a highly insightful critical discussion of this topic.
44 Seligman (2019, p. 5).
45 Frawley (2015, p. 62).
46 For more in-depth discussions, see Haslam et al. (2018), Liu (2011), Smith (2010), and Topor, Ljungqvist, and Strandberg (2016).
47 Bastian (2018).
48 Ehrenreich (2010).
49 Horowitz (2017).
50 For example, see the research of Harvey Whitehouse (e.g., Whitehouse et al. 2014).
51 Gable and Haidt (2005).
52 Gable and Haidt (2005, p. 103).
53 For example, see OECD (2013) and Helliwell, Layard, and Sachs (2013).
54 Easterlin (1974).
55 Sacks, Stevenson, and Wolfers (2012, p. 12).
56 Headey (2019).
57 Marmot (2004), Marmot et al. (1978), Marmot et al. (1991), and Marmot and Wilkinson (2006).
58 For example, see Fryers et al. (2005) and Lund et al. (2010). Also, chapter 2 in Bhugra et al. (2018).
59 For example, Marmot (2015).
60 Belle (1990).
61 Charles et al. (2013).
62 Charles et al. (2013, p. 739).
63 In addition to the research of Marmot (2004), there is a growing research literature linking relative deprivation and health (e.g., Mishra & Carleton 2015; Wickham et al. 2014).

64 See the discussion of 'beyond money' in Diener and Seligman (2004).
65 Lawrence and Kisely (2010).
66 For example, see Brown, Sokal, and Friedman (2014).
67 Diener et al. (2017, p. 182).
68 Diener et al. (2017, p. 168)
69 Myers and Diener (2017, p. 220).
70 Myers and Diener (2017, p. 220).
71 Haushofer and Shapiro (2016).
72 See the report by Ozer et al. (2011), with references to a number of similar studies.
73 Finkelstein et al. (2012).
74 Haushofer and Fehr (2014).
75 For example, see Brown and Rohrer (2020).
76 Wilkinson and Pickett (2011, 2019).
77 See Lindert's (2000) long-term review.
78 Rosenfield (2012).
79 Moghaddam (1987).

9 Looking through the Wrong Side of Prison Bars: The Psychology of Injustice

1 Wakefield and Uggen (2010, p. 401).
2 Reiman and Leighton (2016).
3 The terminology used to discuss incarcerated persons has been changing; see Shalby (2019). I have tried to use terminology that is more neutral.
4 Foster and Hagan (2015).
5 Western and Pettit (2010, p. 9). Mears and Cochran (2018) make the same point: "Individuals in prison have substantially worse educational … histories as compared to the general population" (p. 30).
6 Page, Piehowski, and Soss (2019).
7 Epstein finally met a kind of justice in prison when he (apparently) took his own life, but as chronicled so diligently by Julie Brown (2021) his wealth and influence kept him out of the reaches of the law for decades.
8 De Carvalho and Bantim (2019).
9 For a broader discussion of prison riots, see chapter 12 in Wooldredge and Smith (2018) and Wooldredge (2020).
10 Kulig, Pratt, and Cullen (2017) provide a reasonably balanced discussion, arguing that psychologists should be more demanding regarding replication of results, particularly in the case of studies such as the Stanford prison experiment. Le Texier (2019) provides a more damning discussion of Zimbardo's prison study.
11 Kim, Losen, and Hewitt (2010).
12 Kearney et al. (2014).
13 Scott-Hayward and Fradella (2019).
14 Schweitzer and Nuñez (2017).
15 Franklin (2017).

16 Woolard (in press).
17 Reiman and Leighton (2016).
18 Wheelock and Uggen (2008).
19 Heller, Jacob, and Ludwig (2011).
20 Geller et al. (2009).
21 Carson and Golinelli (2013).
22 Zorbaugh (1929) and Shaw and McKay (1942).
23 Ellen, Lacoe. and Sharygin (2013).
24 Stuckler et al. (2011).
25 Graif, Gladfelter, and Mathews (2014).
26 Graif, Gladfelter, and Mathews (2014, p. 1141).
27 Nikulina, Widom, and Czaja (2011).
28 Freeman (1996) and Lochner (2004).
29 Lally, Mangione, and Honig (1988) and Schweinhart, Montie, and Xiang (2005).
30 Lochner and Moretti (2004).
31 Hjalmarsson, Holmlund, and Lindquist (2014) and Hjalmarsson and Lochner (2012).
32 Carson (2018).
33 Archer (2004).
34 See Choy et al. (2017) and Schwartz, Steffenmeier, and Ackerman (2009).
35 Campbell, Vogel, and Williams (2015, p. 199).
36 Carson (2018, Table 6).
37 Han (2018).
38 Tonry (2014); see also Kearney et al. (2014).
39 Tucker (2014, p. 135)
40 Barnes and Motz (2018).
41 Jan (2017).
42 Kearney et al. 2014).
43 Aizer and Doyle (2015).
44 Aizer and Doyle (2013).
45 Mendel (2011).
46 Sedlak and McPherson (2010).
47 Human Rights Watch (2012).
48 Beck, Harrison, and Guerino (2010).
49 Dierkhising, Lane, and Natsuaki (2014).
50 Dumond (2000).
51 For example, see Trulson et al. (2010) for juveniles and Steiner and Wooldredge (2008) for adults.
52 For a review of this literature, see Foster and Hagan (2015).
53 Lee, Porter, and Comfort (2014).
54 Wildeman, Turney, and Yi (2016).
55 Turney (2015).
56 Amato (2000).

57 Wakefield, Lee, and Wildeman (2016).
58 Wakefield, Lee, and Wildeman (2016, pp. 11–12).
59 Haskins (2014).
60 Geller et al. (2009).
61 Haskins (2014).
62 Ewert, Sykes, and Pettit (2014).
63 Eason (2010).
64 Nance (2016).
65 Katsiyannis et al. (2018).
66 There is a lack of systematic and comparable statistics on recidivism across nations, but Fazel and Wolf (2015) provide a tentative picture.
67 Durose, Cooper, and Snyder (2014).
68 Cullen, Jonson, and Nagin (2011).
69 Foucault (1995).
70 For examples, see Western et al. (2015) and Western (2018).
71 Western et al. (2015, p. 1541).
72 See Gaes (2019) for a discussion of research on prison privatization.
73 See Melossi and Massimo (1981).
74 Katzenstein and Waller (2015, p. 639).
75 Katzenstein and Waller (2015).
76 Van Zyl Smit and Dunkel (2018).
77 For example, see Dyer (2000) and Eiser (2017).
78 Dickens (1970, p. 324).
79 See Alber (2007) for a more comprehensive discussion of how Dickens incorporate the prison in his novels.
80 Surprenant (2019, p. 124).
81 Piff et al. (2012).

10 Psychology for the Masses in Non-Western Societies

1 Ascher (2020).
2 For a standard review of cross-cultural psychology, see Shiraev and Levy (2020).
3 Moghaddam and Studer (1997).
4 Moghaddam and Lee (2006).
5 Save the Children (2019).
6 Wessells (2016, p. 198).
7 Wessells (2017).
8 Moreland (2019).
9 See Götmark and Andersson (2020); Table 1 provides fertility rates for all major countries. The fertility rate for Western European and North American countries ranges from 1.28 to 2.00 (below the 2.1 replacement rate) and for African countries the range is from 2.55 to 7.40 (which means a doubling of the population in some countries every twenty years or so).

10 Table 3 in Cobbinah, Erdiaw-Kwasie, and Amoateng (2015).
11 Cobbinah, Erdiaw-Kwasie, and Amoateng (2015, p. 20).
12 Actually, the global poverty picture would look a lot bleaker if we exclude China, the country where most of the poverty reduction has taken place since the late twentieth century. See the discussions on poverty around the world in Pogge, Köhler, and Cimadamore (2016).
13 Cobbinah, Erdiaw-Kwasie, and Amoateng (2015, Table 2).
14 Korotayev, Goldstone, and Zinkina (2015).
15 Adeola (2001).
16 Alvaredo et al. (2018).
17 Assaad and Krafft (2015).
18 Dupas (2011).
19 Dinsa et al. (2012).
20 Olken and Pande (2012).
21 Moghaddam and Taylor (1986, 1987).
22 For a conventional history of modern psychology, see Goodwin (2015). For a more critical account, see Danziger (1990).
23 For Sherif's legacy, see readings in Dost-Gozkan and Sonmez Keith (2015).
24 Moghaddam and Lee (2006).
25 Moghaddam (1987).
26 Moghaddam (1987).
27 The growth of psychological research in China is reflected in *PsyCh Journal*, China's first international psychology journal (based in the Institute of Psychology, Chinese Academy of Sciences); https://onlinelibrary.wiley.com/journal/20460260
28 The growth of social identity research in Australia came about largely because John Turner (1947–2011) and other British researchers moved from the United Kingdom to Australia. For examples of research in Algeria, see *The Journal of North African Studies*.
29 Kim and Berry (1993, p. 2). See Sun (2013) for examples of themes special to Chinese psychology. In practice, the vast majority of psychological research from China is very similar to psychological research published in North America and Europe. For a critical discussion of indigenous psychology, see Jahoda (2016).
30 For discussions on liberation psychology, see Comas-Diaz and Torres Rivera (2020).
31 Montero (2008). For the very interesting connections being made between liberation psychology and community psychology, see Montero, Sonn, and Burton (2017).
32 Moghaddam and Lee (2006, p. 164)
33 For example, see Spini and Doise (2005).
34 See Moghaddam and Lee (2004, particularly Table 4).
35 For example, Fast et al. (2012) and Sawaoka, Hughes, and Amdaby (2015).
36 Eaton et al. (2011).
37 Eaton et al. (2011, p. 1599).

38 Laungani (2004, p. 2).
39 Bass, Bolton, and Murray (2007).
40 UNHCR (2019).
41 UNHCR (2019).
42 See Vossoughi et al. (2018) for a review.
43 Bruijn (2009).
44 De Carvalho and Pinto (2018).
45 Lukunka (2018).
46 Wessells (2016).
47 See UNICEF (2007) for a discussion on definition.
48 De Silva (2013).
49 Stevens (2014).
50 Kohrt et al. (2016).
51 Warner et al. (2020).
52 Moghaddam (2005).
53 Individuals who eventually become involved in terrorism take on different functions. Nine different specializations within terrorist networks have been identified and these specializations are distributed on the different levels of the staircase to terrorism. For example, 'strategists,' 'networkers,' and 'experts' tend to remain on the third and fourth floors; only 'fodder' (individuals who carry out terrorist attacks) reach the fifth floor. See chapter 8 in Moghaddam (2006).
54 Hawi et al. (2019).
55 Johnson (2018).

Part III   Looking Ahead

1 See Wagoner, Moghaddam and Valsiner (2018).

11   Rethinking Research Methods

1 For examples, see readings in Smith, Harré, and Van Langenhove (1995).
2 For example, Wigginton and Lafrance (2019).
3 For example, Garcia, Lopez, and Velez (2018).
4 For example, Open Science Collaboration (2015).
5 For critical discussions and alternatives of mainstream psychology, see Harré (2002) and Harré, and Moghaddam (2012).
6 Bordens and Abbot (2011, p. 3).
7 Dunstan and Moghaddam (2016).
8 Feist and Rosenberg (2010, p. 7).
9 Sdorow and Rickabaugh (2006, p. 2).
10 See Moghaddam (2005).
11 Huffman (2012, p. 22).
12 Harré and Moghaddam (2016).
13 Harré, and Moghaddam (2012).

14 See Moghaddam (1998), chapter 2 in Moghaddam (2013), and Harré, and Moghaddam (2012) for more in-depth discussions of this issue.

15 For example, see Cambridge, Witton, and Elbourne (2014).

16 Skinner (1971).

17 Attempts to progress beyond causal-reductionism in neuroscience are reflected in discussions in Brook and Akins (2005). However, progress in moving beyond causal-reductionist neuroscience is very limited, with attempts to understand 'collective' activities remaining limited to within-brain processes and the collective activities of neurons (e.g., Breakspear 2017), rather than the relationships of individuals with the social world.

18 A number of authors have discussed different aspects of the relationship between neuroscience and behaviorism (e.g., Machamer 2009).

19 Graham (2017).

20 Haslam and McGarty (2014, p. 14).

21 Pajo (2018, p. 2).

22 Pelham and Blanton (2013, p. 9).

23 Moghaddam and Lee (2006).

24 Milgram (1974).

25 See Moghaddam (1998, p. 247). Also, four decades later Milgram's findings were replicated in the United States; see Burger (2009).

26 Wittgenstein (1958, § 281).

27 Wittgenstein (1958, § 281).

28 For a discussion of the intertwined historical roots of behaviorism and neuroscience, see Clark and Clark (2010).

29 See particularly chapter 3, "The mereological fallacy in neuroscience," in Bennett and Hacker (2003). For further philosophical discussions of neuroscience, see readings in Brook and Akins (2011).

30 For a broad discussion, see Silvers, Buhle, and Ochsner (2014).

31 Denny et al. (2015).

32 As we would expect, some authors have defended neuroscience against such critical attacks. See the lively debates in Bennett et al. (2007).

33 Morling (2017, p. 89).

34 Pajo (2018, p. 18).

35 Haslam and McGarty (2014, p. 426).

36 For examples, see Morling (2018, pp. 98–105), chapter 7 in Bordens and Abbot (2008, pp. 57–65), and chapter 3 in Shaughenessy, Zechmeister, and Zechmeister (2009).

37 Brown (1997, p. 54).

38 Brown (1997, p. 54).

39 Brown (1997, p. 56).

40 Farah (2018) and Tooley et al. (2020).

41 Chetty et al. (2020)., https://doi.org/10.1093/qje/qjaa005

42 McDermott et al. (2019).

43 Power et al. (2018).

12   Revolution and Psychology

1 Taylor and Moghaddam (1994).
2 For collective action research, see Lizzio-Wilson et al. (2021). Much of the intergroup research has been shaped by the social identity research tradition (e.g., van Zomeren, Kutlaca, & Turner-Zwinkels 2018).
3 I am here adopting a strategy inspired by Paulo Freire (1921–1997), who in works such as *Pedagogy of the Oppressed* (2018) encouraged a bottom-up approach and the raising of questions from the perspective of the oppressed.
4 Piketty (2014).
5 "Based on the statistics and information by Statistical Center of Iran, unlike the common trends of the world, absolute poverty is expanding in the country in such a way that it shows an increase from 11% in 2002 to about 30% in 2014." (Salem & Bayat 2018, p. 82)
6 Daniels (2020).
7 Cohen-Chen and van Zomeren (2018) and Van Zomeren, Postmes, and Spears (2008).
8 Grasso et al. (2019); for nonnormative individual action see Greitemeyer and Sagioglou (2017).
9 Reimer et al. (2017).
10 See Moghaddam (2008a) for a broader discussion.
11 For example, see the 'system justification' role of religion as discussed through system justification theory in Jost et al. (2013).
12 See Jost (2019) for a review of system justification research.
13 Davies (1962).
14 Mirabito and Berry (2015).
15 Ardalan (2017).
16 Milan (2015).
17 Gurr (1970).
18 Hill (1972).
19 Yeats's poem 'The Great Day.'
20 For a more in-depth discussion of this trend, see Moghaddam (2013).
21 This is a very apt title about the Iranian revolution by Arjomand (1988).
22 See Campbell and Moghaddam (2018).
23 For a discussion of a more progressive psychology, see Harré and Moghaddam (2012).
24 Moghaddam (2016).
25 Moghaddam and Howard (2017) and Moghaddam (2018).
26 Harré and Moghaddam (2012) and Watzlawick, Weakland, and Fisch (1974).
27 Johnson and de Haan (2015).
28 Moghaddam (2002).
29 Mrazek et al. (2016).
30 For examples, see Costandi (2016), Cunnigham (2016) and Merzenich (2013).

31 For example, see Baroncelli et al. (2010), Costandi (2016), and Cunningham (2016).
32 Le Bon (1894, p. 25).
33 Brinton (1965, p. 277).
34 White, Educated, Industrialized, Rich, Democratic; see Henrich, Heine, and Norenzayan (2010).
35 Moghaddam and Lee (2006).
36 It is beyond the scope of this text to propose what these approaches should be, but some direction is found in Moghaddam (2013, chapter 2), Harré and Moghaddam (2003), and Harré and Moghaddam (2012).
37 Trotsky (1906/2010, p. 109).
38 For a more in-depth discussion of Communist attempts to use behaviorism for social engineering, see Campbell and Moghaddam (2018).
39 See Moghaddam (2005).
40 Quoted in Figes (2002, p. 446–447).
41 Watson (1913).
42 Smith (2017, p. 357).
43 Alt and Alt (1964, p. 19).
44 Willimott (2017, p. 146).
45 Figes (2002, p. 445).
46 Willimott (2017) provides an excellent account of the Communist movement and Soviet socialism.
47 Taylor (1911/1964).
48 See chapter 4 in Moghaddam (1997).
49 For a review of the research literature on social loafing, see Karau and Williams (1993).
50 Earley (1989).
51 Haslam (2004).
52 Van Dick, Tissington, and Hertel (2009).
53 Allen (2003).
54 Johnson and Brooks (1983).
55 Nell (2014, p. 119).
56 Blackey and Paynton (1976, p. 9).
57 See Moghaddam (2013) for a broader discussion of closed societies and corruption. For experimental evidence on power and corruption, see Kipnis (1972), Lammers, Gordijn, and Otten (2008), Lammers, Stapel, and Galinsky (2010), and Whitson et al. (2013). Also, see Runciman (2008).
58 For an example of research showing how our political motivation leads us to biased interpretations, see Tappin, van der Leer, and McKay (2017).
59 Travis and Aronson (2013).
60 Shalvi et al. (2015).
61 Dower (2000).
62 Moghaddam (2016).
63 Atkinson (2015) and Piketty (2014).
64 Scheidel (2017).

65 See Moghaddam (2019) for a discussion of the weakening of democracy and the rise of authoritarian strongmen around the world in the early twenty-first century.

66 The Nobel Prize-winning economist Joseph Stiglitz (2012) has examined the price of this greater inequality with considerable insight.

Afterword: The Path Ahead for Psychology

1 *The Economist* (2018).
2 Ip (2019) in *The Wall Street Journal.*
3 See Streeck's (2016) critical discussion of how capitalism will end.
4 Moghaddam (2019).
5 See Haslam and Kashima (2010)
6 The exportation of psychology from Western nations to non-Western nations has received some critical attention; see Holdstock (2000).
7 There is a small psychological literature on poverty in India; see Mohan and Nalwa (1992), chapters 5, 7, and 8 in Misra (1990), chapters in Mohanty and Misra (2000), and Singh and Pandey (1990).
8 Dhongde and Minoiu (2013).
9 Sen (2006, p. 35).
10 Putnam (2016).
11 For example, see Brown's (2021) analysis of the special economic, social, and other burdens faced by African Americans.

References

Aarts, H., Dijksterhuis, A., & De Vries, P. (2001). On the psychology of drinking: Being thirsty and perceptually ready. *British Journal of Psychology, 92*, 631–642.

Abdullah, S. S. (2018). *Multicultural counseling applications for improved mental healthcare services.* Hershey, PA: IGI Global Publishing. E Book.

Adeola, F. O. (2001). Environmental injustice and human rights abuse: The states, MNCs, and repression of minority groups in the world system. *Research in Human Ecology, 8*, 39–59.

Agarwal, S. (2011). The invisible poor. *World Health Design, 4*, 20–26.

Agmon, M., Zisberg, A., Gil, E., et al. (2017). Adult utilization of psychiatric drugs and differences by sex, age, and race. *Journal of the American Medical Association, 177*, 274–275.

Ainslie, R. C. (1997). *The psychology of twinship.* Northvale, NJ: Jason Aronson.

Aizer, A., & Doyle, J. J. (2013). What is the long-term impact of incarcerating juveniles? *VOX CEPR Policy Portal.* https://voxeu.org/article/what-long-term-impact-incarcerating-juveniles

Aizer, A., & Doyle, J. J. (2015). Juvenile incarceration, human capital, and future crime: Evidence from randomly assigned judges. *Quarterly Journal of Economics, 130*, 759–803.

Alber, J. (2007). *Narrating the prison: Role and representation in Charles Dickens' novels, twentieth-century fiction, and film.* Youngstown, NY: Cambria Press.

Allen, R. C. (2003). *Farm to factory: A reinterpretation of the Soviet industrial revolution.* Princeton, NJ: Princeton University Press.

Allport, G. (1961). *Patterns and growth in personality.* New York: Holt, Rinehart & Winston.

Alt, H., & Alt, E. (1964). *The new Soviet man: His upbringing and character development.* New York: Bookman.

Altermark, N. (2014). The ideology of neuroscience and intellectual disability: Reconstituting the "disordered" brain. *Disability & Society, 29*, 1460–1472.

Alvaredo, F., Chancel, L., Piketty, T., Saez, E., & Zucman, G. (Eds.) (2018). *Inequality report 2018.* Cambridge, MA: The Belknap Press of Harvard University Press.

Alvarez, A. N., Liang, C. T. H., & Nevile, H. A. (Eds.) (2016). *The cost of racism for people of color: Contextualizing experiences of discrimination.* Washington, DC: American Psychological Association Press.

Amato, P. R. (2000). The consequences of divorce for parents and children. *Journal of Marriage and Family, 62*, 1269–1287.

Amis, J. M., Munir, K. A., Lawrence, T. B., Hirsch, P., & McGahan, A. (2018). Inequality, institutions and organizations. *Organization Studies, 39*, 1131–1152.

Anderson, L. A. (2019). Rethinking resilience theory in African American families: Fostering positive adaptations and transformative social justice. *Journal of Family Theory & Review, 11*, 385–397.

Antonopolis, S., & Chen, S. (2020). Time and class: How socioeconomic status shapes conceptions of the future self. *Self and Identity*. DOI: 10.1080/15298868.2020.1789730

Anyon, J. (2017). Social class and the hidden curriculum of work. In G. Handel (Ed.), *Childhood socialization* (pp. 369–394). New York: Routledge.

Appadurai, A. (2004). The capacity to aspire. In V. Rao, & M. Walton (Eds.), *Culture and public action* (pp. 59–84). Washington, DC: The World Bank.

Apple. M. W. (2019). *Ideology and curriculum*. New York: Routledge. 4th ed.

Archer, J. (2004). Sex differences in aggression in real world settings: A meta-analytic review. *Review of General Psychology, 8*, 291–322.

Archer, L., Hutchings, M., & Ross, A. (2003). *Higher education and social class: Issues of exclusion and inclusion*. London: Routledge.

Arcidiacono, P., Kinsler, J., & Ransom, T. (2019). Legacy and athlete preferences at Harvard. Cambridge, MA: National Bureau for Economic Research, Working Paper no. 26316. nber.org/system/files/working_papers/w26316.pdfArdalan, K. (2017). On the Marxian notion of revolution. *Journal of Alternative Perspectives in the Social Sciences, 8*, 424–451.

Argyle, M. (1994). *The psychology of social class*. London: Routledge.

Arjomand, S. A. (1988). *The turban for the crown: The Islamic revolution in Iran*. New York: Oxford University Press.

Aronson, E., & Aronson, J. (2018). *The social animal*. New York: Worth. 12th ed.

Aronson, J., Lustina, M. J., Good, C., et al. (1999). When white men can't do math: Necessary and sufficient factors in stereotype threat. *Journal of Experimental Social Psychology, 35*, 29–46.

Ascher, W. (2020). *The psychology of poverty alleviation: Challenges in developing countries*. New York: Cambridge University Press.

Ashok, A. (2021). The persistent grip of social class on college admission. *New York Times*, May 26. www.nytimes.com/2021/05/26/upshot/college-admissions-essay-sat.html?

Assaad, R., & Krafft, C. (2015). Is free basic education in Egypt a reality or a myth? Cairo: The Egyptian Center for Economic Studies, Working Paper No. 179. www.eces.org.ed/MediaFiles/Uploaded_Files/c86feba.pdf

Atkinson, A. (2015). *Inequality: What can be done?* Cambridge, MA: Harvard University Press.

Auerbach, A. J., Charles, K. K., Coile, C. C., Gale, W., Goldman, D., et al. (2017). How the growing gap in life expectancy may affect retirement benefits and reforms. Cambridge, MA: National Bureau of Economic Research, Working Paper 23329. www.nber.org/papers/w23329

Auld, F. (1952). Influence of social class on personality test responses. *Psychological Bulletin, 49*, 318–332.

Bakker, M., van Dijk, A., & Wicherts, J. M. (2012). The rules of the game called psychological science. *Psychological Science, 7*, 543–554.

Balcetis, E. (2008). Where the motivation resides and self-deception hides: How motivated cognition accomplishes self-deception. *Social and Personality Psychology Compass, 2/1*, 361–381.

Balestri, M., Calati, R., Serreti, A., & De Ronchi, D. (2014). Genetic modulation of personality traits. A systematic review of the literature. *International Clinical Psychopharmacology, 29*, 1–15.

Banerjee, P. A. (2016). A systematic review of factors linked to poor academic performance of disadvantaged students in science and maths in schools. *Cogent Education, 3/1*, 1178441. DOI: 10.1080/2331186X.2016.1178441

Barber, J. S., Yarger, J. E., & Gatny, H. H. (2015). Black-white differences in attitudes related to pregnancy among young women. *Demography, 52*, 751–786.

Barling, J., & Weatherhead, J. G. (2016). Persistent exposure to poverty during childhood limits later leader emergence. *Journal of Applied Psychology, 101*, 1305–1318.

Barlow, D. H., Durand, V. M., & Hofmann, S. G. (2017). *Abnormal psychology: An integrative approach*. Boston: Cengage Learning. 8th ed.

Barnes, J. C., & Motz, R. T. (2018). Reducing racial inequalities in adulthood arrest by reducing inequalities in school discipline: Evidence from the school-to-prison pipeline. *Developmental Psychology, 54*, 2328–2340.

Barnes, J. C., Wright, J. P., Boutwell, B. B., et al. (2014). Demonstrating the validity of twin research in criminology, *Criminology, 52*, 588–626.

Baroncelli, L., Braschi, C., Spolidodo, M., et al. (2010). Nurturing brain plasticity: Impact of environmental enrichment. *Cell Death and Differentiation, 17*, 1092–1103.

Barrett, P. T., Petrides, K. V., Eysenck, S. B. G., & Eysenck, H. J. (1998). The Eysenck Personality Questionnaire: An examination of the factorial similarity of P, E, N and L across 34 countries. *Personality and Individual Differences, 25*, 805–819.

Bass, J. K., Bolton, P. A., & Murray, L. K. (2007). Do not forget culture when studying mental health. *The Lancet, 370*, 918–919.

Bastedo, M. N., & Jaquette, O. (2011). Running in place: Low-income students and the dynamics of higher education stratification. *Educational Evaluation and Policy Analysis, 33*, 318–339.

Bastian, B. (2018). *The other side of happiness: Embracing a more fearless approach to living*. London: Penguin.

Battalora, J. (2013). *Birth of a white nation: The invention of white people and its relevance today*. Houston, TX: Strategic Book Publishing and Rights Co.

Baumeister, R. F., Lau, S., Maranges, H. M., & Clark, C. J. (2018). On the necessity of consciousness for sophisticated human action. *Frontiers in Psychology: Theoretical and Philosophical Psychology*. DOI: 10.3389/fpsyg.2018.01925

Baumeister, R. F., Masicampo, E. J., & Vohs, K. D. (2011). Do conscious thoughts cause behavior? *Annual Review of Psychology, 62*, 331–361.

Bayne, T., Hohwy, J., & Owen, A. M. (2018). Response to 'minimally conscious state or cortically mediated state?' *Brain: A Journal of Neurology, 141*, 1–2.

Beck, A. J., Harrison, P. M., & Guerino, P. (2010). *Sexual victimization in juvenile facilities reported by youth, 2008–09*. Washington, DC: Bureau of Justice Statistics.

Beck, A. T. (1976). *Cognitive therapy and emotional disorders*. New York: A Meridian Book.

Becker, A. E., & Kleinman, A. (2013). Mental health and the global agenda. *The New England Journal of Medicine, 369*, 66–73.

Belgrave, F. Z., & Allison, K. W. (2019). *African American psychology: From Africa to America*. Los Angeles, CA: Sage. 4th ed.

Bell, D. (1990). Poverty and women's mental health. *American Psychologist, 45*, 385–389.

Bellah, R. N., Madsen, R., Sullivan, W. M., Swidler, A., & Tipton, S. M. (1985). *Habits of the heart: Individualism and commitment in American life*. New York: Harper & Row.

Bennett, M., Dennett, D., Hacker, P., & Searle, J. (2007). *Neuroscience & philosophy: Brain, mind & language*. New York: Columbia University Press.

Bennett, M. R., & Hacker, P. M. S. (2003). *The philosophical foundations of neuroscience*. Oxford: Blackwell.

Bernal, G., Trimble, J. E., Burlew, A. K., & Leung, F. T. L. (Eds.) (2002). *Handbook of racial and ethnic minority psychology*. Los Angeles, CA: Sage.

Berns, G. S., Chappelow, J., Zin, C. F., et al. (2005). Neurobiological correlates of social conformity and independence during mental rotation. *Biological Psychiatry, 58*, 245–253.

Bertrand, M., & Morse, A. (2011). Information disclosure, cognitive biases, and payday borrowing. *Journal of Finance, 66*, 1865–1893.

Bertrand, M., & Mullainathan, S. (2004). Are Emily and Greg more employable than Lakisha and Jamal? A field experiment on labor market discrimination. *The American Economic Review, 94*, 991–1013.

Bhatia, S. (2018). *Decolonizing psychology: Globalization, social justice, and Indian youth identities*. New York: Oxford University Press.

Bhugra, D., Bhui, K., Yeung, S., Wong, S., & Gilman, S. E. (Eds.) (2018). *Oxford textbook of public mental health*. Oxford: Oxford University Press.

Biernat, M. (2012). Stereotypes and shifting standards: Forming, communicating, and translating person impressions. In P. Devine, & A. Plant (Eds.), *Advances in experimental social psychology* (vol. 45, pp. 1–59). New York: Academic Press.

Biernat, M., Fuegen, K., & Kobrynowicz, D. (2010). Shifting standards and the inference of incompetence: Effects of formal and informal evaluation tools. *Personality and Social Psychology Bulletin, 36*, 855–868.

Billig, M. (1976). *Social psychology and intergroup relations*. London: Academic Press.

Bishop, D. V. M. (2020). The psychology of experimental psychologists: Overcoming cognitive constraints to improve research: The 47th Sir Frederic Bartlett Lecture. *Quarterly Journal of Experimental Psychology, 73*, 1–19.

Bjerk, D. (2007). Measuring the relationship between youth criminal participation and household economic resources. *Journal of Quantitative Criminology, 23*, 23–39.

Bjorklund, D. F. (2018). Behavioral epigenetics: The last nail in the coffin of genetic determinism. *Human Development, 61*, 54–59.

Bjornsdottir, R. T., & Rule, N. O. (2017). The visibility of social class from facial cues. *Journal of Personality and Social Psychology, 113*, 530–546.

Blackey, R., & Paynton, C. T. (1976). *Revolution and the revolutionary ideal.* Cambridge, MA: Schenkman Publishing Co.

Blair, C., & Raver, C. C. (2016). Poverty, stress, and brain development: New directions for prevention and intervention. *Academic Pediatrics, 16*, S30–S36.

Blair, S. L., Blair, M. C. L., & Madamba, A. B. (1999). Racial/ethnic differences in high school students' academic performance: Understanding the interweave of social class and ethnicity in the family context. *Journal of Comparative Family Studies, 30*, 539–555.

Bobbio, A., Canova, L., & Manganelli, A. M. (2010). Conservative ideology, economic conservativism, and causal attributions for poverty and wealth. *Current Psychology, 29*, 222–234.

Bonilla-Silva, E. (2017). *Racism without racists: Color-blind racism and the persistence of racial inequality in America.* Rowman & Littlefield Publishers. 5th ed.

Bordens, K. S., & Abbott, B. B. (2008). *Research methods and design: A process approach.* New York: McGraw Hill.

Bordens, K. S., & Abbot, B. B. (2011). *Research design and methods: A process approach.* New York: McGraw Hill. 8th ed.

Borsboom, D., Cramer, A. O. J., & Kalis, A. (2019). Brain disorders? Not really: Why network structures block reductionism in psychopathology research. *Behavioral and Brain Sciences, 42*, 1–63.

Bowen, W., & Bok, D. (1998). *The shape of the river: Long-term consequences of consideration of race in college and university admissions.* Princeton, NJ: Princeton University Press.

Braun, M. N., Wessler, J., & Friese, M. (2021). A meta-analysis of Libet-style experiments. *Neuroscience and Biobehavioral Reviews, 128*, 182–198.

Breakspear, M. (2017). Dynamic models of large-scale brain activity. *Nature Neuroscience, 20*, 340–352.

Briggs, A. (1961). *A study of the work of Seebohm Rowntree, 1871–1954.* London: Longmans.

Brinton, C. (1965). *The anatomy of revolution.* New York: Vintage Books. 2nd ed. First published 1938.

Brito, N. H., Fifer, W. P., Myers, M. M., Elliot, A. J., & Noble, K. G. (2016). Associations among family socioeconomic status, EEG power at birth, and cognitive skills during infancy. *Developmental Cognitive Neuroscience, 19*, 144–151.

Brito, N. H., & Noble, K. G. (2018). The independent and interacting effects of socioeconomic status and dual-language use on brain structure and cognition. *Developmental Science, 21,* e12688

Brito, N. H., Piccolo, L. R., & Noble, K. G. (2017). Association between cortical thickness and neurocognitive skills during childhood vary by family socioeconomic factors. *Brain and Cognition, 116,* 54–62.

Brook, A., & Akins, K. (Eds.) (2005). *Cognition and the brain: The philosophy and neuroscience movement.* New York: Cambridge University Press.

Brook, A., & Akins, K. (Eds.) (2011). *Cognition and the brain: The philosophy and neuroscience movement.* New York: Cambridge University Press.

Brown, D. A. (2021). *The whiteness of wealth: How the tax system impoverishes Black Americans – and how we can fix it.* New York: Crown.

Brown, J. K. (2021). *Perversion of justice: The Jeffrey Epstein story.* New York: Dey Street Books.

Brown, L. S. (1997). Ethics in psychology: Cui bono? In D. Fox, & I. Prilleltensky (Eds.), *Critical psychology: An introduction* (pp. 51–67). Thousand Oaks, CA: Sage.

Brown, N. J. L., & Rohrer, J. M. (2020). Easy as (happiness) pie? A critical evaluation of a popular model of the determinants of well-being. *Journal of Happiness Studies, 21,* 1285–1301.

Brown, N. J. L., Sokal, A. D., & Friedman, H. L. (2014). The persistence of wishful thinking: Response to "updated thinking on positivity ratios." *American Psychologist, 69,* 629–632.

Brown, R., & McNeill, D. (1966). The "tip of the tongue" phenomenon. *Journal of Verbal Learning and Verbal Behavior, 5,* 325–337.

Brown-Iannuzzi, J. L., Lundberg, K. B., Kay, A. C., Payne, B. K. (2015). Subjective status shapes political preference. *Psychological Science, 26,* 15–26.

Brown-Iannuzzi, J. L., McKee, S. E. (2019). Economic inequalities and risk-taking behaviors. In J. Jetten, & K. Peters (Eds.), *The social psychology of inequality* (pp. 223–236). Cham, Switzerland: Springer Nature.

Bruijn, B. (2009). *The living conditions and well-being of refugees.* New York: United Nations Development Programme.

Bruner, J. S., & Goodman, C. C. (1947). Value and need as organizing factors in perception. *The Journal of Abnormal and Social Psychology, 42,* 33–44.

Buchmann, C., & DiPrete, T. A. (2006). The growing female advantage in college completion: The role of family background and academic achievement. *American Sociological Review, 71,* 515–541.

Bücker, J., Furrer, O., & Lin, Y. (2015). Measuring cultural intelligence: A new test of the CQ scale. *International Journal of Cross-Cultural Management, 15,* 259–284.

Buckley, P. F., Miller, B. J., Lehrer, D. S., & Castle, D. J. (2009). Psychiatric comorbidities and schizophrenia. *Schizophrenia Bulletin, 35,* 383–402.

Bullock, H. E. (2019). Psychology's contributions to understanding and alleviating poverty and economic inequality: Introduction to the special issue. *American Psychologist, 74,* 635–640.

Bullock, H. E., Wyche, K. F., & Williams, W. R. (2001). Media images of the poor. *Journal of Social Issues, 57,* 229–246.

Burger, J. M. (2009). Replicating Milgram: Would people still obey today? *American Psychologist, 64,* 1–11.

Burkhauser, R. V., Corinth, K., Elwell, J., & Larrimore, J. (2019). Evaluating the success of President Johnson's War on Poverty: Revisiting the historical record using a full-income poverty measure. IZA Institute of Labor Economics, Discussion Paper Series IZA DP No. 12855. http://ftp.iza.org/dp12855.pdf

Byard, R. W. (2013). Frontal lobotomy. *Forensic Science, 13,* 259–264.

Cafiero, C., Viviani, S., & Nord, M. (2018). Food security measurement in a global context: The food insecurity experience scale. *Measurement, 116,* 146–152.

Cain, D. J. (2002). *Humanistic psychotherapies: Handbook of research and practice.* Washington, DC: American Psychological Association Press.

Calvin, C. M., Deary, I. J., Webbink, D., et al. (2012). Multivariate genetic analysis of cognition and academic achievement from two population samples of 174,000 and 166,000 school children. *Behavioral Genetics, 42,* 699–710.

Cambridge, J., Witton, J., & Elbourne, D. R. (2014). Systematic review of the Hawthorne effect: New concepts are needed to study research participation effect. *Journal of Clinical Epidemiology, 67,* 267–277.

Campbell, M. C., Vogel, M., & Williams, J. (2015). Historical contingencies and the evolving importance of race, violent crime, and region in explaining mass incarceration in the United States. *Criminology, 53,* 180–203.

Campbell, S., & Moghaddam, F. M. (2018). Social engineering and its discontents: The case of the Russian Revolution. In B. Wagoner, F. M. Moghaddam, & J. Valsiner (Eds.), *The psychology of radical social change* (pp. 147–171). Cambridge, UK: Cambridge University Press.

Candland, D. K. (1993). *Feral children and clever animals: Reflections on human nature.* New York: Oxford University Press.

Carnevale, A. P., & Rose, S. J. (2003). *Socioeconomic status, race/ethnicity, and selective college admissions.* New York: The Century Foundation.

Carnevale, A. P., & Strohl, J. (2013). Separate & unequal: How higher education reinforces the intergenerational reproduction of White racial privilege. Georgetown Public Policy Institute. https://cew.georgetown.edu/wp-content/uploads/SeparateUnequal.FR_.pdf

Carr, S. C., & Sloan, T. S. (Eds.) (2003). *Poverty and psychology: From global perspective to local practice.* New York: Plenum.

Carriere, K. R., Garney, G., & Moghaddam, F. M. (2018). Terrorism as a form of violence. In A. T. Vazsonyi, D. Flannery, & M. DeLisi (Eds.), *The Cambridge Handbook of Violent Behavior and Aggression.* 2nd ed. (pp. 54–85). Cambridge, UK: Cambridge University Press.

Carroll, W. K. (2010). *The making of a transnational capitalist class: Corporate power in the 21st century.* London: Zen Books.

Carson, E. A. (2018). Prisoners in 2016. U.S. Department of Justice, Office of Justice Programs, Bureau of Justice Statistics. Updated August 7, 2018. www.bjs.gov/content/pub/pdf/p16.pdf.

Carson, E. A., & Golinelli, D. (2013). Prisoners in 2012: Trends in admissions and releases, 1991–2012. U.S. Department of Justice, Office of Justice Programs, Bureau of Justice Statistics NCJ 243920 (Revised September 2, 2014). www.bjs .gov/content/pub/pdf/p12tar9112.pdf

Carvalho, L. S., Meier, S., & Wang, S. W. (2016). Poverty and economic decision-making: Evidence from changes in financial resources at payday. *American Economic Review, 106,* 260–284.

Case, A., & Deaton, D. (2015). Rising morbidity and mortality in midlife among White non-Hispanic Americans in the 21st century. *Proceedings of the National Academy of Science, 112,* 15078–15083.

Cattell, R. B. (1963). Theory of fluid and crystalized intelligence: A critical experiment. *Journal of Educational Psychology, 54,* 1–22.

Cep, C. (2019). The perfecter: A new biography of Thomas Edison recalibrates our understanding of the inventor's genius. *The New Yorker,* October 28, 72–77.

Chalmers, D. (1995). Facing up to the hard problem of consciousness. *Journal of Consciousness Studies, 2,* 200–219.

Chaplin, L. N., Hill, R. P., & John, D. R. (2014). Poverty and materialism: A look at impoverished versus affluent children. *Journal of Public Policy & Marketing, 33,* 78–92.

Charles, S. T., Piazza, J. R., Mogle, J., Sliwinski, M. J., & Almeida, D. M. (2013). The wear and tear of daily stressors on mental health. *Psychological Science, 24,* 733–741.

Chen, Y., Rajabifard, A., Sabri, S., et al. (2020). A discussion of irrational stockpiling behaviour during crisis. *Journal of Safety Science and Resilience, 1,* 57–58.

Chetty, R., Friedman, J. N., Saez, E., Turner, N., Yagan, D. (2020). Income segregation and intergenerational mobility across colleges in the United States. *Quarterly Journal of Economics,* qjaa005. DOI: 10.1093/qje/qjaa005

Chetty, R., Grusky, D., Hell, M., et al. (2017). The fading American Dream: Trends in absolute income mobility since 1940. *Science, 356,* 398–406.

Chetty, R., Stepner, M., Abraham, S., et al. (2016). Mechanisms of deep brain stimulation: Inhibition, excitation, or disruption? *The Neuroscientist, 22,* 313–322.

Chokshi, N. (2019). The New York Times just won 2 Pulitzers. *The New York Times,* April 15, 2019. www.nytimes.com/2019/04/15/business/media/nyt-pulitzer-prize-winners.html

Chomsky, N. (1959). Review of verbal learning by B. F. Skinner. *Language, 35,* 26–58.

Choy, O., Raine, A., Venables, P. H., & Farrington, D. P. (2017). Explaining the gender gap in crime: The role of heart rate. *Criminology, 55,* 465–487.

Cicchetti, D., & Blender, J. (2006). A multiple-levels-of-analysis perspective on resilience. *Annals of the New York Academy of Sciences, 1094,* 248–258.

Clark, R. E., & Clark, V. P. (2010). From neo-behaviorism to neuroscience: Perspectives on the origins and future contributions of cognitive load research. In J. L. Plass, R. Moreno, & R. Brünken (Eds.), *Cognitive load theory* (pp. 203–228). New York: Cambridge University Press.

Clemens, M. A., & Kremer, M. (2016). The new role for the World Bank. *Journal of Economic Perspectives, 30*, 53–76.

Cobbinah, P. B., Erdiaw-Kwasie, M. O., & Amoateng, P. (2015). Rethinking sustainable development within the framework of poverty and urbanization in developing countries. *Environmental Development, 13*, 18–32.

Cohen, A. (2016). *Imbeciles: The Supreme Court, American eugenics, and the sterilization of Carrie Buck.* New York: Penguin.

Cohen, P., & Casselman, B. (2020). Minority workers who lagged in boom are hit hard in a bust. *The New York Times*, June 6. www.nytimes.com/2020/06/06/business/economy/jobs-report-minorities.html?campaign_id=2&emc=edit_th_200606&instance_id=19107&nl=todaysheadlines&regi_id=42059253&segment_id=30245&user_id=e17ed0d9553b6a3f9d56c23c39898150

Cohen-Chen, S., & van Zomeren, M. (2018). Yes you can? Group efficacy beliefs predict collective action, but only when hope is high. *Journal of Experimental Social Psychology, 77*, 50–59.

Collins, P. H., & Bilge, S. (2016). *Intersectionality.* Oxford: Polity Press.

Collins, S. (2017). Social workers and resilience revisited. *Social Work in Action, 29*, 85–105.

Comas-Diaz, L., & Torres Rivera, E. (Eds.) (2020). *Liberation psychology: Theory, method, and social justice.* Washington, DC: American Psychological Association Press.

Comer, R. J., & Comer, J. S. (2019). *Fundamentals of abnormal psychology.* New York: Macmillan Learning. 9th ed.

Conley, D. (2001). Parental assets and postsecondary education. *Sociology of Education, 74*, 59–72.

Cook, J. T., Frank, D. A., Levenson, S. M., et al. (2006). Child food insecurity increases risks posed by household food insecurity to young children's health. *The Journal of Nutrition, 136*, 1073–1076.

Costandi, M. (2016). *Neuroplasticity.* Boston, MA: MIT Press.

Cozzarelli, C., Wilkinson, A. V., & Tagler, M. J. (2001). Attitudes toward the poor and attributions of poverty. *Journal of Social Issues, 57*, 207–227.

Croizet, J. C., & Claire, T. (1998). Extending the concept of stereotype threat to social class: The intellectual underperformance of students from low socioeconomic backgrounds. *Personality and Social Psychology Bulletin, 24*, 588–594.

Croizet, J. C., & Millet, M. (2011). Social class and test performance: From stereotype threat to symbolic violence and vice-versa. In M. Inzlicht, & T. Schmader (Eds.), *Stereotype threat: Theory, process and application (pp. 188–201).* New York: Oxford University Press.

Cullen, F. T., Jonson, C. L., & Nagin, D. S. (2011). Prisons do not reduce recidivism: The high cost of ignoring science. *The Prison Journal, 91*, 48S–65S.

Cunningham, R. (2016). *Neuroplasticity: The brain's way of healing: Ultimate guide to using your brain plasticity and rewiring your brain for change.* New York: CreateSpace.

Cusick, S. E., & Georgieff, M. K. (2016). The role of nutrition in brain development: The golden opportunity of the "first 1000 days." *Journal of Pediatrics, 175,* 16–21.

Cutler, D. (2016). The association between income and life expectancy in the United States, 2001–2014. *The Journal of the American Medical Association, 315,* 1750–1766.

Dalton, P. S., Ghosal, S., & Mani, A. (2014). Poverty and aspirations failure. *The Economic Journal, 126,* 165–188.

Daniels, G. R. (2020). *Uncounted: The crisis of voter suppression in America.* New York: New York University Press.

Danziger, K. (1990). *Constructing the subject: Historical origins of psychological research.* Cambridge, UK: Cambridge University Press.

Dattilio, F. M., & Norcross, J. C. (2006). Psychotherapy integration and the emergence of instinctual territoriality. *Archives of Psychiatry and Psychotherapy, 8,* 5–16.

Davidai, S., & Gilovich, T. (2018). How should we think about Americans' beliefs about economic mobility? *Judgment and Decision Making, 13,* 297–304.

Davies, J. C. (1962). Toward a theory of revolution. *American Sociological Review, 27,* 5–19.

Day, M. V., & Fiske, S. T. (2017). Movin' on up? How perceptions of social mobility affect our willingness to defend the system. *Social Psychology and Personality Science, 8,* 267–274.

De Carvalho, C., & Pinto, M. (2018). Refugee camp as an immediate solution: Response and its psychological meaning. *Peace and Conflict: Journal of Peace Psychology, 24,* 277–282.

De Carvalho, G. P., & Bantim, Y. C. V. (2019). Inmates beheaded in a Brazil prison riot: Human identification by ear individual signs. *Journal of Forensic and Legal Medicine, 68,* 101870.

De Costa, L. P., & Dias, J. G. (2014). Perceptions of poverty attributions in Europe: A multilevel mixture model approach. *Quality & Quantity, 48,* 1409–1419.

Deck, C., & Jahedi, S. (2015). The effect of cognitive load on economic decision making: A survey and new experiments. *European Economic Review, 78,* 97–119.

Dehaene, S., Lau, H., & Koulder, S. (2017). What is consciousness, and could machines have it? *Science, 358,* 486–492.

DeLisi, M., Drury, A. J., Kosloski, A. E., et al. (2010). The cycle of violence behind bars: Traumatization and institutional misconduct among juvenile delinquents in confinement. *Youth Violence and Juvenile Justice, 8,* 107–121.

Dennett, D. C. (2018). Facing up to the hard question of consciousness. *Philosophical Transactions Royal Society B, 373,* 20170342. DOI: 10.1098/rstb.2017.0342

Denny, B. T., Inhoff, M. C., Zerubavel, N., Davachi, L., & Ochsner, K. N. (2015). Getting over it: Long-lasting effects of emotion regulation on amygdala response. *Psychological Science, 26,* 1377–1388.

Derringer, J. (2018). Personality genetics. In C. Johansen (Ed.), *Personality and disease: Scientific proof vs. wishful thinking* (pp. 185–203). Cambridge, MA: Academic press.

Derubeis, R. J., & Lorenzo-Luaces, L. (2017). Recognizing that truth is unattainable and attending to the most informative research evidence. *Psychotherapy Research, 27*, 33–35.

De Silva, D. (2013). The use of child soldiers in war with special reference to Sri Lanka. *Paediatrics and International Child Health, 33*, 273–280.

Dey, N., Hassanien, A. E., Bhatt, C., Ashour, A. S., & Satapathy, S. C. (2018). *Internet of things and big data analytics toward next-generation intelligence.* New York: Springer.

Dhongde, S., & Minoiu, C. (2013). Global poverty estimates: A sensitivity analysis. *World Development, 44*, 1–13.

Dickens, C. (1957). *Oliver Twist.* New York: Washington Square Press. First published 1837.

Dickens, C. (1970). *Bleak House.* New York: Holt, Rinehart and Winston. First published in book form 1853.

Diener, E., & Seligman, M. E. P. (2004). Beyond money: Toward an economy of well-being. *Psychological Science in the Public Interest, 5*, 1–31.

Diener, E., Diener, C., Choi, H., & Oishi, S. (2017). Revisiting "most people are happy" – and discovering when they are not. *Perspectives on Psychological Science, 13*, 166–170.

Diener, E., Seligman, M. E. P., Choi, H., & Oishi, S. (2017). Happiest people revisited. *Perspectives in Psychological Science, 13*, 176–184.

Dierkhising, C. B., Lane, A., & Natsuaki, M. N. (2014). Victims behind bars: A preliminary study of abuse during juvenile incarceration and post-release social and emotional functioning. *Psychology, Public Policy and Law, 20*, 181–190.

Dinsa, G. D., Goryakin, Y., Fumagalli, E., & Suhrcke, M. (2012). Obesity and socioeconomic status in developing countries: A systematic review. *Obesity, 13*, 1067–1079.

DiPrete, T. A., & Buchmann, C. (2014). *The growing gender gap in education and what it means for American schools.* New York: Russell Sage Foundation.

Dobson, D., & Dobson, K. S. (2017). *Evidence-based practice of cognitive-behavioral therapy.* New York: The Guilford Press. 2nd ed.

Doerig, A., Schurger, A., Hess, K., & Herzog, M. H. (2019). The unfolding argument: Why IIT and other causal structure theories cannot explain consciousness. *Consciousness and Cognition, 72*, 49–59.

Dondero, M., & Humphries, M. (2016). Planning for the American Dream: The college-savings behavior of Asian and Latino foreign-born parents in the United States. *Population Research Policy Review, 35*, 791–823.

Dorling, D. (2014). *Inequality and the 1%.* London: Verso.

Dost-Gozkan, A., & D. Sonmez Keith (Eds.) (2015). *Norms, groups, conflict, and social change: Rediscovering Mozafer Sherif's psychology.* London: Transaction Publishers.

Dower, J. W. (2000). *Embracing defeat: Japan in the wake of World War II.* New York: Dover.

Drury, J., Carter, H., Cocking, C., et al. (2019). Facilitating collective psychosocial resilience in the public in emergencies: Twelve recommendations based on the social identity approach. *Frontiers in Public Health, 7,* 141. DOI: 10.3389/fpubh.2019.00141

Dumond, R. W. (2000). Intimate sexual assault: The plague that persists. *The Prison Journal, 80,* 407–414.

Duncan, G. J., Kalil, A., & Ziol-Guest, K. M. (2017). Increasing inequality in parental incomes and children's schooling. *Demography, 54,* 1603–1626.

Duncan, G. J., Magnuson, K., & Votruba-Drzal, E. (2015). Children and socioeconomic status. In M. H. Bornstein, T Leventhal, & R. M. Lerner (Eds.), *Handbook of child psychology and developmental science, Volume 4: Ecological settings and processes* (pp. 534–573). Hoboken, NJ: Wiley. 7th ed.

Dunstan, R., & Moghaddam, F. M. (2016). Causation in introductory psychology texts. In R. Harré, & F. M. Moghaddam (Eds.), *Questioning causality: Scientific explorations of cause and consequence across social contexts* (pp. 53–65). Santa Barbara, CA: Praeger.

Dupas, P. (2011). Health behavior in developing countries. *Annual Review of Economics, 3,* 425–429.

Durante, F., & Fiske, S. T. (2017). How social-class stereotypes maintain inequality. *Current Opinions in Psychology, 18,* 43–48.

Durante, F., Tablante, C. B., & Fiske, S. T. (2017). Poor but warm, rich but cold (and competent): Social classes in the stereotype content model. *Journal of Social Issues, 73,* 138–157.

Durkheim, E. (1953). *Sociology and philosophy* (Trans. D. F. Pocock). New York: The Free Press.

Durose, M. R., Cooper, A. D., & Snyder, H. N. (2014). *Recidivism of prisoners released in 30 states in 2005: Patterns from 2005 to 2010.* Washington, DC: Department of Justice Statistics. https://bjs.gov/content/pub/pdf/rprts05p0510.pdf

Dyer, J. (2000). *The perpetual prisoner machine: How America profits from crime.* Boulder, CO: Westview Press.

Earley, P. C. (1989). Social loafing and collectivism: A comparison of the United States and the People's Republic of China. *Administrative Science Quarterly, 34,* 565–581.

Eason, J. (2010). Mapping prison proliferation: Region, rurality, race and disadvantage. *Social Science Research, 39,* 1015–1028.

Easterbrook, M., Hadden, I., & Nieuwenhuis, M. (2019). Identities in social context: How social class shapes inequalities in education. In J. Jetten, & K. Peters (Eds.), *The social psychology of inequality* (pp. 120–140). Cham, Switzerland: Springer Nature.

Easterlin, R. (1974). Does economic growth improve the human lot? Some empirical evidence. In P. A. David, & M. W. Reder (Eds.), *Nations and households in economic growth: Essays in honor of Moses Abramowitz* (pp. 89–125). New York: Academic Press.

Eaton, J., McCay, L., Semrau, M., et al. (2011). Scale up of services for mental health in low-income and middle-income countries. *The Lancet, 378,* 1592–1603.

Edin, K. J., & Shaefer, H. L. (2015). *$2.00 a day: Living on almost nothing in America.* New York: Houghton, Mifflin, Harcourt.

Ehrenreich, B. (2010). *Bright-sided: How positive thinking is undermining America.* New York: Metropolitan Books.

Ehrenreich, B. (2011). *Nickel and dimed: On (not) getting by in America.* New York: Henry Holt.

Eiser, L. B. (2017). *Inside private prisons: An American dilemma in the age of mass incarceration.* New York: Columbia University Press.

Elcheroth, G., & Drury, J. (2020). Collective resilience in times of crisis: Lessons from the literature for socially effective responses to the pandemic. *British Journal of Social Psychology, 59,* 703–713.

Ellen, I. G., Lacoe, J., & Sharygin, C. A. (2013). Do foreclosures cause crime? *Journal of Urban Economics, 74,* 59–70.

Elliott, A. (2003). *Critical visions: New directions in social theory.* London: Routledge.

Ellis, C. (2017). *Putting inequality in context: Class, political opinion, and representation in the United States.* Ann Arbor, MI: University of Michigan Press.

Engelhardt, L. E., Mann, F. D., Briley, D. A., et al. (2016). Strong genetic overlap between executive functions and intelligence. *Journal of Experimental Psychology: General. 145,* 1141–1159.

Evans, D. M., & Martin, N. G. (2000). The validity of twin studies. *GeneScreen, 1,* 77–79.

Ewert, S., Sykes, B. L., & Pettit, B. (2014). The degree of disadvantage: Incarceration and inequality in education. *The ANNALS of the American Academy of Political and Social Science, 651,* 24–43.

Fancher, R. E. (1983). Biographical origins of Francis Galton's psychology. *Isis. 74,* 227–233.

Farah, M. J. (2018). Socioeconomic status and the brain: Prospects for neuroscience-informed policy. *Nature Reviews Neuroscience, 19,* 428–438.

Fast, N. J., Sivanathan, N., Meyer, N. D., & Galinsky, A. D. (2012). Power and over-confident decision-making. *Organizational Behavior and Human Decision Making, 117,* 249–260.

Fazel, S., & Wolf, A. (2015). A systematic review of criminal recidivism rates worldwide: Current difficulties and recommendations for best practice. *PloS ONE, 10/6,* e0130390. DOI: 10.1371/journal.pone.0130390

Feist, G. J., & Rosenberg, E. L. (2010). *Psychology: Making connections.* New York: McGraw Hill.

Figes, O. (2002). *Natasha's dance: A cultural history of Russia.* New York: Henry Holt.

Finkelstein, A., Taubman, S., Wright, B., et al. (2012). The Oregon health insurance experiment: Evidence from the first year. *The Quarterly Journal of Economics, 127,* 1057–1106.

Frith, C. D. (2019). The neural basis of consciousness. *Psychological Medicine, 51,* 550–562. DOI: 10.1017/S0033291719002204

Fischer, R., Lee, A., & Verzijden, M. N. (2018). Dopamine genes are linked to extraversion and neuroticism personality traits, but only in demanding climates. *Scientific Reports, 8*, 1733. DOI:10.1038/s41598-017-18784-y

Fishbein, M., & Ajzen, I. (1975). *Belief, attitude, intention, and behavior: An introduction to theory and research.* Reading, MA: Addison-Wesley.

Fiske, S. T. (2015). Grolar bears, social class, and policy relevance: Extraordinary agendas for the emerging 21st century. *European Journal of Social Psychology, 45*, 551–559.

Fiske, S. T. (2019). Political cognition helps explain social class divides: Two dimensions of candidate impressions, group stereotypes, and meritocratic beliefs. *Cognition, 188*, 108–115.

Fiske, S. T., Dupree, C. H., Nicolas, G., & Swencionis, J. K. (2018). Status, power, and intergroup relations: The personal is the societal. *Current Opinions in Psychology, 11*, 44–48.

Fiske, S. T., & Markus, H. (Eds.) (2012). *Facing social class: How societal rank influences interaction.* New York: Russell Sage Foundation.

Fitzgerald, S. (1925). *The great Gatsby.* New York: Charles Scribner's Sons.

Flanagan, D. P., & McDonough, E. M. (Eds.) (2018). *Contemporary intellectual assessment: Theories, tests, and issues.* New York: The Guilford Press. 4th ed.

Flynn, J. R. (2007). *What is intelligence? Beyond the Flynn effect.* Cambridge, UK: Cambridge University Press.

Flynn, J. R. (2013). *Intelligence and human progress: The story of what was hidden in our genes.* New York: Academic Press.

Foster, H., & Hagan, J. (2015). Punishment regimes and the multilevel effects of parental incarceration: Intergenerational, intersectional, and interinstitutional models of social inequality and systemic exclusion. *Annual Review of Sociology, 41*, 135–158.

Foucault, M. (1995). *Discipline and punish: The birth of the prison* (Trans. A. Sheridan). New York: Vintage Books. Originally published 1975.

Fox, D., & Prilleltensky, I. (Eds.) (2007). *Handbook of critical psychology.* Newbury Park, CA: Sage.

Fox, S. E., Levitt, P., & Nelson III, C. A. (2010). How the quality and timing of early experiences influence the development of brain structure. *Child Development, 81*, 28–40.

Francis, G. (2012). The psychology of replication and replication in psychology. *Perspectives on Psychological Science, 7*, 585–594.

Franco, J. N. (1985). Intelligence tests and social policy. *Journal of Counselling & Development, 64*, 278–279.

Franklin, T. W. (2017). Sentencing outcomes in U.S. district courts: Can offenders' educational attainment guard against prevalent criminal stereotypes? *Crime & Delinquency, 63*, 137–165.

Frawley, A. (2015). Happiness research: A review of critiques. *Sociology Compass, 9*, 62–77.

Freeman, R. (1996). Why do so many young American men commit crimes and what might we do about it? *Journal of Economic Perspectives, 10*, 25–42.

Freire, P. (2018). *Pedagogy of the oppressed (50th anniversary edition)*. New York: Bloomsbury Academic.

Frey, B. S., & Gallus, J. (2013). Political economy of happiness. *Journal of Applied Economics, 45*, 4205–4211.

Frey, M. C., & Detterman, D. K. (2004). Scholastic assessment or *g*? The relationship between Scholastic Assessment Test and general cognitive ability. *Psychological Science, 15*, 373–378.

Friedman, M., & Rosenman, R. H. (1959). Association of specific overt behavior pattern with blood and cardiovascular findings: Blood cholesterol, blood clotting time, incidence of arcus senilis, and clinical coronary artery disease. *Journal of the American Medical Association, 169*, 1286–1296.

Frierson, H. T., Pearson, W. Jr., & Wyche, J. H. (Eds.) (2009). *Black American males in higher education: Diminishing proportions*. Bingley, UK: Emerald Group Publishing.

Fryers, T., Melzer, D., Jenkins, R., & Brugha, T. (2005). The distribution of common mental disorders: Social inequalities in Europe. *Clinical Practice & Epidemiology in Mental Health, 1*, 14.

Funder, D. C. (2019). *The personality puzzle*. New York: W. W. Norton. 8th ed.

Funk, M., Drew, N., & Knapp, M. (2012). Mental health, poverty and development. *Journal of Public Mental Health, 11*, 166–185.

Gable, S., & Haidt, J. (2005). What (and why) is positive psychology? *Review of General Psychology, 9*, 103–110.

Gaes, G. G. (2019). Current status of prison privatization research on American prisons and jails. *Criminology & Public Policy, 18*, 269–293.

Galton, F. (1869). *Hereditary genius: An inquiry into its laws and consequences*. London: Macmillan and Co. (second edition 1892).

Galton, F. (1883). *Inquiries into human faculty and its development*. London: Macmillan and Co. (second edition 1892).

Gandini, A. (2018). Labour process theory and the gig economy. *Human Relations*. DOI: 10.1177/0018726718790002

Garcia, N. M., Lopez, N., & Velez, V. N. (2018). QuantCrit: Rectifying quantitative methods through critical race theory. *Race, Ethnicity and Education, 21*, 149–157.

Gardner, H. (2004). *Frames of mind: The theory of multiple intelligences in the 21st century*. New York: Basic Books.

Garrett, P. M. (2016). Questioning tales of "ordinary magic": "Resilience" and neo-liberal reasoning. *British Journal of Social Work, 46*, 1909–1925.

Geller, A., Garfinkel, I., Cooper, C. E., & Mincey, R. B. (2009). Parental incarceration and child well-being: Implications for urban families. *Social Science Quarterly, 90*, 1186–1202.

Gerdner, T. L. (2017). *The disciplined, resilient child: 21 tips to get your child to be respectful, responsible, and resilient for a successful future*. New York: Tru Nobilis Publishing.

Gergen, K. J. (1974). Social psychology as history. *Journal of Personality and Social Psychology, 26*, 309–320.

Gest, J. (2016). *The new minority: White working class politics in an age of immigration and inequality.* New York: Oxford University Press.

Gillath, O., Bahns, A. J., Ge, F., & Crandall, C. S. (2012). Shoes as a source of first impressions. *Journal of Research on Personality, 46,* 423–430.

Gillmeister, H. (2017). *Tennis: A cultural history.* Sheffield/Bristol, UK: Equinox.

Godfrey, E. B., & Wolf, S. (2016). Developing critical consciousness or justifying the system? A qualitative analysis of attributions for poverty and wealth among low-income racial/ethnic minority and immigrant women. *Cultural Diversity & Ethnic Minority Psychology, 22,* 93–103.

Goldberg, E. M., & Morrison, S. L. (1963). *Schizophrenia and social class. British Journal of Psychiatry, 109,* 785–802.

Goldrick-Rab, S., & Pfeffer, F. T. (2009). Beyond access: Explaining socioeconomic differences in college transfer. *Sociology of Education, 82,* 101–125.

Goldstein, S., & Brooks, R. B. (2013a). Why study resilience? In S. Goldstein, & R. B. Brooks (Eds.), *Handbook of resilience in children* (pp. 3–14). New York: Springer.

Goldstein, S., & Brooks, R. B. (Eds.) (2013b), *Handbook of resilience in children* (pp. 3–14). New York: Springer.

González-Pardo, H., & Pérez-Álvarez, M. (2013). Epigenetics and its implications for psychology. *Psychothema, 25,* 3–12.

Goodwin, C. J. (2015). *A history of modern psychology.* New York: Wiley. 5th ed.

Goriounova, N. A., & Mansvelder, H. D. (2019). Genes, cells and brain areas of intelligence. *Frontiers in Human Neuroscience, 13,* Article 44. DOI: 10.3389/fnhum.2019.00044

Gorman, T. J. (2017). *Growing up working class: Hidden injuries and the development of angry white men and women.* New York: Palgrave Macmillan.

Gorski, P. C. (2012). Perceiving the problem of poverty and schooling: Deconstructing the class stereotypes that mis-shape education practice and policy. *Journal of Equity & Excellence in Education, 45,* 302–319.

Götmark, F., & Andersson, M. (2020). Human fertility in relation to education, economy, religion, contraception, and family planning programs. *BMC Public Health, 20,* 265. DOI: 10.1186/s12889-020-8331-7

Gøtzsche, P. C., Young, A. H., & Crace, J. (2015). Does long term use of psychiatric drugs cause more harm than good? *BMJ (Clinical research ed.), 350,* h2435. DOI:10.1136/bmj.h2435

Gould, E. (2012). U.S. lags behind peer countries in mobility. Economic Policy Institute. www.epi.org/publication/usa-lags-peer-countries-mobility/

Gould, S. J. (1996). *The mismeasure of man.* New York: Norton.

Graham, G. (2017). Behaviorism. In E. N. Zalta (Ed.), *The Stanford encyclopedia of philosophy* (Spring edition). https://plato.stanford.edu/archives/spr2017/entries/behaviorism

Graif, C., Gladfelter, A. S., & Mathews, S. A. (2014). Urban poverty and neighborhood effects on crime: Incorporating spatial and network perspectives. *Sociological Compass, 8,* 1140–1155.

Grant, B. (2017). Tokenism. In F. M. Moghaddam (Ed.), *The Sage encyclopedia of political behavior* (vol. 2, pp. 834–837). Los Angeles, CA: Sage.

Grasso, M. T., Yoxon B., Karampampas, S., & Temple, L. (2019). Relative deprivation and inequalities in social and political activism. *Acta Politica, 54,* 398–429.

Greenbaum, S. D. (2015). *Blaming the poor: The long shadow of the Moynihan Report on cruel images about poverty.* New Brunswick, NJ: Rutgers University Press.

Greitemeyer, T., & Sagioglou, C. (2017). Increasing wealth inequality may increase interpersonal hostility: The relationship between personal relative deprivation and aggression. *The Journal of Social Psychology, 157,* 766–776.

Grey, A. L. (Ed.) (1969). *Class and personality in society.* London: Routledge.

Grifflin, K. A. (2019). Redoubling our efforts: How institutions can affect faculty diversity. American Council on Education (ACE). www.equityinhighered.org/resources/ideas-and-insights/redoubling-our-efforts-how-institutions-can-affect-faculty-diversity/

Grisold, A., & Theine, H. (2017). How come we know? The media coverage of economic inequality. *International Journal of Communication, 11,* 4265–4284.

Grossi, G. (2017). Hardwiring: Innateness in the age of the brain. *Biology & Philosophy, 32,* 1047–1082.

Gurr, T. (1970). *Why men rebel.* Princeton, NJ: Princeton University Press.

Guthrie, R. V. (2003). *Even the rat was white: A historical view of psychology.* New York: Pearson. 2nd ed.

Hacker, P. M. S. (2012). The brain and consciousness. In R. Harré, & F. M. Moghaddam (Eds.), *Psychology for the third millennium: Integrating cultural and neuroscience perspectives.* (pp. 57–74). Los Angeles, CA: Sage.

Haier, R. J. (2016). *The neuroscience of intelligence.* New York: Cambridge University Press.

Hall, C. C., Zhao, J., & Shafir, E. (2014). Self-affirmation among the poor: Cognitive and behavioral implications. *Psychological Science, 25,* 615–625.

Hall, G. C. N. (2018). *Multicultural psychology.* New York: Routledge.

Han, J. (2018). Who goes to college, military, prison or long-term unemployment? Racialized school-to-labor market transitions among American men. *Population Research and Policy Review, 37,* 615–640.

Hancock, A. M. (2004). *The politics of disgust: The public identity of the Welfare Queen.* New York: New York University Press.

Haney, C. (2018). Restricting the use of solitary confinement. *Annual Review of Criminology, 1,* 285–310.

Hare-Mustin, R. T., & Marecek, J. (1997). Abnormal and clinical psychology: The politics of madness. In D. Fox, & I. Prilleltensky (Eds.), *Critical psychology: An introduction* (pp. 104–120). Thousand Oaks, CA: Sage.

Harlow, H. F., & Harlow, M. K. (1969). Effects of various mother-infant relationships on rhesus monkey behaviors. In B. M. Foss (Ed.), *Determinants of infant behavior* (vol. 4, pp. 15–35). London: Methuen.

Harré, R. (2002). *Cognitive science: A philosophical introduction.* Thousand Oaks, CA: Sage.

Harré, R. (2018). Foreword. In B. Wagoner, F. M. Moghaddam, & J. Valsiner (Eds.), *The psychology of radical social change: From rage to revolution* (pp. xi–xiv). Cambridge, UK: Cambridge University Press.

Harré, R., & Moghaddam, F. M. (Eds.) (2003). *The self and others: Positioning individuals and groups in personal, organizational, political, and cultural contexts.* Westport, CT: Praeger.

Harré, R., & Moghaddam, F. M. (2012). *Psychology for the third millennium: Integrating cultural and neuroscience perspectives.* Los Angeles, CA: Sage.

Harré, R., & Moghaddam, F. M. (Eds.) (2016). *Questioning causality: Scientific explorations of cause and consequence across social contexts.* Santa Barbara, CA: Praeger.

Harré, R., Moghaddam, F. M., Pilkerton-Cairnie, T., Rothbart, D., & Sabat, S. (2009). Recent advances in positioning theory. *Theory & Psychology, 19,* 5–31.

Harris, S. (2012). *Free will.* New York: Free Press.

Harrison, L. A., Stevens, C. M., Monty, A. N., & Coakley, C. A. (2006). The consequences of stereotype threat on the academic performance of White and non-White lower income college students. *Social Psychology of Education, 9,* 341–357.

Haskins, A. R. (2014). Unintended consequences: Effects of paternal incarceration on child school readiness and later special education placement. *Sociological Science, 1,* 141–158.

Haslam, C., Jetten, J., Cruwys, T., Dingle, G. A., & Haslam, A. (2018). *The new psychology of health: Unlocking the social cure.* London: Routledge.

Haslam, N., & Kashima, Y. (2010). The rise and rise of social psychology in Asia: A bibliometric analysis. *Asian Journal of Social Psychology, 13,* 202–207.

Haslam, S. A. (2004). *Psychology in organizations: The social identity approach.* London: Sage.

Haslam, S. A., & McGarty, C. (2014). Research methods and statistics in psychology. Los Angeles, CA: Sage. 2nd ed.

Haushofer, J., & Fehr, E. (2014). On the psychology of poverty. *Science, 344,* 862–867.

Haushofer, J., & Shapiro, J. (2016). The short-term impact of unconditional cash transfers to the poor: Experimental evidence from Kenya. *The Quarterly Journal of Economics, 131,* 1973–2042.

Hausmann, L. R. M., Levine, J. M., & Higgins, E. T. (2008). Communication and group perception: Extending the "saying is believing" effect. *Group Processes & Intergroup Relations, 11,* 539–554.

Hawi, D., Osborne, D., Bulbulia, J., & Sibley, C. G. (2019). Terrorism anxiety and attitudes toward Muslims. *New Zealand Journal of Psychology, 48,* 80–89.

Hayden, E. C. (2013). Taboo genetics. *Nature, 502,* 26–28.

Headey, B. (2019). Wealth influences life satisfaction more than income: A supplement to the Easterlin Paradox. In G. Brulé, & C. Surer (Eds.), *Wealth(s) and subjective well-being* (pp. 167–182). Basingstoke, UK: Springer.

Hearnshaw, L. S. (1974). *Cyril Burt: Psychologist.* Ithaca, NY: Cornell University Press.

Heberle, A. E., & Carter, A. S. (2015). Cognitive aspects of young children's experience of economic disadvantage. *Psychological Bulletin, 141*, 723–746.

Helgeson, V. S. (2016). *Psychology of gender*. New York: Routledge.

Heller, S. B., Jacob, B. A., & Ludwig, J. (2011). Family income, neighborhood poverty, and crime. In P. J. Cook, J. Ludwig, & J. McCrary (Eds.), *Controlling crime: Strategies and tradeoffs* (pp. 419–459). Chicago, IL: University of Chicago Press.

Helliwell, J., Layard, R., & Sachs, J. (2013). *World happiness report*. New York: UN Sustainable Development Solutions Network.

Henrich, J., Heine, S. J., & Norenzayan, A. (2010). The weirdest people in the world. *Behavioral and Brain Sciences, 33*, 61–135.

Herrnstein, R. J., & Murray, C. (1994). *The bell curve: Intelligence and class structure in American life*. New York: Free Press.

Hertz, T., Jayasundera, T., Piraino, P., et al. (2007). The inheritance of educational inequality: International comparisons and fifty-year trends. *The B.E. Journal of Economic Analysis & Policy, 7*, Article 10. www.bepress.com/bejeap/vol7/iss2/art10

Hilger, K., Ekman, M., Fiebach, C. J., & Basten, U. (2017). Efficient hubs in the intelligent brain: Nodal efficiency of hub regions in the salient network is associated with general intelligence. *Intelligence, 60*, 10–25.

Hill, C. (1972). *The world turned upside down: Radical ideas during the English Revolution*. London: Temple Smith.

Hjalmarsson, R., & Lochner, L. (2012). The impact of education on crime: International evidence, CESifo DICE Report, *Journal of Institutional Comparisons, 10*, 49–55.

Hjalmarsson, R., Holmlund, H., & Lindquist, M. J. (2014). The effect of education on criminal convictions and incarceration: Causal evidence from microdata. *The Economic Journal, 125*, 1290–1326.

Hoffer, E. P. (2019). America's health care system is broken: What went wrong and how can we fix it. Part 4: The pharmaceutical industry. *The American Journal of Medicine, 132*, 1013–1016.

Hofstede, G. (2001). *Culture's consequences: Comparing values, behaviors, institutions and organizations across nations*. Thousand Oaks, CA: Sage. 2nd ed.

Holdstock, T. L. (2000). *Re-examining psychology: Critical perspectives and African insights*. London: Routledge.

Holton, R. J. (2014). *Global inequalities*. London: Palgrave Macmillan.

Hooley, J. M., Butcher, J. N., Nock, M., & Mineka, S. M. (2016). *Abnormal psychology*. Harlow, UK: Pearson. 17th ed.

Hopkins, W. D., Li, X., & Roberts, N. (2018). More intelligent chimpanzees (*Pan troglodytes*) have larger brains and increased cortical thickness. *Intelligence, 74*, 18–24.

Horowitz, D. (2017). *Happier? The history of a cultural movement that aspired to transform America*. New York: Oxford University Press.

Horwitz, S. R., Shutts, K., Olson, K. R. (2014). Social class differences produce social group preferences. *Developmental Science, 17*, 991–1002.

Houle, C., & Miller, M. K. (2019). Social mobility and democratic attitudes: Evidence from Latin America and Sub-Saharan Africa. *Comparative Political Studies, 52*, 1610–1647.

Howard, I. P., & Templeton, W. B. (1966). *Human spatial orientation.* New York: Wiley.

Howard, J., Gagné, M., Morin, A. J. S., & Van den Broeck, A. (2016). Motivation profiles at work: A self-determination theory approach. *Journal of Vocational Behavior, 95–96*, 74–89.

Huffman, K. (2012). *Psychology in action.* New York: John Wiley & Sons. 10th ed.

Hughes, B. M. (2018). *Psychology in crisis.* London: Red Globe Press.

Human Rights Watch (2012). *Growing up locked down: Youth in solitary confinement in jails and prisons across the United States.* United States: Human Rights Watch.

Hurtado, A. (2003). *Voicing Chicano feminisms: Young women speak out on sexuality and identity.* New York: NYU Press.

Hutchison, C. B. (Ed.) (2009). *What happens when students are in the minority: Experiences that impact human performance.* Lanham, MD: R&L Education.

Ip, G. (2019). Two capitalists worry about capitalism's future. *The Wall Street Journal*, April 24, p. A2.

Jack, A. A. (2019). *The privileged poor: How elite colleges are failing disadvantaged students.* Cambridge, MA: Harvard University Press.

Jaffrelot, C. (2019). *Modi's India: Hindu nationalism and the rise of ethnic democracy* (Trans. C. Schoch). Princeton, NJ: Princeton University Press.

Jahoda, G. (2016). On the rise and decline of "indigenous psychology." *Culture & Psychology, 22*, 169–181.

Jain, K. K. (2021). *Textbook on personalized medicine.* Cham: Springer Nature. 3rd ed.

Jäkel, F., Singh, M., Wichmann, F. A., & Herzog, M. H. (2016). An overview of quantitative approaches in Gestalt perception. *Vision Research, 126*, 3–8.

James, W. (1890/1981). *The principles of psychology.* Cambridge, MA: Harvard University Press.

Jan, T. (2017). White families have nearly 10 times the net worth of black families. And the gap is growing. *The Washington Post*, September 28. www.washingtonpost.com/news/wonk/wp/2017/09/28/black-and-hispanic-families-are-making-more-money-but-they-still-lag-far-behind-whites/

Janis, I. I. (1982). *Groupthink.* Boston, MA: Houghton Mifflin. 2nd ed.

Jarjoura, G. R., Triplett, R. A., & Brinker, G. P. (2002). Growing up poor: Examining the link between persistent childhood poverty and delinquency. *Journal of Quantitative Criminology, 18*, 159–187.

Jaschik, S. (2014). AP growth and inequalities. *Inside Higher ED.* Insidehighered.com/news/2014/02/11/study-shows-growth-ap-program-continuing-racial-gaps

Jaschik, S. (2018). SAT scores are up, especially for Asians. *Inside Higher ED.* Insidehighered.com/article/2018/20/29/sat-scores-are-gaps-remain-significant-among-racial-and-ethnic-groups

Jetten, J., & Peters, K. (Eds.) (2019). *The social psychology of inequality*. Cham, Switzerland: Springer Nature.

Jindra, I. W., & Jindra, M. (2018). Connecting poverty, culture, and cognition: The bridges out of poverty process. *Journal of Poverty, 22*, 42–64.

Johnson, A. D., & Markowitz, A. J. (2018a). Food insecurity and family well-being outcomes among households with young children. *The Journal of Pediatrics, 196*, 275–282.

Johnson, A. D., & Markowitz, A. J. (2018b). Associations between household food insecurity in early childhood and children's kindergarten skills. *Child Development, 89*, e1–e17.

Johnson, D. G., & Brooks, K. M. (1983). *Prospects for Soviet agriculture in the 1980s*. Bloomington, IN: Indiana University Press.

Johnson, J. (2014). *American lobotomy: A rhetorical history*. Ann Arbor, MI: University of Michigan Press.

Johnson, J. (2018). The self-radicalization of white men: "Fake news" and the effective networking of paranoia. *Communication Culture & Critique, 11*, 100–115.

Johnson, K. R., & Loscocco, K. (2015). Black marriage through the prism of gender, race, and class. *Journal of Black Studies, 46*, 142–171.

Johnson, M. H., & de Haan, M. (2015). *Developmental cognitive neuroscience*. Oxford: Blackwell. 4th ed.

Johnson, P. B., Sears, D. O., & McConahay, J. B. (1971). Black invisibility, the press, and the Los Angeles riot. *American Journal of Sociology, 76*, 698–721.

Jones, M. J., Moore, S. R., & Kobor, M. S. (2018). Principles and challenges of applying epigenetic epidemiology to psychology. *Annual Review of Psychology, 69*, 459–485.

Joseph, J. (2004). *The gene illusion: Genetic research in psychiatry and psychology under the microscope*. New York: Algora.

Joseph, J. (2013). The use of the classic twins method in the social and behavioral sciences: The fallacy continues. *The Journal of Mind and Behavior, 34*, 1–40.

Jost, J. T. (2017). Working class conservatism: A system justification perspective. *Current Opinion in Psychology, 18*, 73–78.

Jost, J. T. (2019). A quarter century of system justification theory: Questions, answers, criticisms, and societal applications. *British Journal of Social Psychology, 58*, 263–314.

Jost, J. T., Gaucher, D., & Stern, C. (2015). "The world isn't fair": A system justification perspective on social stratification and inequality. In M. Mikulincer, & P. R. Shaver (Eds.), *APA Handbook of personality and social psychology* (pp. 317–340). Washington, DC: American Psychological Association Press.

Jost, J. T., Hawkins, C. B., Nosek, B. A., et al. (2013). Belief in a just world (and a just society): A system justification perspective on religious ideology. *Journal of Theoretical and Philosophical Psychology, 34*, 56–81.

Jovchelovitch, S., & Glaveanu, V. P. (2012). Motivation and social representations. In R. Harré, & F. M. Moghaddam (Eds.), *Psychology for the third millennium:*

Integrating cultural and neuroscience perspectives (pp. 166–181). Thousand Oaks, CA: Sage.

Kagan, C., Burton, M., Duckett, P., Lawthom, R., & Siddiquee, A. (2020). *Critical community psychology: Critical action and social change.* New York: Routledge. 2nd ed.

Kahneman, D. (2011). *Thinking fast and slow.* New York: Farrar, Straus and Giroux.

Kalat, J. W. (2017). *Introduction to psychology.* Belmont, CA: Cengage Learning. 11th ed.

Kaminski, J. A., Schlagenhauf, F., Rapp, M., et al. (2018). Epigenetic variance in dopamine D2 receptor: A marker of IQ malleability? *Transactional Psychiatry, 8,* 169.

Karama, S., Colom, R., Johnson, W., et al. (2012). Cortical thickness correlates of specific cognitive performance accounting for the general factor intelligence in healthy children aged 6 to 18. *NeuroImage, 55,* 1443–1453.

Karau, S. J., & Williams, K. D. (1993). Social loafing: A meta-analytic review and theoretical integration. *Journal of Personality and Social Psychology, 65,* 681–706.

Katsiyannis, A., Whitford, D. K., Zhang, D., & Gage, N. A. (2018). Adult recidivism in United States: A meta-analysis 1994–2015. *Journal of Child and Family Studies, 27,* 686–696.

Katz, L. F., & Autor, D. H. (1999). Changes in wage structure and earnings inequality. In O. Ashenfelter, & D. Card (Eds.), *Handbook of labor economics* (pp. 1463–1555). Amsterdam: Elsevier B.V.

Katzenstein, M. F., & Waller, M. R. (2015). Taxing the poor: Incarceration, poverty governance, and the seizure of family resources. *Perspectives on Politics, 13,* 638–656.

Kaufman, M. T., Churchland, M. M., Ryu, S. I., & Shenoy, K. V. (2015). Vacillation, indecision and hesitation in moment-by-moment decoding of monkey motor cortex. *eLife.* cdn.elifesciences.org/articles/04677/elife-04677-v1

Kearney, M. S., Harris, B. H., Jácome, E., & Parker, L. (2014). Ten economic facts about crime and incarceration in the United States. *Policy Memo,* May. www.hamiltonproject.org/assets/legacy/files/downloads_and_links/v8_THP_10CrimeFacts.pdf

Keefer, L. A., Goode, C., & Van Berkel, L. (2015). Toward a psychological study of class consciousness: Development and validation of a social psychological model. *Journal of Social and Political Psychology, 3,* 253–290.

Kell, H. J., Lubinski, D., & Benbow, C. P. (2013). Who rises to the top? Early indicators. *Psychological Science, 24,* 648–659.

Keller, J. (2005). In genes we trust: The biological component of biological essentialism and its relationship to mechanisms of motivated social cognition. *Journal of Personality and Social Psychology, 88,* 686–702.

Kendi, I. X. (2017). *Stamped from the beginning: The definitive history of racist ideas in America.* New York: Nation Books.

Kent, P. (2017). Fluid intelligence: A brief history. *Applied Neuropsychology.* DOI: 10.1080/21622965.2017.1317480

Kettler, T., & Hurst, L. T. (2017). Advanced academic participation: A longitudinal analysis of ethnicity gaps in suburban schools. *Journal for the Education of the Gifted, 40,* 3–19.

Keys, A., Brozek, J., Henschel, A., Mickelsen, O., & Taylor, H. L. (1950). *The biology of human starvation.* Minneapolis: University of Minnesota Press.

Kihlstrom, J. F. (2017). Time to lay the Libet experiment to rest: Commentary on Papanicolaou (2017). *Psychology of Consciousness: Theory, Research, and Practice. 4,* 324–329.

Kim, C. Y., Losen, D. J., & Hewitt, D. T. (2010). *The school-to-prison pipeline.* New York: New York University Press.

Kim, U., & Berry, J. W. (Eds.) (1993). *Indigenous psychologies: Research and experience in cultural context.* Newbury Park, CA: Sage.

Kim, Y., & Raley, R. K. (2015). Race-ethnic differences in non-marital fertility rates 2006–2010. *Population Research and Policy Review, 34,* 141–159.

Kimmel, M. (2017). *Angry White men: American masculinity at the end of an era.* New York: Nation Books.

Kipnis, D. (1972). Does power corrupt? *Journal of Personality and Social Psychology, 24,* 33–41.

Kirkland, K., Jetten, J., & Nielsen, M. (2019). But that's not fair! The experience of economic inequality from a child's perspective. In J. Jetten, & K. Peters (Eds.), *The social psychology of inequality* (pp. 209–222). Cham, Switzerland: Springer Nature.

Knotts, J. D., Odegaard, B., & Lau, H. (2018). Neuroscience: The key to consciousness may not be under the streetlight. *Current Biology, 28,* R749–R752.

Koch, C., Massimini, M., Boly, M., & Tononi, G. (2016). Neural correlates of consciousness: Progress and problems. *Nature Reviews: Neuroscience, 17,* 307–321.

Kohn, M. L. (1969). *Class and conformity: A study in values.* Homewood, IL: The Dorsey Press.

Kohn, M. L., Naoi, A., Schoenbach, C., Schooler, C., & Slomszynski, K. M. (1990). Position in the class structure and psychological functioning in the United States, Japan, and Poland. *American Journal of Sociology, 95,* 964–1008.

Kohrt, B. A., Yang, M., Rai, S., et al. (2016). Recruitment of child soldiers in Nepal: Mental health status and risk factors for voluntary participation of youth in armed groups. *Peace and Conflict: Journal of Peace Psychology, 22,* 208–216.

Kong, F., Ma, X., You, X., & Xiang, Y. (2018). The resilient brain: Psychological resilience mediates the effect of amplitude of low-frequency fluctuations in orbitofrontal cortex on subjective well-being in young healthy adults. *Social Cognitive and Affective Neuroscience, 13,* 755–763.

Korn, M. (2017). ACT test metrics shows wide gap in college readiness. *The Wall Street Journal,* September 7, p. 1.

Kornrich, S., & Furstenberg, F. (2013). Investing in children: Changes in parental spending on children, 1972–2007. *Demography, 50,* 1–23.

Korotayev, A., Goldstone, J. A., & Zinkina, J. (2015). Phases of global demographic transition correlates with phases of the Great Divergence and Great Convergence. *Technological Forecasting and Social Change, 95*, 163–169.

Kozol, J. (1991). *Savage inequalities: Children in America's schools.* New York: Broadway Paperbacks.

Krapohl, E., & Plomin, R. (2016). Genetic link between family socioeconomic status and children's educational achievement estimated from genome-wide SNPs. *Molecular Psychiatry, 21*, 437–443.

Kraus, M. W., & Keltner, D. (2009). Signs of socioeconomic status: A thin-slicing approach. *Psychological Science, 20*, 99–106.

Kraus, M. W., & Keltner, D. (2013). Social class rank, essentialism, and punitive judgment. *Journal of Personality and Social Psychology, 105*, 247–261.

Kraus, M. W., & Mendes, W. B. (2014). Sartorial symbols of social class elicit class-consistent behavioral and physiological responses: A dyadic approach. *Journal of Experimental Psychology – General, 143*, 2330–2340.

Kraus, M. W., & Park, J. W. (2017). The structural dynamics of social class. *Current Opinions in Psychology, 18*, 55–60.

Kraus, M. W., Park, J. W., & Tan, J. J. (2017). Signs of social class: The experience of economic inequality in everyday life. *Perspectives on Psychological Science, 12*, 422–435.

Kraus, M. W., Piff, P. K., & Keltner, D. (2011). Social class as culture: The convergence of resources and rank in the social realm. *Current Directions in Psychological Science, 20*, 246–250.

Kraus, M. W., Piff, P. K., Mendoza-Denton, R., Rheinschmidt, M. L., & Keltner, D. (2012). Social class, solipsism, and contextualism: How the rich are different from the poor. *Psychological Review, 119*, 546–572.

Kraus, M. W., & Stephens, N. M. (2012). A road map for the emerging psychology of social class. *Social and Personality Psychology Compass, 6*, 642–656.

Kraus, M. W., & Tan, J. J. X. (2015). Americans overestimate social class mobility. *Journal of Experimental Psychology, 58*, 101–111.

Kraus, M. W., Torrez, B., Park, J. W., & Ghayebi, F. (2019). Evidence for the reproduction of social class in brief speech. *Proceedings of the National Academy of Sciences.* DOI: 10.1073/pnas.1900500116

Kress, V. E., Minton, C. A. B., Adamson, N. A., Paylo, M. J., & Pope, V. (2014). The removal of the multiaxial system in the DSM-5: Implications and practice suggestions for counselors. *The Professional Counselor, 4*, 191–201.

Kroesen, M., Handy, S., & Chorus, C. (2017). Do attitudes cause behavior or vice versa? An alternative conceptualization of the attitude-behavior relationship on travel behavior modeling. *Transportation Research Part A: Policy and Practice, 101*, 190–202.

Kulig, T. C., Pratt, T. C., & Cullen, F. T. (2017). Revisiting the Stanford prison experiment: A case study in organized skepticism. *Journal of Criminal Justice, Education, 28*, 74–111.

Labov, W. (2006). *The social stratification of English in New York City.* Cambridge, UK: Cambridge University Press.

Lafitte, P. (1958). *Social structure and personality in the factory*. London: Routledge.

Laing, R. D. (1985). *Wisdom, madness and folly*. New York: McGraw-Hill.

Laing, R. D., & Esterson, A. (1970). *Sanity, madness and the family*. Harmondsworth, UK: Pelican. First published 1964.

Lally, J., Mangione, P., & Honig, A. (1988). The Syracuse University Family Development Research Program: Long-range impact of an early intervention with low-income children and their families. In D. Powell (Ed.), *Parent education as early childhood intervention: Emerging directions in theory, research, and practice* (pp. 79–104). Norwood: Ablex.

Lamiell, J. T. (2003). *Beyond individual and group differences: Human individuality, scientific psychology, and William Stern's critical personalism*. Thousand Oaks, CA: Sage.

Lammers, J., Gordijn, E. H., & Otten, S. (2008). Looking through the eyes of the powerful. *Journal of Experimental Social Psychology, 44*, 1229–1238.

Lammers, J., Stapel, D. A., & Galinsky, A. D. (2010). Power increases hypocrisy: Moralizing in reasoning, immorality in behavior. *Psychological Science, 21*, 737–744.

Lamont, M., & Small, M. L. (2010). Cultural diversity and anti-poverty policy. *International Social Science Journal, 61*, 169–180.

Lane, H. (1976). *The wild boy of Aveyron*. Cambridge, MA: Harvard University Press.

Latham, G. P. (2012). *Work motivation: History, theory, research, and practice*. Thousand Oaks, CA: Sage. 2nd ed.

Laungani, P. (2004). *Asian perspectives in counselling and psychotherapy*. New York: Brunner-Routledge.

Laurin, K., Kay, A. C., & Shepherd, S. (2011). Self-stereotyping as a route to system justification. *Social Cognition, 29*, 360–375.

Lawrence, D., & Kisely, S. (2010). Inequalities in healthcare provision for people with severe mental illness. *Journal of Psychopharmacology, 24*, 61–68.

Lawson, G. M., & Farah, M. J. (2017). Executive function as a mediator between SES and academic achievement throughout childhood. *International Journal of Behavioral Development, 41*, 94–104.

Lazarus, R. S. (2003). Does the positive psychology movement have legs? *Psychological Inquiry, 14*, 93–109.

Le Bon, G. (1894). *The psychology of revolution* (Trans. B. Miall). London: Fisher Unwin. First published 1894.

Lee, H., Porter, L., & Comfort, M. (2014). The collateral consequences of family member incarceration: Impacts on civic participation and perceptions of legitimacy and fairness. *The ANNALS of the American Academy of Political and Social Science, 651*, 44–73.

Leong, T. L., Inman, A. G., Ebreo, A., et al. (Eds.) (2006). *Handbook of Asian American psychology*. Los Angeles, CA: Sage. 2nd ed.

Le Roux, G., Vallée, J., & Commenges, H. (2017). Social segregation around the clock in the Paris region. *Journal of Transport Geography, 59*, 134–145.

Le Texier, T. (2019). Debunking the Stanford prison experiment. *American Psychologist, 74*, 823–839.

Lewis, A. J. (2016). "We are certain of our own insanity": Antipsychiatry and the Gay Liberation Movement, 1968–1980. *Journal of the History of Sexuality, 25*, 83–113.

Lewis, O. (1969). The culture of poverty. In D. P. Moynihan (Ed.), *On understanding poverty: Perspectives from the social sciences* (pp. 187–200). New York: Basic Books.

Li, E., Deng, Q., & Zhou, Y. (in press). Livelihood resilience and the generative mechanism of rural households out of poverty: An empirical analysis from Lankao County, Henan Province, China. *Journal of Rural Studies.*

Libet, B., Gleason, C. A., Wright, E. W., & Pearl, D. K. (1983). Time of conscious intention to act in relation to onset of cerebral activity (readiness potential): The unconscious initiation of a freely voluntary act. *Brain, 106*, 623–642.

Lickliter, R., & Witherington, D. C. (2017). Towards a truly developmental epigenetics. *Human Development, 60*, 124–138.

Lightfoot, D. (2020). *Born to parse: How children select their languages.* Cambridge, MA: MIT Press.

Lilienfeld, S. O., & Waldman, I. D. (Eds.) (2017). *Psychological science under scrutiny: Recent challenges and proposed solutions.* Hoboken, NJ: Wiley-Blackwell.

Lindert, P. H. (2000). Three centuries of inequality in Britain and America. In A. B. Atkinson, & F. Bourguignon (Eds.), *Handbook of income distribution* (vol. 1, pp. 167–216). Amsterdam: Elsevier B. V.

Lisanby, S. H. (2007). Electroconvulsive therapy for depression. *The New England Journal of Medicine, 357*, 1939–1945.

Liu, W. (2011). *Classism in the helping professions: Theory, research, and practice.* Los Angeles, CA: Sage.

Lizzio-Wilson, M., Thomas, E. F., Louis, W. R., et al. (2021). How collective action failure shapes group heterogeneity and engagement in conventional and radical action over time. *Psychological Science, 32*, 519–535.

Ljungqvist, I., Topor, A., Forssell, H., Stevensson, I., & Davidson, L. (2016). Money and mental illness: A study of the relationship between poverty and serious psychological problems. *Community Mental Health, 52*, 842–850.

Lochner, L. (2004). Education, work, and crime: A human capital approach. *International Economic Review, 45*, 811–843.

Lochner, L., & Moretti, E. (2004). The effect of education on crime: Evidence from prison inmates, arrests, and self-reports. *American Economic Review, 94*, 155–189.

Locke, E. A., & Latham, G. P. (2004). What should we do about motivation theory? Six recommendations for the twenty-first century. *Academy of Management Review, 29*, 388–403.

Long, H. (2020). Finland's Prime Minister Sanna Marin says the American Dream is best achieved in Nordic countries. *The Washington Post*, February 4.

www.washingtonpost.com/business/2020/02/03/finland-american-dream/?
itid=hp_ed-picks_finland-0204%3Ahomepage%2Fstory-ans

Lopoo, L. M., & London, A. S. (2016). Household crowding during childhood and long-term education outcomes. *Demography, 53*, 699–721.

Lott, B. (2012). The social psychology of class and classism. *American Psychologist, 57*, 100–110.

Lott, B., & Bullock, H. E. (2007). *Psychology and economic injustice: Personal, professional, and political intersections.* Washington, DC: American Psychological Association Press.

Lovenheim, M. E. (2011). The effect of liquid housing wealth on college enrollment. *Journal of Labor Economics, 29*, 741–771.

Lukunka, B. N. (2018). "They call us witches": Exclusion and invisibility in the Burundian returnee reintegration process. *Peace and Conflict: Journal of Peace Psychology, 24*, 315–319.

Lund, C., Breen, A., Flisher, A. J., et al. (2010). Poverty and common mental disorders in low and middle income countries: A systematic review. *Social Science & Medicine, 71*, 517–528.

Luthar, S. S. (2003). The culture of affluence: Psychological costs of material wealth. *Child Development, 74*, 1581–1593.

Lutz, A., & Thompson, E. (2003). Neurophenomenology: Integrating subjective experience and brain dynamics in neuroscience. *Journal of Consciousness Studies, 10*, 31–52.

Machamer, P. K. (2009). Learning, neuroscience, and the return of behaviorism. In J. Bickle (Ed.), *The Oxford handbook of philosophy and neuroscience* (pp. 166–178). New York: Oxford University Press.

Macintyre, A., Ferris, D., Gonçalves, B., & Quinn, N. (2018). What has economics got to do with it? The impact of socioeconomic factors on mental health and the case for collective action. *Palgrave Communications, 4*, 1–5. DOI: 10.1057/s41599-018-0063-21 | www.nature.com/palcomms

MacNeil, M. K., & Sherif, M. (1976). Norm change over subject generations as a function of arbitrariness of prescribed norms. *Journal of Personality and Social Psychology, 34*, 762–773.

Major, L. E., & Machin, S. (2018). *Social mobility and its enemies.* New Orleans, LA: Pelican Books.

Maloutas, T., & Fujita, K. (Eds.) (2016). *Residential segregation in comparative perspective: Making sense of contextual diversity.* London: Routledge. First published 2012.

Mani, A., Mullainathan, S., Shafir, E., & Zhao, J. (2013). Poverty impedes cognitive function. *Science, 341*, 976–980.

Manstead, A. S. R. (2018). The psychology of social class: How socioeconomic status impacts thought, feelings, and behaviour. *British Journal of Social Psychology, 57*, 267–291.

Manzotti, R., & Moderato, P. (2010). Is neuroscience adequate as the forthcoming "mindscience"? *Behavior and Philosophy, 38*, 1–29.

Marcus, D. K., O'Connell, D., Norris, A., & Sawaqdeh, A. (2014). Is the dodo bird endangered in the 21st century? A meta-analysis of treatment comparison studies. *Clinical Psychology Review, 34,* 519–530.

Mare, R. D. (2014). Multigenerational aspects of social stratification: Issues for further research. *Research in Social Stratification and Mobility, 35,* 121–128.

Markus, H. R., & Fiske, S. T. (2012). Introduction: A wide-angle lens on the psychology of social class. In H. R. Markus, & S. T. Fiske (Eds.), *Facing social class: How societal rank influences interaction* (pp. 1–11). New York: Russell Sage Foundation.

Marmot, M. (2015). *The health gap: The challenge of an unequal world.* New York: Bloomsbury.

Marmot, M. G. (2004). *The status syndrome: How social standing affects our health and longevity.* New York: Times Books/Henry Holt.

Marmot, M. G., Rose, G., Shipley, M., & Hamilton, P. J. S. (1978). Employment grade and coronary heart disease in British social servants. *Journal of Epidemiology and Community Health, 32,* 244–249.

Marmot, M.G., Stansfeld, S., Patel, C., et al. (1991). Health inequalities among British civil servants: The Whitehall II study. *The Lancet, 337,* 1387–1393.

Marmot, M. G., & Winkinson, R. G. (Eds.) (2006). *Social determinants of health.* Oxford: Oxford University Press. 2nd ed.

Martinez, S. M., Frongillo, E. A., Leung, C., & Ritchie, L. (2018). No food for thought: Food insecurity is related to poor mental health and lower academic performance among students in California's public university system. *Journal of Health Psychology, 25,*1359105318783028. DOI: 10.1177/1359105318783028

Masterpasqua, F. (2009). Psychology and epigenetics. *Review of General Psychology, 13,* 194–201.

Mayo, A. (2019). The individualism of motivation. *Strategic HR Review, 18,* 96–103.

McCarthy, T. D., & Wolfson, M. (1996). Resource mobilization by local social movement organizations: Agency, strategy, and organization in the movement against drunk driving. *American Sociological Review, 61,* 1070–1088.

McCarthy, T. D., & Zald, M. N. (1977). Resource mobilization and social movements: A partial theory. *American Journal of Sociology, 82,* 1212–1241.

McCrae, R. R., & Costa, P. T. (2003). *Personality in adulthood.* New York: Guilford Press. 2nd ed.

McDermott, C. L., Seidlitz, J., Nadig, A., et al. (2019). Longitudinally mapping childhood socioeconomic status associations with cortical and subcortical morphology. *The Journal of Neuroscience, 39,* 1365–1373.

McPherson, K. S. (1985). On intelligence testing and immigration legislation. *American Psychologist, 40,* 242–243.

Mears, D. P., & Cochran, J. C. (2018). Who goes to prison? In J. Wooldredge, & P. Smith (Eds.), *The Oxford handbook of prisons and imprisonment* (pp. 29–52). New York: Oxford University Press.

Mehta, P. H., Jones, A. C., & Josephs, R. A. (2008). The social endocrinology of dominance: Basal testosterone predicts cortisol changes and behavior following victory and defeat. *Journal of Personality and Social Psychology, 94,* 1078–1093.

Melossi, D., & Massimo, P. (1981). *The prison and the factory: Origins of the penitentiary system.* London: Macmillan.

Mendel, R. A. (2011). *No place for kids: The case for reducing juvenile incarceration.* Baltimore, MD: Annie E. Casey Foundation.

Menger, F. M. (2017). Molecular Lamarckism: On the evolution of human intelligence. *World Futures, 73,* 89–103.

Mertens, D. M. (2020). *Research and evaluation in education and psychology: Integrating diversity with quantitative, qualitative, and mixed methods.* Los Angeles, CA: Sage. 5th ed.

Merzenich, M. (2013). *Soft-wired: How the new science of brain plasticity can change your life.* Nashville, TN: Parnassus Publishing. 2nd ed.

Michaelson, L. E., & Munakata, Y. (2020). Same data set, different conclusions: Preschool delay of gratification predicts later behavioral outcomes in a preregistered study. *Psychological Science, 31,* 193–201.

Mickelson, K. D., & Hazlett, E. (2014). "Why me?": Low-income women's poverty attributions, mental health, and social class perceptions. *Sex Roles, 71,* 319–332.

Milan, S. (2015). From social movements to cloud protesting: The evolution of collective identity. *Information, Communication & Society, 18,* 887–900.

Milgram, S. (1974). *Obedience to authority: An experimental view.* New York: Harper & Row.

Minkov, M., Dutt, P., Schachner, M., et al. (2017). A revision of Hofstede's individualism-collectivism dimension: A new national index from a 56-country study. *Cross Cultural & Strategic Management, 24,* 386–404.

Mirabito, A. M., & Berry, L. L. (2015). You say you want a revolution? Drawing on social movement theory to motivate transformative change. *Journal of Service Research, 18,* 336–350.

Mischel, W. (2014). *The marshmallow test: Why self-control is the engine of success.* New York: Little, Brown and Company.

Mischel, W., Shoda, Y., & Ayduk, O. (2008). *Introduction to personality: Toward an integrative science of the person.* Hoboken, NJ: Wiley.

Mischel, W., Shoda, Y., & Peake, P. K. (1988). The nature of adolescent competencies predicted by preschool delay of gratification. *Journal of Personality and Social Psychology, 54,* 687–696.

Mishra, S., & Carleton, N. (2015). Subjective relative deprivation is associated with poorer physical and mental health. *Social Science & Medicine, 147,* 144–149.

Misra, G. (Ed.). (1990). *Applied social psychology in India.* New Delhi, India: Sage.

Moazed, A., & Johnson, N. L. (2016). *Modern monopolies: What it takes to dominate the 21st-century economy.* New York: St. Martin's Press.

Moffit, T. E., Arseneault, L., Belsky, D., et al. (2011). A gradient of childhood self-control predicts health, wealth, and public safety. *Proceedings of the National Academy of Science, 108,* 2693–2698.

Moghaddam, F. M. (1987). Psychology in the three worlds: As reflected by the crisis in social psychology and the move toward indigenous third world psychology. *American Psychologist, 42*, 912–920.

Moghaddam, F. M. (1997). *The specialized society: The plight of the individual in an age of individualism.* Westport, CT: Praeger.

Moghaddam, F. M. (1998). *Social psychology: Exploring universals across cultures.* New York: Freeman.

Moghaddam, F. M. (2002). *The individual and society: A cultural integration.* New York: Worth.

Moghaddam, F. M. (2004). The cycle of rights and duties in intergroup relations. *New Review of Social Psychology, 3*, 125–130.

Moghaddam, F. M. (2005a). *Great ideas in psychology.* Oxford: Oneworld.

Moghaddam, F. M. (2005b). The staircase to terrorism: A psychological exploration. *American Psychologist, 60*, 161–169.

Moghaddam, F. M. (2006). *From the terrorists' point of view: What they experience and why they come to destroy.* Westport, CT: Praeger Security International Series.

Moghaddam, F. M. (2008a). *Multiculturalism and intergroup relations: Psychological implications for democracy in global context.* Washington, DC: American Psychological Association Press.

Moghaddam, F. M. (2008b). *How globalization spurs terrorism: The lopsided benefits of one world and why that fuels violence.* Westport, CT: Praeger.

Moghaddam, F. M. (2010). Intersubjectivity, interobjectivity, and the embryonic fallacy in developmental science. *Culture & Psychology, 16*, 465–475.

Moghaddam, F. M. (2012). The omnicultural imperative. *Culture & Psychology, 18*, 304–330.

Moghaddam, F. M. (2013). *The psychology of dictatorship.* Washington, DC: American Psychological Association Press.

Moghaddam, F. M. (2016). *The psychology of democracy.* Washington, DC: American Psychological Association Press.

Moghaddam, F. M. (2018). Political plasticity and revolution: The case of Iran. In B. Wagoner, F. M. Moghaddam, & J. Valsiner (Eds.), *The psychology of radical social change* (pp. 122–139). Cambridge, UK: Cambridge University Press.

Moghaddam, F. M. (2019). *Threat to democracy: The appeal of authoritarianism in an age of uncertainty.* Washington, DC: American Psychological Association Press.

Moghaddam, F. M., & Howard, C. (2017). Political plasticity. In F. M. Moghaddam (Ed.), *The Sage encyclopedia of political behavior* (vol. 2, pp. 625–627). London & Thousand Oaks, CA: Sage.

Moghaddam, F. M., & Lee, N. (2006). Double reification: The process of universalizing psychology in the three worlds. In A. Brock (Ed.), *Internationalizing the history of psychology* (pp. 163–182). New York: New York University Press.

Moghaddam, F. M., & Riley, C. J. (2005). Toward a cultural theory of human rights and duties in human development. In N. J. Finkel, & F. M. Moghaddam

(Eds.), *Human rights and duties: Empirical contributions and normative commentaries* (pp. 75–104). Washington, DC: American Psychological Association Press.

Moghaddam, F. M., & Studer, C. (1997). Cross-cultural psychology: The frustrated gadfly's promises, potentialities, and failures. In D. Fox, & I. Prilleltensky (Eds.), *Handbook of Critical Psychology* (pp. 185–201+refs). Newbury Park, CA: Sage.

Moghaddam, F. M., & Taylor, D. M. (1986). What constitutes an "appropriate psychology" for the developing world? *International Journal of Psychology, 21,* 253–267.

Moghaddam, F. M., & Taylor, D. M. (1987). Toward appropriate training for developing world psychologists. In C. Kagitcibasi (Ed.), *Growth and progress in cross-cultural psychology* (pp. 66–75). Lisse: Swets & Zeitlinger Publishers.

Mohan, V., & Nalwa, K. (1992). Delinquency proneness as related to deprivation. *Journal of Criminology, 2,* 93–98.

Mohanty, A. K., & Misra, G. (Eds.) (2000). *Psychology of poverty and disadvantage.* New Delhi, India: Concept Publishing Company.

Mohaupt, S. (2009). Review article: Resilience and social exclusion. *Social Policy & Society, 8,* 63–71.

Montejo, A. L., Montejo, L., & Navarro-Cremades, F. (2015). Sexual side-effects of antidepressant and antipsychotic drugs. *Current Opinion in Psychiatry, 28,* 418–423.

Montero, M. (2008). An insider's look at the development and current state of community psychology in Latin America. *Journal of Community Psychology, 36,* 661–674.

Montero, M., Sonn, C. C., & Burton, M. (2017). Community psychology and liberation psychology: A creative synergy for an ethical and transformative praxis. In M. A. Bond, I. Serrano-Gracia, C. B. Keys, & M. Shinn (Eds.), *APA handbook of community psychology: Theoretical foundations, core concepts, and emerging challenges.* (pp. 149–167). Washington, DC: American Psychological Association Press.

Moore, D. S. (2003). *The dependent gene: The fallacy of "nature vs. nurture."* New York: Henry Holt.

Moreland, P. (2019). *The human tide: How population shaped the modern world.* New York: PublicAffairs.

Morey, L. C., & Hopwood, C. J. (2019). Expert preferences for categorical, dimensional, and mixed/hybrid approaches to personality disorders and diagnosis. *Journal of Personality Disorders* (not yet in print) DOI: 10.1521/pedi_2019_33_398

Morgan, M. S. (2019). *Charles Booth's London poverty maps: A landmark reassessment of Booth's social survey.* London: Thames & Hudson.

Morling, B. (2018). *Research methods in psychology.* New York: Norton. 3rd ed.

Morris, L. (2002). *Dangerous class: The underclass and social citizenship.* London: Routledge.

Moscovici, S. (1981). On social representations. In J. Forgas (Ed.), *Social cognition: Perspectives on everyday understandings* (pp. 181–210). New York: Academic Press.

Mrazek, M. D., Mooneyham, B. W., Mrazek, K. L., & Schooler, J. W. (2016). Pushing the limits: Cognitive, affective, and neural plasticity revealed by an intensive multifaceted intervention. *Frontiers in Human Neuroscience, 10,* 117. https://doi.org/10.3389/fnhum.2016.00117

Mullainathan, S., & Shafir, E. (2013). *Scarcity: Why having too little means so much.* New York: Times Books.

Mullen, A. L. (2009). Elite destinations: Pathways to attending an Ivy League university. *British Journal of Sociology of Education, 30,* 15–27.

Mulvihill, J. J., Capps, B., Joly, Y., et al. (2017). Ethical issues of CRSPR technology and gene editing through the lens of solidarity. *British Medical Bulletin, 122,* 17–29.

Mumtaz, Z., Salway, S., Bhatti, A., & McIntyre, L. (2014). Addressing invisibility, inferiority, and powerlessness to achieve gains in maternal health for ultra-poor women. *The Lancet, 383,* 1095–1097.

Muntaner, C., Borrell, C., & Chung, H. (2007). Class relations, economic inequality and mental health: Why social class matters to the sociology of mental health. In W. R., Avison, J. D. McLeod, & B. A. Pescosolido (Eds.), *Mental health, social mirror* (pp. 127–141). Boston: Springer.

Muntaner, C., Ng, E., Vanroelen, C., Christ, S., & Eaton, W. W. (2012). Social stratification, social closure, and social class as determinants of mental health disparities. In C. S. Aneshensel, J. C. Phelan, & A. Bierman (Eds.), *Handbook of the sociology of mental health* (pp. 2015–2227). New York: Springer.

Murali, V., & Oyebode, F. (2004). Poverty, social inequality and mental health. *Advances in Psychiatric Treatment, 10,* 216–224.

Murnane, R., & Duncan, G. (Eds.) (2011). *Whither opportunity? Rising inequality and the uncertain life chances of low-income children.* New York: Russell Sage Foundation.

Myers, D. G., & Diener, E. (2017). The scientific pursuit of happiness. *Perspectives on Psychological Science, 13,* 218–225.

Nam, Y., & Huang, J. (2009). Equal opportunity for all? Parental economic resources and children's educational attainment. *Children and Youth Services Review, 31,* 625–634.

Nance, J. P. (2016). Students, police, and the school-to-prison pipeline. *Washington University Law Review, 93,* 919–987.

Narayan, D., Chambers, R., Shah, M. K., & Petesch, P. (2000). *Voices of the poor: Crying out for change.* New York: Oxford University Press.

Narayan, D., Patel, R., Schafft, K., Rademacher, A., & Koch-Schulte, S. (1999). *Can anyone hear us? Voices from 47 countries. Voices of the poor.* New York: Oxford University Press.

Nastasi, B. K. (2014). *Multicultural issues in school psychology.* Taylor & Francis. E-book.

Nell, G. L. (2014). *Spontaneous order and the utopian collective.* New York: Palgrave Macmillan.

Nguyen, J., Hinojosa, M. S., Strickhouser Vega, S., et al. (2017). Family predictors of child mental health conditions. *Journal of Family Issues,* 1–25. DOI: 10.1177/0192513X16684891

Niemann, Y. F. (2016). The social ecology of tokenism in higher education. *Peace Review: A Journal of Social Justice, 28*, 451–458.

Nikulina, V., Widom, C. S., & Czaja, S. (2011). The role of childhood neglect and childhood poverty in predicting mental health, academic achievement and crime in adulthood. *American Journal of Community Psychology, 48*, 309–321.

Noam, E. L. (2016). *Who owns the world's media? Media concentration and ownership around the world.* New York: Oxford University Press.

Noble, K. G., Engelhardt, L. E., Brito, N. H., et al. (2015). Socioeconomic disparities in neurocognitive development in the first two years of life. *Developmental Psychobiology, 57*, 535–551.

Nollenberger, N., Rodríguez-Planas, N., & Sevilla, A. (2016). The math gender gap: The role of culture. *American Economic Review: Papers & Proceedings, 106*, 257–261.

Nook, E. C., & Zaki, J. (2015). Social norms shift behavioral and neural responses to foods. *Journal of Cognitive Neuroscience, 27*, 1412–1426.

Norman, W. T. (1963). Toward an adequate taxonomy of personality attributes: Replicated factor structure in peer nomination personality ratings. *Journal of Abnormal and Social Psychology, 66*, 574–583.

Notten, G., & de Neubourg, C. (2011). Monitoring absolute and relative poverty: "Not enough" is not the same as "much less." *The Review of Income and Wealth, 57*, 247–269.

O'Connor, C., Rees, G., & Joffe, H. (2012). Neuroscience in the public sphere. *Neuron, 74*, 220–226. DOI: 10.1016/j.neuron.2012.04.004

OECD (2013). *OECD guidelines on measuring subjective well-being*, Paris: OECD Publishing. DOI: 10.1787/9789264191655-en

OECD (2018). *A broken social elevator? How to promote social mobility.* Paris: OECD Publishing.

Ogaki, M., Ostry, J. D., & Reinhart, C. M. (1996). Saving behavior in low- and middle-income developing countries. *Staff Paper (International Monetary Fund), 43*, 38–71.

Ogunwole, S. U., Drewery, M. P. Jr., & Rios-Vargas, M. (2012). The population with a bachelor's degree or higher by race and Hispanic origin: 2006–2010. www.census.gov/prod/2012pubs/acsbr10-19.pdf

Okbay, A., Beauchamp, J. P., Fontana, M. A., et al. (2016). Genome-wide association study identifies 74 loci associated with educational attainment. *Nature, 533*, 539–542.

Olken, B. A., & Pande, R. (2012). Corruption in developing countries. *Annual Review of Economics, 4*, 479–509.

Open Science Collaboration (2015). Estimating the reproducibility of psychological science. *Science, 349*, aac4716.

Orr, A. J. (2003). Black-White differences in achievement: The importance of wealth. *Sociology of Education, 76*, 281–304.

Osborne, D., Sengupta, N. K., & Sibley, C. G. (2018). System justification theory at 25: Evaluating a paradigm shift in psychology and looking toward the future. *British Journal of Social Psychology, 58*, 340–361.

Osborne, D., & Weiner, B. (2015). A latent profile analysis of attributions for poverty: Identifying response patterns underlying people's willingness to help the poor. *Personality and Individual Differences, 85,* 149–154.

Ostrove, J. M., & Cole, E. R. (2003). Privileging class: Toward a critical psychology of social class in the context of education. *Journal of Social Issues, 59,* 677–692.

Ottersen, O. P., Dasgupta, J., Blouin, C., Buss, P., Changsuvivatwong, V., et al. (2014). The political origins of health inequity: Prospects for change. *Lancet, 383,* 630–667.

Owen, A. M., Coleman, M. R., Boly, M., et al. (2006). Detecting awareness in the vegetative state. *Science, 313,* 1402.

Owens, A., Reardon, S. F., & Jencks, C. (2016). Income segregation between schools and school districts. *American Educational Research Journal, 53,* 1159–1197.

Oxfam (2017). Just 8 men own same wealth as half the world. www.oxfam.org/en/pressroom/pressreleases/2017-01-16/just-8-men-own-same-wealth-half-world

Oxfam (2018). Reward work, not wealth. www.oxfamitalia.org/wp-content/uploads/2018/01/tb-reward-work-not-wealth-methodology-note-220118-en_EMBARGO-1.pdf

Oxfam (2019). An economy for the 99%. https://d1tn3vj7xz9fdh.cloudfront.net/s3fs-public/file_attachments/bp-economy-for-99-percent-160117-en.pdf

Oxfam (2021). The inequality virus. https://oxfamilibrary.openrepository.com/bitstream/handle/10546/621149/bp-the-inequality-virus-250121-en.pdf

Ozer, E. J., Fernald, L. C. H., Weber, A., Flynn, E. P., & VanderWeele, T. J. (2011). Does alleviating poverty affect mothers' depressive symptoms? A quasi-experimental investigation of Mexico's *Oportunidades* programme. *International Journal of Epidemiology, 40,* 1565–1576.

Paas, G. W. C., & Van Merriënboer, J. J. G. (1994). Instructional control of cognitive load in the training of complex cognitive tasks. *Educational Psychology Review, 6,* 351–371.

Page, J., Piehowski, V., & Soss, J. (2019). A debt of care: Commercial bail and the gendered logic of. criminal justice predation. *The Russell Sage Foundation Journal of the Social Sciences, 5,* 150–172.

Pajo, B. (2018). *Introduction to research methods: A hands-on approach.* Los Angeles, CA: Sage.

Pareto, V. (1935). *The mind and society: A treatise on general sociology* (vols. 1–4). New York: Dover.

Parker, P. (2015). The historical role of women in higher education. *Administrative Issues Journal, 5,* Article 3. http://dc.swosu.edu/aij/vol5/iss1/3

Paterson, LL., & Gregory, L. N. (2019). *Representations of poverty and place: Using geographical text analysis to understand discourse.* Cham, Switzerland: Palgrave Macmillan.

Payne, K. (2017). *The broken ladder: How inequality affects the way we think, live, and die.* New York: Viking.

Pelham, B. W., & Blanton, H. (2013). *Conducting research in psychology: Measuring the weight of smoke.* Belmont, CA: Wadsworth. 4th ed.

Pereira, J. G., Gonçalves, J., & Bizzari, V. (2019). The roots and seeds of human-istic psychiatry. In J. G. Pereira., J. Gonçalves., & V. Bizzari (Eds.), *The neu-robiology-psychotherapy-pharmacology intervention triangle* (pp. 1–20). Delaware: Vernon Press.

Peters, K., Fonseca, M. A., Haslam, S. A., Steffens, N. K., & Quiggin, J. (2019). Fat cats and thin followers: Excessive CEP pay may reduce ability to lead. In J. Jetten, & K. Peters (Eds.), *The social psychology of inequality* (pp. 33–48). Cham, Switzerland: Springer Nature.

Pettit, B., & Western, B. (2004). Mass imprisonment and the life course: Race and class inequality in U.S. incarceration. *American Sociological Review, 69,* 151–169.

Pfeffer, F. T. (2014). Multigenerational approaches to social mobility: A mul-tifaceted research agenda. *Research in Social Stratification and Mobility, 35,* 1–12.

Pfeffer, F. T. (2018). Growing wealth gaps in education. *Demography, 55,* 1033–1068.

Phillips, J. D. (2018). The culture of poverty: On individual choices and infantiliz-ing bureaucracies. In C. Frisby, & W. O'Donohue (Eds.), *Cultural competence in applied psychology* (pp. 383–401). New York: Springer.

Phillips, L. T., & Lowery, B. S. (2018). Herd invisibility: The psychology of racial privilege. *Current Directions in Psychological Science, 27,* 156–162.

Pickett, K. E., & Wilkinson, R. G. (2010). Inequality: An underacknowledged source of mental illness and distress. *The British Journal of Psychiatry, 197,* 426–428.

Pickett, K. E., & Wilkinson, R. G. (2015). Income inequality and health: A causal review. *Social Science & Medicine, 128,* 316–326.

Pietschnig, J., Penke, L., Wicherts, J., Zeiler, M., & Voracek, M. (2015). Meta-analysis of associations between human brain volume and intelligence differ-ences: How strong are they and what do they mean? *Neuroscience Biobehavior Review, 57,* 411–432.

Piff, P. K., Kraus, M. W., & Keltner, D. (2018). Unpacking the inequality para-dox: The psychological roots of inequality and social class. In J. M. Olson (Ed.), *Advances in experimental social psychology, 57,* 53–124.

Piff, P. K., Stancato, D. M., Cote, S., Mendoza-Denton, R., & Keltner, D. (2012). Higher social class predicts increased unethical behavior. *Proceedings of the National Academy of Sciences, 109,* 4086–4091.

Piketty, T. (2014). *Capital in the twenty-first century* (Trans. A. Goldhammer). Cambridge, MA: The Belknap Press of Harvard University press.

Piketty, T., & Saez, E. (2014). Inequality in the long run. *Science, 344,* 838–843.

Plomin, R., & Deary, I. J. (2015). Genetics and intelligence differences: Five spe-cial findings. *Molecular Psychiatry, 20,* 98–108.

Plomin, R., & von Stumm, S. (2018). The new genetics of intelligence. *Nature Review Genetics, 19,* 148–159.

Pockett, S., & Miller. A. (2007). The rotating spot method of timing subjective events. *Consciousness and Cognition, 16,* 241–254.

Pogge, T., Köhler, G., & Cimadamore, A. D. (Eds.) (2016). *Poverty & the millennium development goals (MDGs): A critical assessment and a look forward.* London: Zed Books.

Power, S. A., Vellez, G., Qadafi, A., & Tennant, J. (2018). The SAGE model of social psychological research. *Perspectives on Psychological Science, 13,* 359–372.

Prilleltensky, I. (1994). *The morals and politics of psychology: Psychological discourse and the status quo.* New York: SUNY Press.

Prilleltensky, I. (2020). Mattering at the intersection of psychology, philosophy, and politics. *American Journal of Community Psychology, 65,* 16–34.

Putnam, R. D. (2000). *Bowling alone: The collapse and revival of American community.* New York: Simon & Schuster.

Putnam, R. D. (2016). *Our kids: The American dream in crisis.* New York: Simon & Schuster.

Radel, R., & Clément-Guillotin, C. (2012). *Psychological Science, 23,* 232–234.

Raphael, D. (2011). Poverty in childhood and adverse outcomes in adulthood. *Maturitas, 69,* 22–26.

Raver, C. C. (2012). Low-income children's self-regulation in the classroom: Scientific inquiry for social change. *American Psychologist, 67,* 681–689.

Rauscher, E. (2016). Passing it on: Parent-to-adult child financial transfers for school and socioeconomic attainment. *The Russell Sage Foundation: Journal of the Social Sciences, 2,* 172–196.

Rauscher, E., Friedline, T., & Banerjee, M. (2017). We're not rich, but we're definitely not poor: Young children's conceptions of social class. *Children and Youth Services Review, 83,* 101–111.

Reilly, P. R. (2015). Eugenics and involuntary sterilization: 1907–2015. *The Annual Review of Genomics and Human Genetics, 16,* 351–368.

Reiman, J., & Leighton, P. (2016). *The rich get richer and the poor get prison.* London: Routledge. 10th ed.

Reimer, N. K., Becker, J. C., Benz, A., et al. (2017). Intergroup contact and social change: Implications of negative and positive contact for collective action in advantaged and disadvantaged groups. *Personality and Social Psychology Bulletin, 43,* 121–136.

Resnick, B. (2011). The relationship between resilience and motivation. In B. Resnick, L. P. Gwyther, & K. A. Roberto (Eds.), *Resilience in aging: Concepts, research and outcomes* (pp. 199–216). New York: Springer.

Revelle, W. (2009). Personality structure and measurement: The contribution of Raymond Cattell. *British Journal of Psychology, 100,* 253–257.

Revilla, J. C., Martin, P., & de Castro, C. (2017). The reconstruction of resilience as a social and collective phenomenon: Poverty and coping capacity during the economic crisis. *European Societies.* DOI: 10.1080/14616696.2017.1346195

Rietveld, C. A., Medland, S. E., Derringer, J., et al. (2013). GWAS of 126,559 individuals identifies genetic variants associated with educational attainment. *Science, 340,* 1467–1471.

Riis, J. (1890/2016). *How the other half lives: Studies among the tenements of New York. Reprinted by Benediction Classics*, Oxford, UK.

Rogers, C. R. (1965). *Client-centered therapy*. Boston: Houghton Mifflin. First published 1951.

Roll, S., Grinstein-Weiss, M., & Despard, M. (2019). Long-term impacts of online tax-savings interventions: Effects among persistently poor and resource-constrained households. *Consumer Interests Annual, 65*, 1–7. consumerinterests.org/assets/docs/CIA/CIA2019/RollCIA19.pdf

Rosen, M. L., Sheridan, M. A., Sambrook, K. A., Meltzoff, A. N., & McLaughlin, K. A. (2018). Socioeconomic disparities in academic achievement: A multi-modal investigation of neural mechanisms in children and adolescents. *NeuroImage, 173*, 298–310.

Rosenfield, S. (2012). Triple jeopardy? Mental health at the intersection of gender, race, and class. *Social Science & Medicine, 74*, 1791–1801.

Roy, A. L., Raver, C. C., Masucci, M. D., & DeJoseph, M. (2019). "If they focus on giving us a chance in life we can actually do something in this world": Poverty, inequality and youths' critical consciousness. *Developmental Psychology, 55*, 550–561.

Rubin, M., Evans, O., & McGuffog, R. (2019). Social class differences in social integration at university: Implications for academic outcomes and mental health. In J. Jetten, & K. Peters (Eds.), *The social psychology of inequality* (pp. 103–119). Cham, Switzerland: Springer Nature.

Runciman, D. (2008). *Political hypocrisy: The mask of power, from Hobbes to Orwell and beyond*. Princeton, NJ: Princeton University Press.

Runciman, W. G. (1966). *Relative deprivation and social justice*. Harmondsworth, England: Penguin.

Russell, W. (1980). *Educating Rita*. London: Methuen Drama.

Ryan, C. L., & Bauman, K. (2016). Educational attainment in the United States: 2015, population characteristics. www.census.gov/content/dam/Census/library/publications/2016/demo/p20-578.pdf

Sacks, D. W., Stevenson, B., & Wolfers, J. (2012). *The new stylized facts about income and subjective well-being. IZA Discussion Papers*, No. 7105, Institute for the Study of Labor (IZA), Bonn. Econstor.eu/bitstream/10419/68372/1/733999808.pdf

Sacks, P. (2007). *Tearing down the gates: Confronting the class divide in American education*. Oakland, CA: University of California Press.

Saez, E., & Zucman, G. (2019). *The triumph of injustice: How the rich dodge taxes and how to make them pay*. New York: Norton.

Salem, A. A., & Bayat, N. (2018). Factors influencing poverty in Iran using a multilevel approach. *Journal of Money and Economy, 13*, 81–106.

Sampson, E. E. (1977). Psychology and the American ideal. *Journal of Personality and Social Psychology, 35*, 767–782.

Sampson, E. E. (1981). Cognitive psychology as ideology. *American Psychologist, 36*, 730–743.

Santiago, C. D., Kaltman, S., & Miranda, J. (2012). Poverty and mental health: How do low-income adults and children fare in psychotherapy? *Journal of Clinical Psychology: In Session, 69*, 115–126.

Savage, J. E., Jansen, P. R., Stringer, S., et al. (2018). Genome-wide association meta-analysis in 269,867 individuals identifies new genetic and functional links to intelligence, *Nature Genetics, 50*, 912–919.

Save the Children (2019). Stop the war on children: Protecting children in 21st century conflict. www.savethechildren.org/content/dam/usa/reports/ed-cp/stop-the-war-on-children-2019.pdf

Sawaoka, T., Hughes, B. L., & Ambady, N. (2015). Power heightens sensitivity to unfairness against the self. *Personality and Social Psychology Bulletin, 41*, 1023–1035.

Scarr, S., & Carter-Saltzman, L. (1979). Twin method: Defense of a critical assumption. *Behavior Genetics, 9*, 527–542.

Scheidel, W. (2017). *The great leveler: Violence and the history of inequality from the stone age to the twenty-first century*. Princeton, NJ: Princeton University Press.

Schilbach, F., Schofield, H., & Mullainathan, S. (2016). The psychological lives of the poor. *American Economic Review, 106*, 435–440.

Schurger, A., Sitt, J. D., & Dehaene, S. (2012). An accumulator model for spontaneous neural activity prior to self-initiated movement. *PNAS*, E2904–E2913. DOI: 10.1073/pnas.1210467109

Schwartz, J., Steffensmeier, D. J., Zhong, H., & Ackerman, J. (2009). Trends in the gender gap in violence: Reevaluating NVCS and other evidence. *Criminology, 47*, 401–425.

Schweinhart, L. J., Montie, J., Xiang, Z., et al. (2005). *Lifetime effects: The High/Scope Perry Preschool study through age 40* (Monographs of the High/Scope Educational Research Foundation, 14). Ypsilanti: High/Scope Press.

Schweitzer, K., & Nuñez, N. (2017). Victim impact statements: How victim social class affects juror decision making. *Violence and Victims, 32*, 521–532.

Scott-Hayward, C. S., & Fradella, H. F. (2019). *Punishing poverty: How jail and pretrial detention fuel inequalities in the criminal justice system*. Oakland, CA: University of California Press.

Sdorow, L. M., & Rickabaugh, C. A. (2006). *Psychology*. Cincinnati, OH: Atomic Dog Publishing. 6th ed.

Searle, J. R. (2013). Can information theory explain consciousness? Consciousness: Confessions of a romantic reductionist by C. Koch. *The New York Review of Books, 60*, 54–58.

Seccombe, K. (1999). *"So you think I drive a Cadillac?" Welfare recipients' perspectives on the system and its reform*. Needham Heights, MA: Allyn and Bacon.

Sedlak, A. J., & McPherson, K. S. (2010). *Conditions of confinement: Findings from the survey of youth in residential placement. Juvenile Justice Bulletin*. Washington, DC: Office of Juvenile Justice and Delinquency Prevention. http://rhyclearinghouse.acf.hhs.gov/siles/default/files/docs/19590-Conditions_of_Confinement-findings.pdf

Seligman, C. K. (2012). Rich man, poor man: Developmental differences in attributions and perceptions. *Journal of Experimental Child Psychology, 113*, 415–429.

Seligman, M. E. P. (2011). Building resilience. *Harvard Business Review, 89*, 100–106.

Seligman, M. E. P. (2019). Positive psychology: A personal history. *Annual Review of Clinical Psychology, 15,* 1–23.

Sen, A. (2006). Conceptualizing and measuring poverty. In D. B. Grusky, & S. M. R. Kanbur (Eds.), *Poverty and inequality* (pp. 30–46) Stanford, CA: Stanford University Press.

Sewell, W. H. (1961). Social class and childhood personality. *Sociometry, 24,* 340–356.

Shafir, E. (2017). Decisions in poverty contexts. *Current Opinion in Psychology, 18,* 131–136.

Shah, A., Mullainathan, S., & Shafir, E. (2012). Some consequences of having too little. *Science, 338,* 682–685.

Shah, A. K., Zhao, J., Mullainathan, S., and Shafir, E. (2018). Money in the mental lives of the poor. *Social Cognition, 36,* 4–19.

Shalby, C. (2019). No more "convict" or "felons" if San Francisco passes criminal justice language proposal. *Los Angeles Times,* August 22. www.latimes .com/california/story/2019-08-22/words-like-convict-and-felon-would-be-out-in-new-san-francisco-criminal-justice-language-proposal

Shalvi, S., Gino, F., Barkan, R., & Ayal, S. (2015). Self-serving justification: Doing wrong and feeling moral. *Current Directions in Psychological Science, 24,* 125–130.

Shapiro, D., Dunbar, A., Huie, F., et al. (2017). *A national view of student attainment rates by race and ethnicity – Fall 2010 cohort* (Signature Report No. 12b). April. Herndon, VA: National Student Clearinghouse Research Center.

Shaughnessy, J. J., Zechmeister, E. B., & Zechmeister, J. S. (2009). *Research methods in psychology.* New York: McGraw Hill. 8th ed.

Shaw, C., & McKay, H. (1942). *Juvenile delinquency and urban areas.* Chicago, IL: University of Chicago Press.

Sheldon, W. H., & Stevens, S. S. (1942). *The varieties of temperament: A psychology of constitutional differences.* Oxford: Harper.

Sherif, M. (1936). *The psychology of group norms.* New York: Harper.

Sherif, M. (1966). *Group conflict and cooperation: Their social psychology.* London: Routledge & Kegan Paul.

Shiraev, E. B. (2017). *Personality theory: A global view.* Thousand Oaks, CA: Sage.

Shiraev, E. B., &. Levy, D. A. (2020). *Cross-cultural psychology: Critical thinking and contemporary applications.* New York: Routledge. 7th ed.

Shonkoff, J. P., & Phillips, D. A. (Eds.) (2000). *From neurons to neighborhoods: The science of early childhood development.* Washington, DC: National Academy Press.

Shrout, P. E., & Rodgers, J. L. (2018). Psychology, science, and knowledge construction: Broadening perspectives from the replication crisis. *Annual Review of Psychology, 69,* 487–510.

Shweder, R. A. See a collection of his writings at https://humdev.uchicago.edu/ directory/richard-shweder

Shweder, R. A., & Bourne, E. J. (1984). Does the concept of the person vary cross-culturally? In R. A. Shweder, & R. A. LeVine (Eds.), *Culture theory: Essays on mind, self, and emotion* (pp. 158–199). Cambridge, UK: Cambridge University Press.

Silvers, J. A., Buhle, J. T., & Ochsner, K. N. (2014). The neuroscience of emotion regulation: Basic mechanisms and their role in development, aging, and psychopathology. In K. N. Ochsner, & S. M. Kosslyn (Eds.), *The Oxford handbook of cognitive neuroscience. Vol. 2 The cutting edges* (pp. 52–78). New York: Oxford University Press.

Singh, K., & Pandey, J. (1990). Psychology of poverty. *Indian Journal of Social Work, 51*, 623–632.

Sirin, S. R. (2005). Socioeconomic status and academic achievement: A meta-analytic review. *Review of Educational Research, 75*, 417–453.

Skinner, B. F. (1948). *Walden two.* New York: Macmillan paperbacks edition (1962).

Skinner, B. F. (1971). *Beyond freedom & dignity.* Cambridge, MA: Hackett Publishing Co.

Small, M. L., Harding, D. J. & Lamont, M. (2010). Reconsidering culture and poverty. *The Annals of the American Academy of Political and Social Science, 629*, 6–27.

Smith, J. A., Harré, R., & Van Langenhove, L. (Eds.) (1995). *Rethinking methods in psychology.* London: Sage.

Smith, L. (2010). *Psychology, poverty, and the end of social exclusion: Putting our practice to work.* New York: Teachers College, Columbia University.

Smith, S. A. (2017). *Russian revolution 1890–1928: An empire in crisis.* New York: Oxford University Press.

Social Mobility Index (2018). Opportunity through US higher education. www.socialmobilityindex.org/

Spearman, C. G. (1904). "General intelligence," objectively determined and measured. *American Journal of Psychology, 15*, 201–292.

Spencer, B., & Castano, E. (2007). Social class is dead. Long live social class! Stereotype threat among low socioeconomic status individuals. *Social Justice Research, 20*, 418–432.

Spencer, S. J., Steele, C. M., & Quinn, D. M. (1999). Stereotype threat and women's math performance. *Journal of Experimental Social Psychology, 35*, 4–28.

Spini, D., & Doise, W. (2005). Universal rights and duties as normative social representations. In N. Finkel, & F. M. Moghaddam (Eds.), *The psychology of rights and duties* (pp. 21–48). Washington, DC: American Psychological Association Press.

Stanley, M. L., Moussa, M. N., Paolini, B. M., et al. (2013). Defining nodes in complex brain networks. *Frontiers in Computational Neuroscience, 7*, 169. DOI: 10.3389/fncom.2013.00169

Steele, C. (1997). A threat in the air: How stereotypes shape the intellectual identities and performance of women and African Americans, *American Psychologist, 52*, 613–629.

Steele, C. (2011). Stereotype threat and African-American student achievement. In D. B. Grusky, & S. Szelényi (Eds.), *The inequality reader: Contemporary and foundational readings in race, class, and gender* (pp. 276–281). Boulder, CO: Westview Press. 2nd ed.

Steiner, B., & Wooldredge, J. (2008). Inmate versus environmental effects on prison rule violations. *Criminal Justice and Behavior, 35*, 438–456.

Stephens, N. M., Markus, H. R., & Phillips, L. T. (2014). Social class culture cycles: How three gateway contexts shape selves and fuel inequality. *Annual Review of Psychology, 65*, 611–634.

Stephens, N. M., Townsend, S. S. M., & Dittmann, A. G. (2019). Social-class disparities in higher education and professional workplaces: The role of cultural mismatch. *Current Directions in Psychological Science, 28*, 67–73.

Sternberg, R. J. (2015). Successful intelligence: A model for testing intelligence beyond IQ tests. *European Journal of Education and Psychology, 8*, 76–84.

Stevens, A. J. (2014). The invisible soldiers: Understanding how the life experiences of girl child soldiers impacts upon their health and rehabilitation needs. *Archives of Disease in Childhood, 99*, 458–462.

Stevens, F. G., Plaut, V. C., & Sanchez-Burks, J. (2008). Unlocking the benefits of diversity: All-inclusive multiculturalism and positive organizational change. *The Journal of Applied Behavioral Science, 44*, 116–133.

Stewart, F. (2014). Against happiness: A critical appraisal of the use of measures of happiness for evaluating progress in development. *Journal of Human Development Capabilities, 15*, 293–307.

Stiglitz, J. E. (2012). *The price of inequality: How today's divided society endangers our future*. New York: W. W. Norton.

Stoppard, T. (2015). *The hard problem*. London: Faber and Faber.

Streeck, W. (2016). *How will capitalism end?* New York: Verso.

Strenze, T. (2007). Intelligence and socioeconomic success: A meta-analytic review of longitudinal research. *Intelligence, 35*, 401–426.

Stuckler, D., Basu, S., Suhrcke, M., Coutts, A., & McKee, M. (2011). Effects of the 2008 recession on health: A first look at European data. *The Lancet, 378*, 124–125.

Sumner, A., Hoy, C., & Ortiz-Juarez, E. (2020). Estimates of the impact of COVID-19 on global poverty. WIDER Working Paper 2020/43, United Nations University. www.indiaenvironmentportal.org.in/files/file/Estimates-of-the-impact-of-COVID-19-on-globalpoverty.pdf

Sun, T. L. C. (2013). *Themes in Chinese psychology*. Singapore: Cengage Learning Asia. 2nd ed.

Surprenant, C. W. (2019). Policing and punishment for profit. *Journal of Business Ethics, 159*, 119–131.

Sutton, A., Langenkamp, A. G., Muller, C., & Schiller, K. S. (2018). Who gets ahead and who falls behind during the transition to high school? Academic performance at the intersection of race/ethnicity and gender. *Social Problems, 65*, 154–173.

Sverdlik, A. (2011). Ill-health and poverty: A literature review on health in informal settlements. *Environment & Urbanization, 23*, 123–155.

Sweller, J. (1988). Cognitive load during problem solving: Effects on learning. *Cognitive Science, 12*, 257–285.

Sylvestre, J., Notten, G., Kerman, N., Polillo, A., & Czechowki, K. (2018). Poverty and serious mental illness: Toward action on a seemingly intractable problem. *American Journal of Community Psychology, 61*, 153–165.

Szasz, T. S. (1961). *The myth of mental illness: Foundations of a theory of personal conduct.* New York: Dell Publishing.

Tajfel, H., Flament, C., Billig, M. G., & Bundy, R. F. (1971). Social categorization and intergroup behaviour. *European Journal of Social Psychology, 1*, 149–177.

Tajfel, H., & Turner, J. C. (1979). An integrative theory of intergroup conflict. In W. G. Austin, & S. Worchel (Eds.), *The social psychology of intergroup relations* (pp. 33–47). Monterey, CA: Brooks/Cole.

Tanaka, T., Camerer, C. F., & Nguyen, Q. (2010). Risk and time preference: Linking experimental and survey data from Vietnam. *The American Economic Review, 100*, 557–571.

Tappin, B. M., van der Leer, L., & McKay, R. T. (2017). The heart trumps the head: Desirability bias in political belief revision. *Journal of Experimental Psychology: General, 146*, 1143–1149.

Tatum, B. D. (2017). *Why are all the Black kids sitting together in the cafeteria? And other conversations about race.* New York: Basic Books.

Taylor, D. M., & de la Sablonniére, R. (2014). *Toward constructive change in Aboriginal communities.* Montreal, Canada: McGill-Queens University Press.

Taylor, D. M., & Moghaddam, F. M. (1994). *Theories of intergroup relations: International social psychological perspectives.* New York: Praeger.

Taylor, F. D. (1964). *The principles of scientific management.* New York: Harper & Row. First published 1911.

Taylor, K. Y. (2016). *From #BlackLivesMatter to Black Liberation.* Chicago: Haymarket Books.

The Economist (2018). The next capitalist revolution. November 17–23, p. 13.

The Economist (2020a). Measuring the 1%: As inequality rises further up the political agenda, some economists are rethinking the numbers. November 30–December 6, pp. 21–24.

The Economist (2020b). Covid-19 and global poverty: The great reversal. May 23–29, pp. 46–48.

The Economist (2021a). Waiting: Time and money. May 6–14, pp. 30–31.

The Economist (2021b). Special report: The Chinese Communist Party. June 26, pp. 1–12.

Thornton, P. (2018). Opinion: Trump prefers immigrants from Norway over "shithole" countries? He must not know anything about Norway's history. *Los Angeles Times,* January 11. www.latimes.com/opinion/opinion-la/la-ol-norway-trump-immigration-20180111-story.html

Tilly, C. (1998). *Durable inequality.* Berkeley, CA: University of California Press.

Tomalski, P., Moore, D. G., Ribeiro, H., et al. (2013). Socioeconomic status and functional brain development – associations in early infancy. *Developmental Science, 16*, 676–687.

Tononi, G., & Koch, C. (2015). Consciousness: Here, there, everywhere? *Philosophical Transactions Royal Society B, 370,* 20140167. DOI: 10.1098/rstb.2014.0167

Tonry, M. (2014). Why crime rates are falling throughout the Western world. *Crime and Justice, 43,* 1–63.

Tooley, U. A., Mackey, A. P., Ciric, R., et al. (2020). Associations between neighborhood SES and functional brain network development. *Cerebral Cortex, 30,* 1–19.

Topor, A., Ljungqvist, I., & Strandberg, E. L. (2016). Living in poverty with severe mental illness coping with double trouble. *Nordic Social Work Research.* DOI: 10.1080/2156857X.2015.1134629

Trampush, J. W., Yang, M. I., Yu, J., et al. (2017). GWAS meta-analysis reveals novel loci and genetic correlates for general cognitive function: A report from the COGENT consortium. *Molecular Psychiatry, 22,* 336–345.

Travis, C., & Aronson, E. (2013). *Mistakes were made (but not by me): Why we justify foolish beliefs, bad decisions and hurtful acts.* London: Pinter & Martin. 2nd ed.

Tricomi, E., Rangel, A., Camerer, C. F., & O'Doherty, J. P. (2010). Neural evidence for inequality-averse social preferences. *Nature, 463,* 1089–1092.

Tripathi, R. C. (2010). Poverty alleviation: Is it only tilting at the windmills? *Psychology & Developing Societies, 22,* 201–220.

Tronick, E., Als, H., Adamson, L., Wise, W., & Brazelton, T. B. (1978). The infant's response to entrapment between contradictory messages in face-to-face interaction. *Journal of the American Academy of Child Psychiatry, 17,* 1–13.

Trotsky, L. (2010). *The permanent revolution and results and prospects.* Seattle, WA: Red Letter Press. First published 1906.

Trudeau, P. E. (1992). Statement by the Prime Minister in the House of Commons, October 8, 1971. In *Multiculturalism in Canada: The challenge of diversity* (pp. 281–283). Scarborough, Canada: Nelson Canada (Original work published 1971).

Trulson, C. R., DeLisi, M., Caudill, J. W., Belshaw, S., & Marquart, J. W. (2010). Delinquent careers behind bars. *Criminal Justice Review, 35,* 200–219.

Trzaskowski, M., Yang, J., Visscher, P. M., & Plomin, R. (2014). DNA evidence for strong genetic stability and increasing heritability of intelligence from age 7 to 12. *Molecular Psychiatry, 19,* 380–384.

Tucker, R. (2014). The color of mass incarceration. *Ethnic Studies Review, 37–38,* 135–149.

Turney, K. (2015). Liminal men: Incarceration and relationship dissolution. *Social Problems, 62,* 499–528.

United Nations High Commissioner for Refugees (UNHCR) (2019). Forced displacement in 2018. www.unhcr.org/globaltrends2018/

United Nations International Children's Emergency Fund (UNICEF) (2007). *Paris principles.* New York: UNICEF.

Van der Horst, E. C. P., LeRoy, H. A., & Van der Veer, R. (2008). "When strangers meet": John Bowlby and Harry Harlow on attachment behavior. *Integrative Psychological Behavioral Science, 42,* 370–388.

Van Dick, R., Tissington, P. A., & Hertel, G. (2009). Do many hands make light work? How to overcome social loafing and gain motivation in work teams. *European Business Review, 21*, 233–245.

Van Zomeren, M., Kutlaca, M., &. Turner-Zwinkels, F. (2018). Integrating who "we" are with what "we" (will not) stand for: A. further extension of the *Social Identity Model of Collective Action. European Review of Social Psychology, 29*, 122–160.

Van Zomeren, M., Postmes, T., & Spears, R. (2008). Toward an integrative social psychological model of collective action: A quantitative research synthesis of three social-psychological perspectives. *Psychological Bulletin, 134*, 504–535.

Van Zyl Smit, D., & Dunkel, F. (Eds.) (2018). *Prison labour: Salvation or slavery?* New York: Routledge. Originally published 1999.

Vargas-Salfate, S., Paez, D., Liu, J. H., Pratto, F., & de Zuñiga, H. G. (2018). A comparison of social dominance theory and system justification: The role of social status in 19 nations. *Personality and Social Psychology Bulletin, 44*, 1060–1076.

Vazquez, J. J., Panadero, S., & Zuniga, C. (2018). Attributions about homelessness in homeless and domiciled people in Madrid, Spain: "Why are they homeless people?" *American Journal of Orthopsychiatry, 88*, 236–247.

Vein, A. A., & Maat-Schieman, M. L. C. (2008). Famous Russian brains: Historical attempts to understand intelligence. *Brain, 131*, 583–590.

Vossoughi, N., Jackson, Y., Gusler, S., & Stone, K. (2018). Mental health outcomes for youth living in refugee camps: A review. *Trauma, Violence, & Abuse, 19*, 528–542.

Votanopoulos, K. I., Forsythe, S., Sivakumar, H., et al. (2020). Model of patient-specific immune-enhanced organoids for Immunotherapy screening: Feasibility study. *Annals of Surgical Oncology, 27*, 1956–1967.

Vygotsky, L. S. (1962). *Thought and language* (Trans. E. Hanfmann, & G. Vakar). Cambridge, MA: MIT Press.

Vygotsky, L. S. (1978). *Mind in society* (Trans. M. Cole). Cambridge, MA: Harvard University Press.

Wagoner, B., Moghaddam, F. M., & Valsiner, J. (Eds.) (2018). *The psychology of radical social change: From rage to revolution*. Cambridge, UK: Cambridge University Press.

Wakefield, S., Lee, H., & Wildeman, C. (2016). Tough on crime, tough on families? Criminal justice and family life in America. *ANNALS of the American Academy of Political and Social Science, 665*, 8–21.

Wakefield, S., & Uggen, C. (2010). Incarceration and stratification. *Annual Review of Sociology, 36*, 387–406.

Walder, A. G. (2015). *China under Mao: A revolution derailed*. Cambridge, MA: Harvard University Press.

Wallerstein, M., & Western, B. (2000). Unions in decline? What has changed and why. *Annual Review of Political Science, 3*, 355–377.

Wang, Y., Zhang, L., Kong, X., et al. (2016). Pathway to neural resilience: Self-esteem buffers against deleterious effects of poverty on the hippocampus. *Human Brain Mapping, 37*, 3757–3766.

Warner, J., O'Farrell, R., Nsaibia, H., & Cummings, R. (2020). Outlasting the Caliphate: The evolution of the Islamic State threat in Africa. *CTS Sentinel, 13.* https://ctc.usma.edu/outlasting-the-caliphate-the-evolution-of-the-islamic-state-threat-in-africa/

Watson, J. B. (1913). Psychology as a behaviorist views it. *Psychological Review, 20,* 157–177.

Watts, T. W., Duncan, G. J., & Quan, H. (2018). Revisiting the marshmallow test: A conceptual replication investigating links between early delay of gratification and later outcomes. *Psychological Science, 29,* 1159–1177.

Watzlawick, P., Weakland, J. H., & Fisch, R. (1974). *Change: Principles of problem formation and problem resolution.* New York: Norton.

Waugh, M. H., Hopwood, C. J., Krueger, R. F., et al. (2017). The poverty of the neuroscience of poverty: Policy payoff or false promise? *Jurimetrics, 57,* 239–187.

Waugh, M. H., Hopwood, C. J., Krueger, R. F., et al. (2017). Psychological assessment with the DSM-5 alternative model for personality disorders: Tradition and innovation. *Professional Psychological Research, 48,* 79–89.

Webb, P. (2018). Hunger and malnutrition in the 21st century. *British Medical Journal.* www.bmj.com/content/bmj/361/bmj.k2238.full.pdf

Wegner, D. M. (2003). *The illusion of conscious will.* Cambridge, MA: MIT Press.

Weiner, B., Osborne, D., & Rudolph, U. (2011). An attributional analysis of reactions to poverty: The political ideology of the giver and the perceived morality of the receiver. *Personality and Social Psychology Review, 15,* 199–213.

Weiner, I. B., & Greene, R. L. (Eds.) (2017). *Handbook of personality assessment.* Hoboken, NJ: Wiley. 2nd ed.

Wessells, M. G. (2016). Children and armed conflict: Introduction and overview. *Peace and Conflict: Journal of Peace Psychology, 22,* 198–207.

Wessells, M. G. (2017). Children and armed conflict: Interventions for supporting war-affected children. *Peace and Conflict: Journal of Peace Psychology, 23,* 4–13.

Western, B. (2018). *Homeward: Life in the year after prison.* New York: Russell Sage Foundation.

Western, B., Braga, A. A., Davis, J., & Sirois, C. (2015). Stress and hardship after prison. *American Journal of Sociology, 120,* 1512–1547.

Western, B., & Pettit, B. (2010). Incarceration & social inequality. *Daedalus, 139,* 8–19.

Wheelock, D., & Uggen, C. (2008). Punishment, crime, and poverty. In A. C. Lin, & D. R. Harris (Eds.), *The colors of poverty: Why racial and ethnic disparities persist* (pp. 261–292). New York: Russell Sage Foundation.

Whitehouse, H., Jong, J., Buhrmester, M. D., & Swann, W. B. (2014). Brothers in arms: Libyan revolutionaries bond like family. *Proceedings of the National Academy of Sciences, 111,* 17783–17785.

Whitson, J. A., Liljenquist, K. A., Galinsky, A. D., et al. (2013). The blind leading: Power reduced awareness of constraints. *Journal of Experimental Social Psychology, 49,* 579–582.

Wickham, S., Shryane, N., Lyons, M., Dickins, T., & Bentall, R. (2014). Why does relative deprivation affect mental health? The role of justice, trust and social rank in psychological wellbeing and paranoid ideation. *Journal of Public Mental Health, 13*, 114–126.

Wigginton, B., & Lafrance, M. N. (2019). Learning critical feminist research: A brief introduction to feminist epistemologies and methodologies. *Feminism & Psychology, 29*, 534–552.

Wildeman, C., Turney, K., & Yi, Y. (2016). Paternal incarceration and family functioning: Variation across federal, state, and local facilities. *ANNALS of the American Academy of Political and Social Science, 665*, 80–97.

Wilkinson, R., & Pickett, K. (2011). *The spirit level: Why equality is better for everyone.* London: Bloomsbury Press.

Wilkinson, R., & Pickett, K. (2019). *The inner level: How more equal societies reduce stress, restore sanity and improve everyone's well-being.* New York: Penguin Press.

Williams, W. R. (2009). Struggling with poverty: Implications for theory and policy of increasing research on social class-based stigma. *Analysis of Social Issues and Public Policy, 9*, 37–56.

Williams, W. R. (2019). Considering Carnegie's legacy in the time of Trump: A science and policy agenda for studying social class. *Journal of Social Issues, 75*, 356–382.

Willimott, A. (2017). *Living the revolution: Urban communes & Soviet socialism, 1917–1932.* New York: Oxford University Press.

Windelband, W. (1894/1998). History and natural science (Trans. J. T. Lamiell). *Theory & Psychology, 8*, 5–22.

Winship, S. (2018). *Economic mobility in America: A state-of-the-art primer. Part 2: The United States in comparative perspective.* Washington DC: Archbridge Institute. www.archbridgeinstitute.org/wp-content/uploads/2018/12/Archbridge-Economic-Mobility-primer-part2-US-in-perspective.pdf

Witelson, S. F., Kigar, D. L., & Harvey, T. (1999). The exceptional brain of Alfred Einstein. *The Lancet, 353*, 2149–2153.

Wittgenstein, L. (1958). *Philosophical investigations* (Trans. G. E. G. Anscombe). Upper Saddle River, NJ: Prentice Hall. 3rd ed.

Wolfe, B. (2011–2012). Poverty and poor health: Can health-care reform narrow the rich-poor gap? *Focus, 28*, 25–30.

Woolard, J. (2022). The injustices of crimmigration: Discretion, detention, and deportation. In F. M. Moghaddam, & M. J. Hendricks (Eds.), *Contemporary immigration: Psychological perspectives to address challenges and inform solutions (pp. 203–221).* Washington, DC: American Psychological Association Press.

Wooldredge, J. (2020). Prison culture, management, and in-prison violence. *Annual Review of Criminology, 3*, 165–188.

Wooldredge, J., & Smith, P. (Eds.) (2018). *The Oxford handbook of criminology and criminal justice.* New York: Oxford University Press.

Yaddanapudi, L. N. (2016). The American Statistical Association statement on P-values explained. *Journal of Anaesthesiology Clinical Pharmacology, 32*, 421–423.

Yeung, W. J., & Conley, D. (2008). Black-White achievement gap and family wealth. *Child Development, 79*, 303–324.

Yoshikawa, H., Aber, J. L., & Beardslee, W. R. (2012). The effects of poverty on the mental, emotional and behavioral health of children and youth. *American Psychologist, 67*, 272–284.

Yu, L., & Suen, H. K. (2005). Historical and contemporary exam-driven education fever in China. *KEDI Journal of Educational Policy, 2*, 17–33.

Zeanah, C. H., Berlin, L. J., & Boris, N. W. (2011). Practitioner review: Clinical applications of attachment theory and research for infants and young children. *The Journal of Child Psychology and Psychiatry, 52*, 819–833.

Zimbardo, P. (2007). *The Lucifer effect: Understanding how good people turn evil.* New York: Random House.

Zorbaugh, H. W. (1929). *The Gold Coast and the slum: A sociological study of Chicago's Near North Side.* Chicago, IL: University of Chicago Press.

Index

Printed in the USA
CPSIA information can be obtained
at www.ICGtesting.com
CBHW072130280324
6039CB00006B/410